Buffy Goes Dark

Buffy Goes Dark

Essays on the Final Two Seasons of Buffy the Vampire Slayer *on Television*

Edited by
LYNNE Y. EDWARDS,
ELIZABETH L. RAMBO and
JAMES B. SOUTH

Foreword by David Lavery

McFarland & Company, Inc., Publishers
Jefferson, North Carolina, and London

LIBRARY OF CONGRESS CATALOGUING-IN-PUBLICATION DATA

Buffy goes dark : essays on the final two seasons of Buffy the vampire slayer on television ; edited by Lynne Y. Edwards, Elizabeth L. Rambo and James B. South ; foreword by David Lavery.
    p.   cm.
Includes bibliographical references and index.

ISBN 978-0-7864-3676-7
softcover : 50# alkaline paper ∞

1. Buffy, the vampire slayer (Television program) I. Edwards, Lynn Y., 1966– II. Rambo, Elizabeth L., 1954– III. South, James B., 1960–
PN1992.77.B84B82   2009
791.45'7 — dc22   2008033623

British Library cataloguing data are available

©2009 Lynne Y. Edwards, Elizabeth L. Rambo and James B. South. All rights reserved

No part of this book may be reproduced or transmitted in any form or by any means, electronic or mechanical, including photocopying or recording, or by any information storage and retrieval system, without permission in writing from the publisher.

On the cover: Sarah Michelle Gellar as Buffy Summers in *Buffy the Vampire Slayer* (FOX/Photofest)

Manufactured in the United States of America

McFarland & Company, Inc., Publishers
Box 611, Jefferson, North Carolina 28640
www.mcfarlandpub.com

Table of Contents

Foreword by David Lavery — 1
Preface: At Sixes and Sevens in Sunnydale — 5

Section 1. Auteurs
(Writers, Directors, Producers)

Marti Noxon: *Buffy*'s Other Genius   DAVID PERRY   13
Understanding the Espensode   DAVID KOCIEMBA   23

Section 2. Characters
(Lovers, Fans and Heroes)

Evil, Skanky, and Kinda Gay: Lesbian
   Images and Issues   ALISSA WILTS   41
"It's complicated ... because of Tara": History, Identity Politics,
   and the Straight White Male Author   BRANDY RYAN   57
The Candide of Sunnydale: Andrew Wells as Satire
   of Pop Culture and Marketing Trends
   IRA SHULL AND ANNE SHULL   75

Section 3. Story
(Flesh, Style and Purpose)

Buffy and the Death of Style   MICHAEL ADAMS   83

"Set on This Earth Like a Bubble": Word as Flesh in
the Dark Seasons   RHONDA V. WILCOX   95

Bodies and Narrative in Crisis: Figures of Rupture and
Chaos in Seasons Six and Seven   GREGORY ERICKSON
AND JENNIFER LEMBERG   114

Reality Bites: *Buffy* in the UPN Years   LYNNE Y. EDWARDS
AND CARLY HAINES   130

Section 4: Seasons
(At Sixes and Sevens)

"Just a Family Legend": The Hidden Logic of *Buffy*'s
"Chosen Family"   AGNES B. CURRY AND JOSEF VELAZQUEZ   143

Yeats's Entropic Gyre and Season Six   ELIZABETH L. RAMBO   167

Season Six and the Supreme Ordeal   PAUL HAWKINS   183

Kiss Kiss, Stake Stake: Storytelling and the Philosophical
Pleasures of Season Seven   JAMES B. SOUTH   198

Appendix: Episode Guides for Buffy the Vampire Slayer
and Angel   211

About the Contributors   219

Index   223

Foreword

DAVID LAVERY

In the summer of 2003, only two months after *Buffy the Vampire Slayer* had aired its final episode in the United States, Rhonda Wilcox and I traveled to Australia to speak on *BtVS* in Adelaide and Melbourne. At "Staking a Claim: Exploring the Global Reach of Buffy" at the University of South Australia, we experienced first hand to what extent Joss Whedon's creation had become a world-wide, multi-[JR1]hemispheric phenomenon (and this was back in the day before books in Italian on Buffy and a conference — "Buffy Hereafter: From the Whedonverse to the Whedonesque"— in Istanbul!).

As we gave our talks, we needed to be extra-cautious with spoilers, for "Empty Places," "Touched," "End of Days," and "Chosen" had not yet aired Down Under, and this was an audience that did not want to be spoiled. (A "spoiler whore" myself, I had found PDFs of the scripts of the last five episodes in my in-box prior to their airing in the U.S.) We announced spoiler warnings emphatically during our talks, and the result, on more than one occasion, was a mass exodus of our audience, their hands clamped over their ears, running from the auditorium.

On the last days of "Staking," the individual who had programmed Buffy for Australian television (where it ran late in the evening and garnered a substantially larger market share than in the U.S.), generously offered to send for the final episodes so that everyone might experience what Rhonda Wilcox and I already had: the end of Buffy. That evening we sat in an auditorium and watched over four hours of Buffy in a way television is almost never experienced: on a big screen with a crowd. As the scythe was secured, Angel came to the rescue, Caleb split, Dawn was slow on the uptake concerning pierced tongues, a young girl faced a pitcher with true fearlessness, Anya and Spike died, Sunnydale cratered, and Buffy saved the world — again — we found ourselves sometimes watching the watchers as much as the screen. We knew what would come next; we didn't know how they would react. And then, at last, it was over, and more than a few tears were shed at the sight of that slight smile breaking out on Buffy Summers' face, crying inspired not just by an ending worthy of a great television series but also by the shocking realization that *Buffy the Vampire Slayer* had come to end.

We did not know then that, in 2007, there would be a Season Eight, at least in comic book form, to partially placate us. But we had already begun to grasp yet another way in which *Buffy* would continue to exist: the unprecedented wave of scholarly and critical writing about the show, aka *Buffy* Studies, a phenomenon recently assessed by Rhonda Wilcox,[1] that would keep the series vibrantly in our minds and imaginations for a long time to come.

With over twenty books and hundreds of essays on Buffy now in print, it remains nevertheless clear that there is still much to be done, and the wonderfully diverse and insightful essays in this book allow us to check off several items from the Buffy Studies "To Do" list:

To do:	Contributions in *Buffy Goes Dark*:
careful examinations of the sometimes underestimated contributors of Joss Whedon's collaborators	Perry's essay on Marti Noxon and Kociemba's on Jane Espenson
more studies of major and minor BtVS characters	Ryan and Wilts on Tara, the Shulls on Andrew
investigations into the narratology of the Buffyverse	the wide-ranging essays of Adams, Erickson and Lemberg, and Wilcox
examinations of single seasons of Buffy, considered in their entirety	the ambitious essays of Curry, Rambo, Hawkins, and South

In a sense, of course, the entire book you are about to read is seasonal criticism, constituting as it does a multi-faceted look at two of Buffy's most controversial years. The last words of BtVS were a question (Dawn's "What are you gonna do now?"), and 6 and 7 provoked many more: Did *Buffy* change in the UPN years? Did *Buffy* decline as Whedon's involvement in the series diminished? Did *Buffy* end at the right time? Was the Troika as "nemeseses" a mistake? Was the killing of Tara an act of bad faith? These are some of the many questions this book pursues.

These essays are by newcomers to Buffy Studies and seasoned veterans, by Mr. Pointy Award winners, the annual award for the best Buffy scholarship (Adams, Wilcox, Kociemba) and the authors and editors of several books (Adams, South, Wilcox, Edwards), by philosophy, religion, and English professors, graduate students, and independent scholars (the field has always inspired a complex, interdisciplinary demographic). Glen Creeber made the case recently for the edited collection as the natural critical venue for consideration of complex, many-voiced television series — quintessential examples of Bakhtin's dialogism in action.[2][r2] The many voices of *Buffy Goes Dark* wonderfully confirm his argument, offering us multiple takes on what may be the most polysemic television text of them all.

To read these pages, of course, is to recollect in tranquility the powerful emotions we felt when we were at sixes and sevens in real time, experiencing a kind of critical pathos in which Buffy ends all over again. But then, thanks to DVDs, thanks to books like this (and more yet come), Buffy will never die (even if Buffy did die twice).

Notes

1. "In 'The Demon Section of the Card Catalogue': Buffy Studies and Television Studies." *Critical Studies in Television* 1, no. 1 (Spring 2006): 37–48.
2. "The Joy of Text? Television and Textual Analysis." *Critical Studies in Television* 1, no.1 (Spring 2006): 81–88.

Preface: At Sixes and Sevens in Sunnydale

In May 2001, Buffy the Vampire Slayer sacrificed herself to save the world (again) and *Buffy the Vampire Slayer* ended its fifth season on the WB television network. Buffy's death in "The Gift" would have been crushing to the show's most devoted fans if they had not known that *BtVS*, and presumably Buffy herself, would rise again on another fledgling network, UPN — United Paramount Network. In one of his rare but always memorable postings to the WB's *BtVS* online discussion board, "The Bronze," Joss Whedon wrote about the transition from Season Five to Season Six and the change in networks:

> How will we bring her back? With great difficulty, of course. And pain and confusion. Will it be cheezy? I don't think so.... The fact is, we've had most of next season planned before we ever shot this ep.... Different network. But we've never been controlled by the network — WB was great about that, UPN has already shown they will be too. The only difference is that Marti will share exec prod credit with me, and it's about time she did. I'm in charge.

Whedon also promised the Bronzers that there would be a musical in Season Six. Fans buzzed with excitement and speculation throughout the summer.

And then, finally, it was October, and *Buffy* Season Six opened on UPN with the two-part "Bargaining." We saw how grim the consequences of a Sunnydale — or a world — without the Slayer could be, not to mention Sunnydale without Giles, and just how far Willow would go to bring Buffy back to life. Where were Buffy's smiles and puns? Controversy increased when the fourth episode, "Flooded," unveiled the season's theme, "life as the big bad," with three hapless villain-wannabes and home-repair bills as Buffy's worst nightmares. Doug Petrie, who wrote and directed this episode, insisted that nothing had changed with the move to UPN: "I'm told ... that the censorship is lighter, but we've gotten away with *unbelievable* things on the WB. I don't see that we've ever done anything gratuitously, so I don't see any change at all. I think the good news for *Buffy* fans is that we're doing exactly the show that we wanted to be doing all along." Easily said, but Season Six was already more controversial than any event in the Buffyverse since, perhaps, the departure of Oz (Seth Green) in Season Four.

Many of the contentious issues raised by fans and scholars during Seasons Six and Seven and in the years since the series ended may be found in the essays collected here: Are these seasons too dark? Why doesn't Buffy love Spike? What about Tara and Willow? Are the villains lame? Are we even sure who the villains are? Why is Dawn still such a "young, delicate pain in [the] butt"? ("Blood Ties," 5.13). Is "Once More, with Feeling" (6.7) the best episode ever? Do these seasons lack structure and thematic coherence? Can everything be blamed on co–executive-producer Marti Noxon? Is Joss Whedon really the only "genius behind *Buffy*," or can we give some credit to other Mutant Enemy staff writers such as Jane Espenson as well?

We wanted to explore all these questions and more, because, honestly, the three of us actually liked *Buffy*'s UPN seasons a lot. We thought they deserved some special attention, while also, perhaps, demonstrating how they remain, in some ways, at least "exactly the show we wanted ... all along" (Petrie). We met and began talking about this project at the first Slayage Conference on *BtVS* in 2004, a year after the end of the series. At that time, we agreed that among the elements that made the final seasons both fascinating and controversial were the intensifying contrasts and conflicts in the narrative and character arcs, and in the viewers' responses. At the same time, these elements, surely, had always been essential to the series. At the heart of *BtVS* from Season One has been the use of metaphor to explore the conflicts of growth, power, and transgression: characters have dual identities or shadow characters, the show's style, setting, and plots lend themselves to thematic dualities, and, at last, fortuitously, to the program's network duality. After moving from the WB to UPN, however, *Buffy* became so intense and provocative that fan response split as well.

Ordinary viewers or fans often rank Season Six (and less frequently, Season Seven) among their favorite seasons, or they hate it. It has become commonplace to refer to Season Six as "dark." Entire fan-sites became largely devoted to disappointed discussions of *BtVS* and Mutant Enemy writers and producers or revisionist fan-fiction during the original broadcast years of Seasons Six and Seven. Two examples: (1) Membership in The Kittens, the Witches, and the Bad Wardrobe, "the only and largest exclusive Willow and Tara Message Board," grew explosively in 2002, evidently coinciding with the last half of Season Six, but the board's rules currently forbid discussion of anything beyond episode 6.19 "Seeing Red"—the episode in which Tara was killed (xita). (2) The Web site BTVS-Tabula Rasa—"We believe in Spike's redemption"—includes an FAQ "to respond to criticisms that have been made of Spike or of Spike and Buffy's relationship" ("Bunker"). The UPN years polarized *Buffy* fans, in many cases. Web sites or discussion boards dedicated to praising the final two seasons of *BtVS* are much rarer, if they exist at all, but defenses of the show during these years came from media critics such as Stephanie Zacharek and Emily Nussbaum, or some of the fans known as Existential Scoobies of the All Things Philosophical on BtVS & AtS discussion board (Shaffer). Although Thomas Hibbs of *National Review Online* found the Season Seven finale, "Chosen," disappointing, he concluded that it "does not diminish the remarkable dramatic achievements of *Buffy the Vampire Slayer* over seven seasons."

In addition, the final two seasons of *BtVS* aroused more intense scrutiny from viewers who perhaps had previously considered a show called *Buffy* too frivolous to be a threat. In 2000, Kathleen McConnell examined one of the earliest examples of this kind of response in her study of the repercussions of the Columbine High School massacre on *Buffy*, particularly with respect to the Season Three episodes "Earshot" and "Graduation Day, part 2." The increased attention the show garnered from these coincidental events was followed, two years later, by the entertainment media and fan frenzy accompanying the shift from WB to UPN (P. Graham, par. 30). Conservative media watchdog groups and even the Federal Communications Commission turned on the show they had earlier ignored, decrying it as "sacrilegious," "violent," and even "flirting with kiddie porn" (Bozell), suggesting that the uproar about Seasons Six and Seven was actually a real world response to the same kind of dualities that *Buffy* has always been about.

The first episodes of Season Six premiered in October 2001, less than a month after the stunning September 11 terrorist attacks on New York City and the Pentagon. Although Joss Whedon had stated that plans for *Buffy*'s sixth season were mapped out as the fifth season ended, viewers may have been expecting their favorite show to provide an escape or antidote to the real world horror and devastation the daily news brought closer every day. In a 2007 interview, Marti Noxon acknowledges the impact of these events even as the Mutant Enemy writers had already planned a less "fanciful" sixth season:

> I'll never forget the day, 9/11, going down to the set and telling people to leave and driving through the streets. I mean we'd been joking about the apocalypse for years but suddenly it felt more real than a joke.... We did know, for instance, that in season six we wanted to explore that post-collegiate, toxic taste of adulthood where you kind of try all of the bad stuff to see if that's you. I mean the darkness and the nastiness was definitely a reflection of our own fatigue and we didn't feel the need to be quite as fanciful. We'd done that.

Although some viewers found their escape in identifying with Buffy's attempts to regain her difficult balance in a hellish world after being torn away from heavenly peace, and others reveled in seeing Spike and Buffy tear various places apart with passion, vocal numbers were not pleased with the story as it unfolded.

Similarly, Season Seven disturbed some viewers' expectations as they watched from the real-world context of the period leading up to and following the U.S.–UK invasion of Iraq. Helen Graham argues that "in this new context *Buffy*'s once polysemic representational cycle was shifted, creating explicit, and unpleasurable, ideological signification.... Buffy's fighting and rhetoric start to signify ideologically as a result of the newly felt 'real contradiction' between leadership and democracy." An alternative perspective on this question is Chambers and Williford's "Anti-Imperialism in the Buffyverse: Challenging the Mythos of Bush as Vampire Slayer," which argues that the moral world-view of *BtVS* turns out to be more "sophisticated" than the "mythos of Bush as vampire-killer" in which "the horror of 9/11 and its complex history is reduced to a stock horror story where paladins arrayed in white defend American life from soulless parasites shrouded in black" (par. 38).

Although scholars of popular culture certainly began taking good hard looks at *Buffy* early in the show's history — Susan A. Owen published "Vampires, Postmodernity, and Postfeminism: *Buffy the Vampire Slayer*" in the *Journal of Popular Film and Television* in 1999, and a University of Toronto Ph.D. dissertation was registered in 2000 (Byers) — "*Buffy* studies" or "buffyology" may be said to have coalesced as a specific focus within pop-culture studies with the debut of *Slayage: The Online International Journal of Buffy Studies* in January 2001 (coinciding with the last half of Season Five), the 2002 publication of *Fighting the Forces: What's at Stake in Buffy the*

Vampire Slayer (edited by Rhonda Wilcox and David Lavery), and the first international scholarly conference devoted to *Buffy*, "Blood, Text and Fears" at the University of East Anglia, in October 2002. Initially planned as a one-day local event, BT&F made headlines when organizers received more than 100 paper proposals from the UK, USA, Europe, and Australia, and were obliged to expand to two days for sixty presentations. The academic interest in *Buffy*— and *Angel* and *Firefly*— which followed these events may be related to their coinciding with the controversial UPN seasons of *Buffy*.

We wish this collection could cover every issue that set fans, scholars, and media pundits at sixes and sevens in *Buffy*'s final two seasons. But, of course, that is impossible. Readers interested in additional analysis of *Buffy*'s UPN years may wish to refer to *Slayage* for Claire Fossey's "Never Hurt the Feelings of a Brutal Killer: Spike and the Underground Man," Richard S. Albright's " '[B]reakaway pop hit or book number?': 'Once More, with Feeling' and Genre," Caroline Ruddell's " 'I am the law' 'I am the magics': Speech, Power, and the Split Identity of Willow," Angie Burns's "Passion, Pain and 'bad kissing decisions': Learning about Intimate Relationships from *Buffy* Season Six," Elizabeth Rambo's " 'Lessons' for Season Seven," James South's "On the Philosophical Consistency of Season Seven," and Arwen Spicer's " 'It's Bloody Brilliant!' The Undermining of Metanarrative Feminism in the Season Seven Arc Narrative." When Joss Whedon heard about the "Blood, Text and Fears" conference, and noticed that it included papers about Season Six, he said, "I'm psyched, because [Season Six] is the bastard child that everyone's mean to. We had a purpose. And for people to take it seriously and not just to say, 'That season was depressing and the villains were nerds,' makes me feel good" ("Buffy 101"). We take Season Six and Season Seven seriously, and hope this book will encourage more thoughtful consideration of *Buffy*'s dark seasons. As Thomas Hibbs says, " '*Buffy the Vampire Slayer* saved TV, a lot'" and she's not done yet. In 2007, *Time* Magazine named *BtVS* among its Top 100 television shows of all time, and Marc Berman of *Media Week* noted that college students named *Buffy* as the show they miss most. The Dark Horse "Season 8" comics have been amazingly successful. So the only question is, "Where do we go from here?"

Works Cited

"The 100 Best TV Shows of All-TIME." *Time*, 7 Sept. 2007. 12 Sept. 2007. http://www.time.com/time/specials/2007/completelist/0,,1651341,00.html.

Albright, Richard S. "'[B]reakaway pop hit or book number?': 'Once More, with Feeling' and Genre." *Slayage: The Online International Journal of Buffy Studies* 5.1 (June 2005). 30 July 2007. http://www.slayageonline.com/Numbers/slayage17.htm.

Berman, Marc. "The Programming Insider." *Media Week*, 7 Sept. 2007. 12 Sept. 2007. http://www.mediaweek.com/mw/search/article_display.jsp?vnu_content_id=1003636739.

Bozell, L. Brent, III. "'Buffy': Call It Irresponsible." Cybercast News Service CNSNEWS.com. 13 Feb. 2002. 30 July 2007. http://www.cnsnews.com/bozell column/archive/2002/col20020213.asp.

"Buffy 101: Slaying Gets Serious." *TV Guide*, 19–25 Oct. 2002. 6–7.

"The Bunker of Debunking." BTVS-Tabula Rasa, 18 Feb. 2002. 30 July 2007. http://www.btvs-tabularasa.net/faq/bunker/index.html.

Burns, Angie. "Passion, Pain and 'Bad Kissing Decisions': Learning about Intimate Relationships from *Buffy* Season Six." *Slayage: The Online International Journal of Buffy Studies* 6.1, August 2006. 30 July 2007. http://www.slayageonline.com/Numbers/slayage21.htm.

Byers, Michelle. "'Buffy the Vampire Slayer': The Insurgence of Television as a Performance Text." *Dissertation Abstracts International—Section A (DAIA)* 61.11, May 2001.

Chambers, Samuel A., and Daniel Williford. "Anti-imperialism in the Buffyverse: Challenging the Mythos of Bush as Vampire Slayer." *POROI: An Interdisciplinary Journal of Rhetorical Analysis and Invention* 3.2, December 2004. 30 July 2007. http://inpress.lib.uiowa.edu/poroi/papers/chambers041001_outline.html.

Fossey, Claire. "Never Hurt the Feelings of a Brutal Killer: Spike and the Underground Man." *Slayage: The Online International Journal of Buffy Studies* 2.4, March 2003. 30 July 2007. http://www.slayageonline.com/Numbers/slayage8.htm.

Graham, Helen. "Post-pleasure: Representations, Ideologies and Affects of a Newly-Post 9/11 'Feminist' Icon." *Feminist Media Studies* 7.1, March 2007: 1–15. *Communication & Mass Media Complete*. EbscoHost. Campbell University, Carrie Rich Memorial Library. 30 July 2007. http://web.ebscohost.com.

Graham, Paula. "Buffy Wars: The Next Generation." *Rhizomes: Cultural Studies Emerging* 4 (2002). 30 July 2007. http://www.rhizomes.net/issue4/graham.html.

Hibbs, Thomas. "Forget about the World ... *Buffy* Saved TV." *National Review Online*, 22 May 2003. 30 July 2007. http://www.nationalreview.com/comment/comment-hibbs052203.asp.

McConnell, Kathleen. "Chaos at the Mouth of Hell: Why the Columbine High School Massacre Had Repercussions for *Buffy the Vampire Slayer*." *Gothic Studies* 2.1, April 2000: 119–35. *MLA International Bibliography/Academic Search Premier*. EbscoHost. Campbell University, Carrie Rich Memorial Library. 30 July 2007. http://search.ebscohost.com.

Noxon, Marti. Interviewed by "Jackal." Stakes and Salvation: A Complete Encyclopedia to the Buffyverse 11 Sept. 2007. 12 Sept. 2007 http://www.stakesandsalvation.com/2007/09/interview-with-marti-noxon.html.

Nussbaum, Emily. "Sick of 'Buffy' Cultists? You Ain't Seen Nothing Yet." *New York Times*, 8 Jun 2003, late edition (East Coast): 2.24. Proquest. Campbell University, Carrie Rich Memorial Library. 30 July 2007. http://proquest.umi.com.

Owen, Susan A. "Vampires, Postmodernity, and Postfeminism: *Buffy the Vampire Slayer*." *Journal of Popular Film and Television* 27.2, Summer 1999: 24–31. *MLA International Bibliography/Academic Search Premier*. EbscoHost. Campbell University, Carrie Rich Memorial Library. 30 July 2007. http://search.ebscohost.com.

Petrie, Douglas. Interview. BBC — Cult — Buffy. 30 July 2007. http://www.bbc.co.uk/cult/buffy/interviews/petrie_clips/clip3.shtml.
Rambo, Elizabeth. "'Lessons' for Season Seven." *Slayage: The Online International Journal of Buffy Studies* 3.3–4, April 2004. 30 July 2007. http://www.slayageonline.com/Numbers/slayage11_12.htm.
Ruddell, Caroline. "'I am the law,' 'I am the magics': Speech, Power, and the Split Identity of Willow." *Slayage: The Online International Journal of Buffy Studies* 5.4, May 2006. 30 July 2007. http://www.slayageonline.com/Numbers/slayage20.htm.
Shaffer, Nancy, ed. "All Things Philosophical on *Buffy the Vampire Slayer* and *Angel the Series*." Existential Scoobies Web site. 1 June 2006. 30 July 2007. http://www.atpobtvs.com/existentialscoobies/.
South, James. "On the Philosophical Consistency of Season Seven." *Slayage: The Online International Journal of Buffy Studies* 4.3, December 2004. 30 July 2007. http://www.slayageonline.com/Numbers/slayage15.htm.
Spicer, Arwen. "'It's Bloody Brilliant!' The Undermining of Metanarrative Feminism in the Season Seven Arc Narrative." *Slayage: The Online International Journal of Buffy Studies* 4.3, December 2004. 30 July 2007. http://www.slayageonline.com/Numbers/slayage15.htm.
Whedon, Joss. Online posting. 23 May 2001. Bronze VIP Archive. 30 July 2007. http://www.cise.ufl.edu/cgi-bin/cgiwrap/hsiao/buffy/get-archive?date=20010523.
xita. "FAQ." The Kittens, the Witches and the Bad Wardrobe. 30 July 2007. http://thekittenboard.com/board/viewtopic.php?t=3674.
Zacharek, Stephanie. "Willow, Destroyer of Worlds." *Salon.com*. 22 May 2002. 30 July 2007. http://dir.salon.com/story/ent/tv/feature/2002/05/22/buffy/index.html?.

SECTION 1. AUTEURS
(WRITERS, DIRECTORS, PRODUCERS)

Marti Noxon:
Buffy's *Other Genius*

DAVID PERRY

Introduction

I clearly remember being very excited to hear the WB promo refer to "Joss Whedon's *Buffy the Vampire Slayer*" for the first time. Not only was I happy for Mr. Whedon's justly deserved accolade, but also I saw the incident as illustrative of the bigger picture in our film and television landscape. Much has been said and written about the maligned role of the screenwriter (Charlie Kaufman not withstanding) in feature film production; take David Kipen's *Schreiber Theory* as a recent example.[1] The successful writer gets a good paycheck and credits and awards, but not nearly as much as the stars or the director, and sometimes not as much as cinematographers or special effects artists. In television production the writer can fare much better. Certainly, the star still reigns, but often the chief writer of a TV series is also the creator and executive producer, and these are the artistic architects, the receivers of hefty paychecks, and the ones mentioned in the press. In short, on TV, the writer really can be a star. Steven Bochco, David Chase, David E. Kelley, Aaron Sorkin, and Chris Carter are just a few of the prominent writer-executive producers who have gained notoriety and success in recent years. And to this list we add Joss Whedon. However, as Roz Kaveney has pointed out, the writing for *Buffy* is a team effort, with Joss plotting out the season's arc and then helping writers pitch ideas and flesh out individual episodes (Kaveney, 3–4). "Hercules T. Strong"—who has for years offered news, reviews, and spoilers on the Buffyverse at aintitcoolnews.com — refers to the Mutant Enemy writing staff as Team Whedon. It was a promising proposition for the young screenwriter to be drafted by Team Whedon. We have seen staff writers like Jane Espenson, Tim Minear, Douglas Petrie, and David Fury rise through the ranks of Mutant Enemy from staff writer to story editor to associate producer to executive producer. Some of these mere writers have actually been allowed to direct an episode or two.

The first writer to begin this ascent, and the writer who would become Joss Whedon's right-hand *person* and Number Two, is Marti Noxon. It was during the second season of *Buffy* that the WB first started referring to "Joss Whedon's *Buffy the Vampire Slayer*," and it was also during Season Two that Marti's writing first appeared on *Buffy* and began having an immediate impact. Themes and imagery that would later be associated with her writing were evident from the outset.

This essay will focus on four basic aspects of Marti Noxon's contributions to *Buffy*. First, I will look at Marti's immediate impact in Season Two with her first episodes, "What's My Line, part 1 (co-written with Howard Gordon) and part 2," demonstrating that these are iconic episodes for several reasons. Second, I will explore the themes and imagery that Marti consistently brings to her work. Third, I will briefly address the scurrilous and unfounded accusations of Marti's alleged mishandling of the controversial sixth season. Finally, I will examine how Joss Whedon expressed his admiration for Marti Noxon by rewarding her with choice assignments.

Evidently there exists some animosity towards Marti, especially in the online community. "The love is intense, and the hate is intense" (Spicuzza) and Marti "has felt the heat" (Walton). Online critic Joe Steiff's concern over Season Seven is typical: "When Joss Whedon first turned over the [reins] to Marti Noxon a while ago ... I refrained from expressing my fears that a person credited with some of the series' most awkwardly written episodes would be calling the shots.... She has surpassed my worst fears." I find this somewhat amazing since it can be shown that her thematic concerns are, if not overriding, then certainly central to the overall thrust of the series. It can also be shown by virtue of her increasingly important and powerful role in the writing and production of the series that Joss Whedon holds her in high esteem. So to the Marti bashers I say, "Ha!"

Ground Zero: "What's My Line"

"What's My Line, parts 1 and 2," (2.09 and 2.10) are important episodes for a variety of reasons. First, this story sets a heightened level of melodrama and intensity that continue for the rest of Season Two and, frankly, for the rest of the series' run. Consider what has come before: Season One consists of twelve episodes, six of which can be considered stand-alone installments. While the recurring threat of The Master lends the season a sense of an arc, and an episode such as "Nightmares" (1.10) is anchored with the very serious theme of child abuse, the first season is largely episodic and fun. It is relatively easy to explain the series plot to a non-fan who is tuning in for the first time: Buffy's a vampire slayer, those are her friends, this is the Hellmouth, that's the main vampire, enjoy the show. The season finale ends on a positively toe-tapping note: The Master is defeated, the Scoobies bounce off to party, and Giles makes a joke. Season Two's first eight episodes largely split the difference between monster-of-the-week stories and the twin arcs of the threat from Spike and Dru and Buffy's growing relationship with Angel. With the "What's My Line" episodes, the complexity and dramatic intensity grow. The arc becomes more evident, as stand-alone episodes become more and more rare. After "What's My Line," there are three more stand-alone episodes in Season Two, only one in Season Three, and virtually none for the remainder of the series. Within the "What's My Line" episodes, enough plot development for half a season of many television series occurs. Buffy's longing for a normal life is exacerbated by the career fair at school. She also argues with Giles about her work ethic after updating him about the previous night's patrol. Buffy finds herself growing closer to Angel in two important scenes. First, in her bedroom, as they discuss their relationship and Buffy's fondness for ice skating, their attraction for each other is palpable. Second, at the skating rink after an attack, their embrace and kiss express a physicality and desire that will manifest itself quite dramatically later in the season. Similarly, a despairing Buffy sneaks into Angel's empty apartment and lies down in his bed, looking forward to passion and despair to come. Mirroring Buffy and Angel, Spike and Drusilla grow more kinky and menacing. Spike's frustration at his failure to deal effectively with Buffy causes him to recruit assassins to murder her. Spike's spell to cure Drusilla of her illness necessitates the torture and attempted ritual murder of Angel, a scene that foreshadows their vampire love triangle. All the while, Spike and Drusilla seem to grow more in love with each other. "What's My Line" features other season- and series-defining events. Oz and Willow finally meet at the career fair, survive an assassin's attack, and flirt over animal crackers. Xander and Cordelia snipe at each other constantly, make out in the Summers' basement while under attack from Worm Guy, argue some more, and then start kissing again. The concept of a second Slayer is introduced in the form of Kendra. Angel is caged by Kendra, and then tortured by Drusilla. Finally, unbeknownst to the Scoobies, Spike is merely critically injured rather than killed and Drusilla is returned to full strength. The rest of the season is set up by "What's My Line," as is at least the next several seasons. The importance of "What's My Line" lies not in mere plot points, but in the intensity of the emotions felt by the characters and, by extension, the audience. *Buffy* is not a show that its fans simply watch; it inspires obsession. Fans fall in love with the show, and they fall in love with the characters. If Joss Whedon succeeded in his "master plan ... to create an icon" (Noxon, quoted in Walton), significant credit goes to Marti Noxon's writing in the "What's My Line" episodes, among others.

These episodes do not deal with entirely new ideas and themes, but they deal with familiar ideas and themes with much stronger consequences for our beloved characters. Prior to these episodes, Buffy felt an attraction to Angel; they dated but she was somewhat tentative about what to do next. Now, as Hillary Leon has noted, Angel and Buffy are "giving in to their passions" (par. 26). She loves him, and she will defend him at all costs. Before "What's My Line," Spike and Drusilla were the new vamps in town and they had to be stopped. Now, Spike and Drusilla are Buffy's mortal enemies trying to kill her and hers by any means necessary. The remainder of Season Two is anchored by "What's My Line" and two other iconic two-part episodes: "Surprise" (2.13, also by Noxon) and "Innocence" (2.14, by Joss Whedon) and "Becoming, parts 1 and 2" (2.21 and 2.22, by Joss Whedon). Again, consider the Season One finale, and compare it to the Season Two slugfest. Sweet relief, jokes, and skipping off to the Bronze versus this litany of disaster: Willow is in a wheelchair, Xander's arm is broken, Giles has been tortured, Kendra is dead, Spike and Dru have escaped, Buffy has outed herself to her mom to disastrous results, Buffy has stabbed Angel and sent him to hell, and Buffy has left town without telling her friends what's going on. She saved the world again, but that seems like a small consolation. This dire season finale, set in motion in large part by Noxon's "What's My Line," sets the tone for all seasons and season finales to come. In the second half of Season Two, after "What's My Line," *BtVS* is no longer simple to synopsize. It is not an easy entry show; however, it is an even more engrossing and enriching viewing experience than before.

Themes: Dangerous Love

Marti Noxon is credited by other Mutant Enemy writers for being the passionate and pained heart of the show and for capturing the sometimes deliberately cruel aspects of love (Spicuzza). Marti explores these ideas repeatedly in episode after episode. In "What's My Line" Angel and Buffy grow much closer. Xander and Cordelia pounce on each other, and Oz and Willow begin their courtship. However, all three couples are directly threatened by Spike and Dru's malevolent desires. Angel's taunting of Spike while suffering Dru's torture hints at the tense vamp love triangle to come. In 2.13, "Surprise," The Judge contemptuously points out Spike and Dru's undemonlike affection for each other. Buffy and Angel's love swells more with each new attack, until they finally, and tragically, consummate their love and banish Angel's soul. Marti's take on Valentine's Day is scathing and blackly hilarious in 2.16, "Bewitched, Bothered, and Bewildered." Giles frosts Jenny Calendar when she attempts reconciliation. Angel taunts Buffy with flowers and a menacing note. An anxious Xander is crushed by Cordelia's Valentine's kiss-off, and he resorts to blackmailing Amy the witch for a love spell. When the spell misfires and causes all the women of Sunnydale to pathologically desire him, Xander's dilemma is the nightmare vision of getting what every teen boy thinks he wants. "I Only Have Eyes For You" (2.19) expresses Marti's idea that young love is doomed to fail ("You"), and it mirrors "Beauty and The Beasts" (3.4) in its exploration of the horrific violence often inflicted by males on the ones they claim to love. Marti has stated, "The connection between sex and violence lies for me in our basic animal nature" ("You"). This concept is played out dramatically in "Wild at Heart" (4.6) as Oz's lycanthropy is spun out of control by fellow werewolf Veruca's amorous advances. A suspicious Willow discovers them sleeping together and is distraught. When Oz decides to leave Sunnydale, she is positively devastated, illustrating once again that, as fellow Mutant Enemy writer Jane Espenson says, "Marti writes the best heartbreak scenes ever" (Dumars). In "New Moon Rising" (4.19), Willow's return to happiness, enriched by her growing relationship with Tara, is shattered by Oz's return. When Oz smells Willow's scent on Tara, he loses his new-found control and goes all wolfy. The Initiative bags him, but thanks to Riley's final break with his bosses, Oz is released so he can leave Willow to her bliss with Tara. It is worth noting that Alyson Hannigan's performance in these Oz break-up episodes is exceptionally moving. Ian Shuttleworth comments, "As an actress she is a perfect interpreter in particular of the bare emotional directness which is the specialty of writer Marti Noxon" (242). In 5.1 "Buffy vs. Dracula," Buffy comes face to face with classic embodiment of the erotic love–dangerous love dichotomy. Also, Buffy continues to come to terms with the darkness that resides within her as well as the recurring darkness in men to which she is so often attracted. This Noxon episode, which opens Season Five, also launches Buffy and Riley's drifting apart, which culminates in 5.10, "Into the Woods." Buffy catches Riley whoring around with his crack vamp, this scenario an obvious yet dead-on metaphor for men dallying with hookers or strippers. Buffy is too late to stop Riley from leaving town with the military, and Marti Noxon has yet again broken Buffy's heart. Other episodes continue this tradition of frustration and angst: "The Wish" (3.9) is the direct result of Cordelia's disgust with Xander and his interlude with Willow; in 3.15, "Consequences," Xander reveals that he's slept with Faith, which leaves Willow crying in the bathroom; in 3.20, "The Prom," Angel finally breaks it off with Buffy, who then collapses, wracked with sobs, in Willow's arms; and in "Wrecked" (6.10) and "Villains" (6.20), Willow's disastrous abuse of dark majick is her reaction to her break-up with and, later, to the death of Tara. In fact, all of Season Six can be seen as the culmination of Marti Noxon's idea that "Sunnydale romance just rarely goes well" ("Online Chat").

Themes: S & M

Joss Whedon calls Marti Noxon the "pain and chains girl" (quoted in Spicuzza). He has credited her with introducing an S& M element to the show (Noxon, "You"). A brief overview of some of her scripts reveals Marti's need to not only break your heart but to beat your ass. "What's My Line" features Angel being caged by Kendra and strung up and tortured by Drusilla. Then, Spike ties Angel and Drusilla each and stabs their hands together with the du Lac Cross in the ceremony to heal Dru. Deborah Thomas argues persuasively that Noxon's "concern with the relationship between love and pain — and their thematic links with issues around trust and power — is so integral to the series as a whole that it is extremely unlikely that this is simply a maverick interest of her own with no substantial connection to the concerns of other series collaborators" (226). In 2.16, "Bewitched, Bothered, and Bewildered," Willow tells Xander that "force is okay" before biting his ear. Buffy tries to seduce Xander wearing nothing but a leather jacket. As the botched spell tightens its grip, Xander and Cordelia are almost torn to pieces by the murderously amorous mob. In 3.15, "Consequences," Faith pushes Xander onto her bed. Instead of merely boinking him (as she did in 3.13, "The Zeppo"), Faith chokes him, and she seems to enjoy it until Angel knocks her out. When she comes to, Angel has Faith chained up at his place. Before long, Wesley shows up with some Watcher's Council heavies who subdue Angel and cart Faith off in — yes, you guessed it — chains. In 4.6, "Wild at Heart," Willow wears leather pants in an attempt to turn Oz on. Oz cages himself, turns into a wolf, breaks out, has wild wolf sex with Veruca that leaves scars all over each of them, and then they have more wild scarring wolf sex ... in a cage. In 6.10, "Wrecked," Willow's addiction to Rack's services is an obvious metaphor for drug dependence. However, the way he enjoys toying with Amy and Willow is the very image of kinky, domineering sex, especially when Rack tells Willow she "tastes like strawberries." In 6.20, "Villains," Willow transforms herself into the ultimate image of a world-destroying bondage queen, ties up Warren, and skins him. No other single episode embodies Marti Noxon's sadomasochistic vision like "The Wish" (3.9) Vamp Xander co-opts Spike's punk-leather look, and Vamp Willow's goth dominatrix is bored, cruel, and really hot. The Bronze is now the vampire lair where victims-to-be are tied to pool tables and suspended in more cages. Vamp Willow begs the Master to let her "play with the puppy." Of course, "the puppy" is Angel, who is chained up in a cage and still wounded from his last torture session. Vamp Willow teases him before preparing to burn him with some matches, while Vamp Xander strokes the bars of the cell and just watches. If vampirism is a metaphor for erotic love, then what is to be made of the Master's industrial blood removal machine? Perhaps it is the ultimate vampire sex toy.

Season Six

The only thing that can top "The Wish" for raw kink is the entirety of Season Six. Marti Noxon was the chief day-to-day executive producer for this season because Joss Whedon was busy launching *Firefly*. Her dark touch can be seen in everything from Spike and Buffy's raw and destructive sexual encounters to Willow's addiction to magic, from The Nerds of Doom murdering Warren's ex-girlfriend to the literal ripping to pieces of the Buffybot. Season Six also contains perhaps the most disturbing and divisive incident in the Buffyverse: Spike's attempted rape of Buffy. Evidently the online debates among Bronzers about this scene were quite heated ("Fandom II"). Some fans have speculated (not always intending praise) that Noxon drew on some autobiographical elements in creating this scene, but the only definite support for such speculation is what Noxon herself has said: "I had a pretty dark past myself. As a teenager, I was pretty self-destructive. Thank God, I came through that. But I do think the dark part of my personality is where my creativity comes from" (Dumars). This season is dirty and it is disturbing, and it is consistently dark in its outlook on virtually every front. This resulted, at least initially, in many fans claiming to dislike the Sixth Season and to resent Marti's alleged mishandling thereof. Among many other things, *BtVS* has always been about passion getting out of control, dealing with the consequences of one's actions, and acknowledging one's own darker impulses. It is also worth noting that prior to Season Six, most of the characters' romantic motives were relatively upstanding: Buffy and Angel obviously really do love each other, but so do Xander and Cordelia, Giles and Jenny, Willow and Oz, Willow and Tara, Xander and Anya, Spike and Drusilla: everyone's in it for the allegedly right reasons. As the characters grow into their twenties, it makes sense that some of them will hook up for the wrong reasons. Marti has pointed out that Season Six was largely plotted out by the staff, with Joss Whedon, at the end of Season Five. She has also stated that he was still "very involved in the story breaking; he just won't walk away" (quoted in Blumberg and Ferrante, part 2). Obviously, if one sees Season Six as a failure, the blame cannot be placed solely on Marti.

Assignments

Joss Whedon's reliance on Marti Noxon's expertise is illustrated in the choice writing assignments her gives her. When Joss writes or directs an episode, it is usually a special event. It's a tough act to follow and you would want your top person for the job. The most telling instance of this occurs with "Forever" (5.17), which Marti not only wrote but also directed. "Forever" also immediately follows "The Body" (5.16), a pivotal episode for Season Five and in many ways for the entire series, and an episode we know is very important to Joss Whedon, from interviews and his DVD commentary on it. Certainly, he would want the episode that followed it to be strong as well. Both "Living Conditions" (4.2) and "Dead Man's Party" (3.2) are the next episodes after Joss had written and directed the season premieres. "Dead Man's Party" is also an interesting assignment because it is the "Night of the Living Dead" episode. As a genre show, *BtVS* has tackled many of the "classic" monsters — the Gill Men in "Go Fish" (2.20), Adam as Frankenstein's monster, "Inca Mummy Girl" (2.4) — and it is not unlikely that getting to write one of these episodes would be a somewhat coveted task. Getting to write an actual Dracula episode in a series titled *Buffy the Vampire Slayer* is obviously a reward and a challenge, and it was also a season premiere. "Beauty and the Beasts" (3.4) can be seen as a Jekyll and Hyde episode, and with "Wild at Heart" (4.6) and "New Moon Rising" (4.19), Marti addresses the Wolf Man. In that latter episode, Willow comes out to Buffy, and this is revealed to be a personal issue with Marti because she has stated that her own mother is in fact gay (Mangels). Many other choice assignments occur in Marti's resume: in "Surprise" (2.13) Buffy and Angel sleep together, it's part one of a hugely important two-part episode, and it was the last episode to air on Mondays; Joss Whedon's commentary on "Innocence" (2.14) notes "the idea of love and torture and pain and power — and bondage — and all of these things working together in the minds of these people. Marti really brought a lot of cool, twisted sexuality to the characters that fit really well" (quoted in Thomas, 227). "Bewitched, Bothered, and Bewildered" (2.16) is a very special Buffy Valentine's episode; "I Only Have Eyes For You" (2.19) was the first episode of May sweeps in Season Two; and "Into The Woods" (5.10), written and directed by Marti, is not only Riley's exit but also the first instance of a Mutant Enemy writer other than Joss stepping into the director's role.

Two additional, valuable contributions by Marti Noxon to the general success of Buffy must be noted: In "The Wish" (3.9) she created the character of Anya (Emma Caulfield) who becomes increasingly significant to the ensemble from Season Four onward; and she was responsible for casting Amber Benson as Tara (Whedon, "Hush"). I'll conclude with this last fact: in the last seasons of Buffy, when an episode's last scene cuts to black, the credits read: Executive Producers ... Joss Whedon and Marti Noxon.

Notes

1. Kipen's thesis is that the film-studies auteur theory gives too much credit to directors for the success of their movies. Instead, he says, in many cases, we should give more credit to the script-writer, the schreiber.

Works Cited

Blumberg, Arnold T., and Anthony C. Ferrante. "Marti the Vampire Producer, part 2." *Mania: Beyond Entertainment*, 12 March 2002. 10 May 2007. http://www.mania.com/33389.html.
Dumars, Denise. "Heartbreaker: *Buffy* Writer Marti Noxon." *Mania: Beyond Entertainment*, 2 May 2000. 10 May 2007. http://www.mania.com/20918.html.

"Fandom II: The Bronze." Session 4C. SC1: The Slayage Conference on *Buffy the Vampire Slayer*. Middle Tennessee State University. Nashville, Tennessee, 28–30 May 2004.

Kaveney, Roz. "'She Saved the World, A Lot': An Introduction to the Themes and Structures of Buffy and Angel." In *Reading the Vampire Slayer: The New, Updated, Unofficial Guide to Buffy and Angel*, Roz Kaveney, ed. New York: Tauris Parke, 2004. 1–82.

Kipen, David. *The Schreiber Theory: A Radical Rewrite of American Film History*. Hoboken, NJ: Melville House Publishing, 2006.

Leon, Hillary M. "Why We Love Monsters: How Anita Blake, Vampire Hunter, and Buffy the Vampire Slayer Wound Up Dating the Enemy." *Slayage, The Online International Journal of Buffy Studies* 1.1 (January 2001). 10 November 2006. http://www.slayageonline.com.

Mangels, Andy. "'Nasty' Noxon." *Dreamwatch* 90 (March 2002). 10 November 2006. http://fanficcafe.ifrance.com/interview/interview.html.

Noxon, Marti. "Marti Noxon Online Chat." Buffy the Vampire Slayer in the UK on BBC2. October 2001. 10 November 2006. www.bbc.co.uk/cult/buffy/interviews/noxonchat.

_____. "You and ... Marti Noxon." 24 February 2000. *The Breakup Girl*. 10 November 2006. http://www.breakupgirl.net/guest/000224.html.

Shuttleworth, Ian "They Always Mistake Me For the Character I Play: Transformation, Identity and Role-Playing in the Buffyverse (and a Defence of Fine Acting)." In *Reading the Vampire Slayer: The New, Updated, Unofficial Guide to Buffy and Angel*, edited by Roz Kaveney. New York: Tauris Parke, 2004. 233–276.

Spicuzza, Mary. "The Lady and The Vamps." *ChosenTwo.com: The Grr in Grrl*. 10 November 2006. http://www.chosentwo.com/marti/.

Steiff, Joe. "Buffy the Vampire Slayer: The 2002/03 Season." *On The Box, Netfirms*. 3 November 2002. 10 November 2006. http://onthebox.netfirms.com/Articles/Buffy2002/Buffy2002.html.

Strong, Hercules T. "Coaxial News." *Ain't It Cool News*. 4 March 2001. 10 November 2006. http://www.aintitcool.com/node/8315.

Thomas, Deborah. "Reading Buffy." In *Close-Up 01*, edited by Ian Garwood and Douglas Pye. London: Wallflower Press, 2006. 167–244.

Walton, Andy. "Bye-bye, Buffy: Cult Hit Rides into Its Last Sunset." CNN.com. 28 February 2004. 12 July 2007. http://www.cnn.com/2003/SHOWBIZ/TV/05/19/buffy.finale.

Whedon, Joss. "Hush" Commentary. *Buffy the Vampire Slayer Season Four DVD Collection*. 20th Century–Fox, 2003.

_____. "The Body" Commentary. *Buffy the Vampire Slayer Season Five DVD Collection*. 20th Century–Fox, 2003.

Understanding the Espensode

David Kociemba

"Joss directs, but to me, no, I'm a writer. That's what I love best."
— Jane Espenson (Bratton)
"I have people with whom I trust my artistic *life*."
— Joss Whedon (Wilcox, 7)[1]

When we think of an artist, we think of a single mind expressing a personal vision by asserting control over the creative work of the craftspeople under the artist's direction. In film, we think of Alfred Hitchcock as the artist who made *Psycho* (1960). That can be an accurate description of the creative process when you're dealing with dominating directors like Hitchcock, especially when they become producers.

Under this approach, called auteurism, Jane Espenson could never be considered an artist in her own right. She'd be a craftsperson working under Joss Whedon's direction, and nothing more.

After all, Espenson has never created a series. The executive producer assigns her episodes. Espenson co-wrote several of her best episodes, although Joss Whedon wrote the clock tower scene between Jonathan and Buffy in "Earshot" (3.18). He came up with the idea for "Superstar" (4.17) and "Storyteller" (7.16) (which starred Jonathan and Andrew, respectively). Whedon even suggested kittens as the monsters' poker stakes in her "Life Serial"(6.5). For many series, most of the writing staff brainstorms the plot of each episode. Espenson doesn't have final say in the casting of actors and she has not directed an episode. She doesn't write the shooting draft version of the script, nor does she control the final edit of the episode. From concept to broadcast, there can be as many as nine different realizations of the original idea for the story; the fact that one of Espenson's monsters ended up looking like "an enormous penis" came as a surprise to her ("Jane Espenson: Succubus Club").

If Espenson is to be considered a worthwhile artist to study through the lens of auteur theory, the central question is whether she uses similar writing techniques and themes across the body of her writing on various series. If she demonstrates some internal consistency in her artistic choices over time and in working with different people and narratives, then such work shows that she imprints her worldview and artistic values on her scripts. So how is it that you know an Espensode when you see one?

Alternative Authorship

In *Why* Buffy *Matters*, Rhonda Wilcox argues that some cases merit using a different model of authorship:

> For years now, when I have thought of the art of a television series, I have thought of the master builder of a cathedral and his workers: a cathedral is a creation which is certainly accepted as art, but which was worked on by many differing people over many years ... *Buffy* itself ... has taught me to envision the interaction in a much livelier and less one-way, top-down fashion [5–6].

The creative process can be marked by more than just a dynamic of control and ownership; it can include influence and sharing, too. The artisans can influence the designer such that the values and choices of the artisans leave traces on the final work. They become artists in their own right. This obsessive focus on the artist-hero's rallying of the artisan-minions to eventual victory against the network barbarians and the forces of middlebrow culture misses one of the traits that made them artist-heroes in the first place: the ability to follow as well as lead. It's best to think of creators like Joss Whedon as catalysts to other artists' creations as well as creators in their own right. They are both a muse and an artist.

In short, what defines a series like *Buffy the Vampire Slayer* is not just the big moments in narrative arcs that are most directly tied to individual creators like Joss Whedon. A series is also defined by how it gets to the end of those narrative arcs: by its dialogue, its voices, and its tone. And that's where Jane Espenson shines.

There are several places where Espenson carves out some artistic autonomy and influences others in the creative process. While she does not control what episodes she writes or how they're shot and edited, that does not mean that she does not have influence over how her ideas are realized. Starting with Season Five, Espenson wrote a preliminary set of notes on the edit of her episodes, provided non-technical guidance to the director about how she pictured a scene, and she sat in on the casting sessions, which she had done on other shows prior to *BtVS* (Bratton).

Espenson indirectly influences what episodes she writes on *BtVS* and elsewhere through her track record as a writer. By Season Six, for example, Espenson was third in the writing rotation behind Marti Noxon and David Fury for the episode "Afterlife" (6.3). Because Fury and Doug Petrie also wanted to write a comic episode that season, she wrote "Afterlife" (6.3), which became her first completely non-zany episode ("Jane Espenson: Succubus Club"). She then co-wrote the more comic episodes "Flooded" (6.4) with Petrie and "Life Serial" (6.5) with Fury. Her early success with "Band Candy" (3.6) may explain why she was assigned so many episodes featuring doppelgangers and shadow selves, ranging from the teen versions of the adults in "Band Candy," the monstrous exterior of Giles in "A New Man" (4.12), and Xander's halved selves in "The Replacement" (5.3), to fakes like the Buffybot in "Intervention" (5.18) and Wesley's impersonation of Angel in "Guise Will Be Guise" (*Angel* 2.6) to the fan-fic alternate representations of the Buffyverse in "Superstar" (4.17) and "Storyteller"(7.16). [2] Her writing outside of the Buffyverse, however, does not continue to explore this vein.

Espenson's choice to work on these series at all best illustrates her values as a writer. She wrote of going to *BtVS* from *Ellen*, "I was widely told not to make the jump, that I'd be starting over on the drama side, that I'd lose all the status I'd established in comedy. But I did it anyway, and haven't looked back" (Strong). Espenson made the jump not just because she admired *BtVS* but also because she was less suited to the writing process behind comedies than dramas:

> I don't think it fits my skills very well.... I am much funnier on the page than I am in person. The way a traditional sit-com is run, you have to say your jokes out loud in a room full of people and that's where my non-acting personality hinders me a little bit, [laughs], because I'm a little too shy. And I find it very hard to think when there's 11 other people shouting out their jokes. It's just not a system that allows me to work at my best [Bratton].

The process behind writing TV drama is not only a better fit to her personality; it also provides more autonomy to the writer. Episodes on a sitcom are communally authored. Espenson, who got her start with the sitcom *Dinosaurs*, says,

> Every line is evaluated as a group, and most jokes get rewritten.... Drama writing is much more of an individual pursuit, and often the show runner is the only one who changes your lines. Some drama shows don't even have a writers'

room at all — the writers rarely or never assemble to discuss stories together.... When a change is mandated, the writer goes home (or to her office) and makes the change herself [*Jane in Progress*, 10 September 2006].

Espenson forges a middle path. The communal laying out of the act breaks and scenes in each episode on *BtVS* and the debates around major plot points gives writers the sense of collective series ownership that marks the creation of the comedy. This sense of collective ownership must have some appeal for Espenson, who collaborated on eight of her 25 episodes for *Angel* and *BtVS*. With "Earshot" (3.18) she sets up Joss Whedon's moving clock tower scene between Jonathan and Buffy nicely. Her "kitten poker" and Magic Box storylines blend with David Fury's work in "Life Serial" (6.05). Wilcox writes that "it is not just the talent of each individual that matters here, but the synergy invoked by the central figure — Joss Whedon. And one can imagine it growing — The more good people were working well, the more good people would want to join in" (7–8). One defining trait of Espenson's artistry is that she makes this kind of virtuous circle possible.

Yet, Espenson has said that the key to such collaboration is that "we've all learned to write in the same style" and that "the best shows on TV are usually those in which the original voice of the show's creator is allowed to shine through with minimal interference" ("Jane Espenson: The Writing Process"; "*Jane in Progress*," 27 February 2006). Her facility with writing secondary characters (like Jonathan, Andrew, Anya, and Spike on *BtVS*, Kaylee on *Firefly*, or Kat on *Battlestar Galactica*) maximizes her influence in *creating* voices in the series. Her skill in writing them expands their role in the narrative, affecting the arc of the series indirectly. Espenson needed Whedon to become the well-rounded writer she is, but Whedon needed writers like Espenson to craft series with such complexly rendered ensembles.

This skill was not limited to her time on Whedon's three series. Espenson shares writing credit on more than half of the episodes she has written since working with Whedon, ranging in genre from three sci-fi and fantasy shows to a police procedural to an animated series to a sitcom to three relationship melodramas. Espenson seeks out these opportunities ("Jane Espenson: Succubus Club"). In an auteurist approach, such frequent collaboration may raise suspicions of insufficient independence and power. Here, it's one of her defining traits as a writer.

Espenson retains a distinctive voice while enabling others to put their voices to best use. She values the greater autonomy often afforded by dramatic television. She left *Gilmore Girls* for *Tru Calling* after just one season, despite adoring the staff and citing series creator Amy Sherman Palladino as an important influence on her writing. Palladino's system, however, broke stories in great detail. "It is a system," Espenson says, "that emphasizes using the writers heavily for story construction and less for writing of dialogue. I found that I missed the writing" (Jozic). The system on *Gilmore Girls* ran against one of Espenson's strengths as a writer: her facility at capturing the voice of the character through her attention to their distinctive rhythms and word choices. Espenson elaborates on the importance of having autonomy in writing the draft:

> People outside the writing process are sometimes disappointed to learn that we are following a detailed outline. They feel that there can be little creative work left to do in the actual writing, but this is not the case. This is, in fact, the most exciting and freeing part of the process ... every word spoken, every punch thrown, is spelled out by the writer at this stage. For me, this, more than during filming, is when the episode actually becomes *real* ["Jane Espenson: The Writing Process"].

Even when a script is co-written, writers typically split the script by act or by storyline rather than write each scene together. When she and Doug Petrie didn't split the script for "Flooded" (6.4), "both of us would throw out all the other person's stuff and write our own version. And then the next person would get and throw out all the other person's stuff and rewrite" ("Jane Espenson: Succubus Chat").

Anatomy of the Espensode

If the Espensode is strictly a feature of Jane Espenson's work with Whedon, then she is simply an adept craftswoman. Fortunately, that is not the case. Espenson makes use of the following writing techniques in her scripts, independent of the series for which she writes:

(1) **Off-the-Nose Dialogue:** Espenson avoids having characters say exactly what they feel or precisely conveying information. She feels that such "on the nose" dialogue creates characters that are palpably constructed and shockingly self-aware. Espenson writes, "Characters who always grasp the situation instantly, who understand each other's most obscure questions and who follow each other's logical leaps aren't behaving like the rest of us do" (*Jane in Progress*, 15 December 2006). Worse, they're lacking in vulnerability. To craft sympathetically flawed characters, she'll have them hesitate or trail off, use embarrassed over-or understatement, anticipate other characters, and interrupt themselves. "I love this trick. It's easy and

efficient. It reveals character without a bunch of words.... But only use it when a character is REALIZING something, because that's when they're distracted, when their censor is not engaged, when things can slip out" (*Jane in Progress*, 23 February 2006").

(2) **The Blurt**: Off-the-nose dialogue often sets up a blurt of true feeling in Espenson's scripts. In her blog, "Jane in Progress," Espenson observes "people get inarticulate when they have to tell the truth. I don't mean all truths. I mean here the kind of truth that either makes the speaker vulnerable, like a proclamation of love, or the kind that has the potential to hurt the listener" (*Jane in Progress*, 3 October 2006). An example of this dynamic can be found in her *Tru Calling* episode, "In the Dark," when she has Davis confess to a woman that he's attracted to that "I think that maybe I, I, I could help you." Doesn't that sound like Giles? Here, the truth is painful not only because his expressing his feelings for her makes him vulnerable, but also because revealing how he knows she needs help might reveal Tru's secret. (Tru has the power to relive days to prevent unjust deaths.) Knowledge of the existence of the supernatural might scare or endanger this woman. Espenson observes "one natural reaction to suddenly finding oneself inarticulate is to push too hard to get through it. And then you get the blurt. Also effective, and also all wrapped up with the truth. You don't blurt a lie" (*Jane in Progress*, October 2006).

(3) **Acing the Written**: Despite her use of imprecision in her dialogue, overly precise dialogue is another feature of the Espensode. One manifestation is her affection for puns. "Punny writing has been called 'Espensonian,' which just makes [me] giggle with delight," Espenson writes. "That kind of thing is inevitable as you get to know the writing preferences of people you spend long hours with" (*Jane in Progress*, 6 April 2006). Just a few of her more notable puns will indicate her taste. In "Life Serial" (6.5), Jonathan begs his fellow nerds to please stop touching his "magic bone." His unknowing use of language contrasts nicely with Espenson's very knowing use of same. More of her puns are of the intentional brand. In the *Gilmore Girls* episode she co-wrote with Amy Sherman Palladino, "Chicken or Beef," Lorelai has to deal with an overly sensitive motion detector alarm that she can't turn off. So she creates a path on the floor with yellow markings that will enable her and Rory to avoid it, prompting Rory to ask, "So I should follow the yellow-stick road?" "We'll be here all week, ladies and gentlemen. Enjoy the veal," Lorelai replied.

Espenson's comic use of overly precise language was not restricted to punning. Anya was the queen of using "written" dialogue. Here she is, pointing out the fact that she is jealous: "Observe my bitter ranting! Hear the shrill edge of hysteria in my voice!" This is not naturalistic speech. This character was distinguished by her ability to produce dialogue like this. And that in itself is the joke — the notion that anyone would speak like that (*Jane in Progress*, 9 May 2006).

Of course, Espenson once remarked, "Anya, for example, usually says what I would say in any situation" ("Carl"). And Espenson has also stated, "I hate causing confusion" ("Popgurls.com: Interviews"). Espenson has Kaylee "ace the written" in her *Firefly* episode "Shindig" when she wins over a crowd of suitors at a ball by nattering on about the relative merits of various spaceship engines. This moment is designed to produce Espenson's preferred result: a laugh of recognition grounded in the appreciation of character, not event. As she once observed, "If you can write people, you can write comedy" (*Jane in Progress*, 15 May 2006).

(4) **Analogies**: Espenson uses analogies as a basic tool in her comedy arsenal. Buffy remarks after a "Doublemeat Palace" training video that their burger's union of beef and chicken was like "*Sleepless in Seattle* if Tom and Meg were, like, minced" (6.12). She has Willow explore the symbolic militarism of marching bands in "Band Candy" (3.6) by musing that they are "Like an army. With music instead of bullets and usually no one dies." Espenson's exploration of the analogy here expresses Willow's immense intellect and voracious curiosity. These lines start out attempting to explain or make sense of the world, but the wayward logic of the simile forces the character to choose between being true to his or her witticism or to the subject of the observation. In short, these characters flirt with being writers with such observational comedy even while the writer emphasizes something about their character. In her blog, Espenson was surprised to discover at least one example in every one of her scripts. She explains, "I find it quite powerful. Comparisons, like pictures, are worth a thousand words. They're part of how we understand the world, by conceptualizing things in terms of other things" (*Jane in Progress*, 28 April 2006).

(5) **Repetition**: Callbacks reference an earlier joke. A runner is a series of nonadjacent callbacks that build off each other. These echoes make for a more complex structure, as the attentive viewer makes connections across scenes, acts, episodes, or even seasons. In "Afterlife," Anya bluntly asks if Buffy if she's a zombie (6.3). The humor's based in part on Buffy's withdrawn behavior and Anya's unique worldview. It's also a callback to prior comic episodes like "Dead Man's Party" (3.2) (zombies attack the Summers home) and "The Zeppo" (3.13) (Xander vs. the zombie gang). Espenson's joke (and Anya's question) gets its edge, however, from its call-

back to the deadly serious moments involving the unseen spirit of Joyce Summers brought back by Dawn in "Forever" (5.17). The question is both absurdly rude and perfectly valid. By momentarily revealing the underlying craft of the series, Espenson highlights the importance of play and active viewing in *BtVS*.

When characters repeat words in a single line of dialogue, however, their lack of verbal ability highlights the character's excitement, as in Espenson's "Shindig" episode of *Firefly*, an inexperienced suitor endearingly tells Inara, "I understand that your time on our planet is limited. And if you've selected my proposal to hear, then the honor that you do me flatters my... my honor."

Espenson puts callbacks, runners, and other forms of repetition to more complex use. One use is pure misdirection. In Espenson's episode of *Tru Calling*, "In the Dark," she uses a runner to distract the audience from the possibility of a surprise birthday party for Tru. The use of the joke as a distraction, however, is itself a red herring. The runner's real purpose is to hide the identity of the victim-to-be whom Tru must save by day's end, which is the maintenance man, who isn't at the party. Here's how it works. In the teaser to Espenson's *Tru Calling* episode, Tru (played by Eliza Dushku) talks about buying herself jewelry for her birthday. Her brother's remark that men never notice a woman's jewelry produces a playful sibling squabble. In the next scene, her female lab partner complements Tru on her new necklace, only to make the same observation as Tru's brother. Later, Tru passes a maintenance man, who complements her on her jade necklace. The momentary surprise disguises the inevitable "surprise" birthday party that immediately follows. Once the surprise birthday party scene occurs, the viewer thinks no more about the runner. It has served its purpose. In fact, its purpose really is to maintain the suspense of trying to identify which person is unjustly marked for death. The victim-to-be was the one person not at the party, whose presence in the episode seemingly was just to deliver the final joke in the runner about men's lack of appreciation for jewelry. Espenson nicked this technique from her time with *BtVS*: "We did this, at Joss's direction, in my *Buffy* episode "Earshot" (3.18). Xander made a joke, early on, about the ultimate identity of the would-be-killer, which turned out later to be correct. The fact that it was done as a joke was especially nice since audiences tend to dismiss jokes anyway. It kept the moment from calling too much attention to itself" (*Jane in Progress*, 17 May 2006).

Espenson grew more audacious in her use of repeated images since *BtVS*. In "Storyteller" (7.16), Andrew badly sings, "We are as gods!" four times in a ridiculous fantasy sequence featuring a unicorn, harps, togas, and seemingly the set of the *Teletubbies*. She then has Andrew briefly recall that same shot later. Espenson evidently believes that one recall of an absurd image is not nearly enough. She remarked on her blog, "Tell a joke once, it's funny. Twice, it's not funny. Eight times ... it gets funny again" (*Jane in Progress*, 7 August 2006). In the *Andy Barker, PI* episode that she co-wrote, "Fareway, My Lovely," Andy plays a round of golf with an obese client who runs a fast food chain, Doublemeat Industries — a reference to Buffy's place of work in Espenson's "Doublemeat Palace" (6.12) episode. This fat businessman dies of a heart attack during a footrace. Espenson returns to the slow-motion shot of this fat man running while waving his snack (a sub with "three kinds of ham") at least four more times in the half-hour episode.

(6) **The Two Percent Solution**: The fact that Doublemeat Palace actually sold meatless burgers — and not meat-stuffed subs — is an example of a specialized type of callback. Espenson calls it

> a two-percenter, [which] is a joke that the writers estimate will be understood and enjoyed by two percent of the audience. Sometimes the number cited varies, but the idea is the same, it means you're dealing with a fairly obscure reference. As an audience member, when you're part of the two percent that gets it, there's nothing better than this kind of joke because it feels like the writer is reaching into your own personal brain. In a good way [*Jane in Progress*, 3 December 2006].

Justine Larbalestier writes that *BtVS* "invites a specialized reading" in its use of reflexivity to communicate with its fandom, specifically citing Espenson's "Superstar" (4.17) as investigating the meaning of fandom (Larbalestier, 228). For Marianne Cantwell, such reflexive moments are one vital explanation for the intense connection between the authors and the audience of *BtVS*. The fact that "these references are not only made, but made without explanation and further played with, is an acknowledgement of the fans' own knowledge and awareness: Espenson plays *with* them" (Cantwell). The only people who would get the *Andy Barker* Doublemeat reference would be *BtVS* viewers, viewers who were most likely watching this sitcom about an accountant moonlighting as a detective because they were hoping for an Espensode.

Family Guy and *The Simpsons* are known for their referential comedy, too. An Espensode's references, however, are used differently. They tend to point inwards, fostering a greater appreciation of the series, the character, or her other episodes. Espenson writes,

> *Family Guy* does absolutely brilliant and hilarious things with these jokes....
> And yet, [they] are not my faves. They sound written, and they don't lend them-

selves very easily to exposing character or to forwarding the story. They're about an event separate from the events of the script, and they're about as spontaneous as the analogy section of the SAT [*Jane in Progress*, 18 May 2006].

Cantwell argues that Espenson's reflexive jokes in "Storyteller" (7.16) tacitly acknowledge the defects of Season Seven, a technique Espenson calls "hanging a lantern" on it (*Jane in Progress*, 25 December 2006). Cantwell argues that this technique restores faith in the series. Espenson's sense of humor forges a community among fans and between fans and the writers.

(7) **Clichés**: Espenson breathes new life into clichés by reversing the intent. Her example from *BtVS* is when Buffy remarks that a monster has "a face even a mother could hate." She likes to work with clichés because "it's a fun type of joke. Breezy, a little dry, kind of smart" (*Jane in Progress*, 19 April 2006). Alternatively, she'll take the common idiom and make it literal. She tended use these jokes to express Anya's hard-headed practicality and inexperience with finer human etiquette, as when she decides in "Harsh Light of Day" (4.3) that having sex with Xander will help her put him behind her: "Behind me, figuratively. I'm thinking face-to-face for the event itself."

(8) **Throw-Away Lines**: Aspiring writers are often taught to end their jokes on the funniest word to avoid having audience laughter mar the line. Espenson occasionally will take the pressure off the joke by having the line continue. She finds that it makes the exchange feel "more confident, less rimshotty, less desperate," especially as it allows the actor to casually toss out the joke (*Jane in Progress*, 29 April 2006). She uses this technique in "Rm w/ a Vu" in *Angel* to express Cordelia's surge of confidence at getting rid of the ghost haunting her perfect apartment: "This is easy! Little old lady ghost. Probably hanging around 'cause she thinks she left the iron on. Let's get us a nice cleansing spell and do this thing!" (*Angel* 1.5).

(9) **Crickets**: These jokes use the character's delayed or absent response as the punch line (*Jane in Progress*, 2 May 2006). Espenson tended not to use humor based on a delayed reaction until she wrote for *Firefly*. There, it was much more common either to end an act with a moment of stunned silence (such as when the camera holds on Inara's open-mouthed reaction when she realizes that Mal's fooled her into thinking that he's about to declare his love for her at the end of "Our Mrs. Reynolds") or to begin an act with one (such as the stunned speechless staring at the statue of Jayne in "Jaynestown"). Espenson adapted the technique, marrying it to some off-the-nose dialogue in her lone episode in the series, "Shindig." She has Mal, having just learned that the hateful fop Atherton has lured him into a formal duel with swords, express his shock at the weapon choice

by saying, "Use of a ... s'what?" The camera lingers on Mal frozen with his mouth agape for just a beat past the last line before cutting to commercial.

(10) **Put-downs:** Espenson prefers not to mock her characters. She commented, "We don't want to say mock so much because we don't make fun of the show or our characters, but we do sometimes go ... look at that funny thing" ("Jane Espenson: Succubus Club"). She does use them, however, to illustrate the tension between Anya and Willow. This use is especially prominent in "Afterlife" (6.3), when Anya acidly wonders why Willow didn't consider the possibility that Buffy might not "get over" her death or Xander's false optimism that a week is all that Buffy might need to recover from what he thought was a sojourn in Hell. Rather than just revealing something about the butt of the put-down, Espenson argues, "almost all of them are flashlights trained on the character that says them," too; namely, that Anya deals with her anxiety through joking aggression (*Jane in Progress*, 9 March 2006). Nor is this bitter sarcasm intended to be particularly funny. Espenson uses these jokes when characters are trying and failing to relieve their own tension, attempting to placate someone, or when they're engaged in self-loathing. She writes, "The interesting thing about these jokes is that they aren't funny. They look funny, and some part of your brain gives them credit for having joke content. What they convey is bravery and intelligence in the face of anger or pain or fear. They're endearing. Heart-crushing. But they're not funny. And they're great" (*Jane in Progress*, 16 October 2006).Espenson tries to use put-downs to foster understanding, not gall or hate.

(11) **Trait-Based Humor:** Espenson opposes comedy based on race or gender, arguing that "a joke that pokes fun at a person is sharpest, funniest, when it finds that perfect detail, the most subtle observation of what sets that person apart. Someone's race or gender is unlikely to be the most subtle thing about them, and certainly it's not the most specific" (*Jane in Progress*, 19 January 2006). Yet, in the *Andy Barker, PI* episode she co-wrote, the repeated slow-motion shot of the client's final sprint is based on the character's least subtle quality: his weight. Arguably, this runner is used to question Andy's (and the viewer's) assumptions about conventional standards of sexual appeal. Four other characters find the client attractive, even irresistible. When Andy observes that the client stinks, Andy's wife shoots back, "It's called pheromones!" Indeed, one of the client's lovers found his "boobs" central to the man's appeal. Espenson likes jokes that invert audience assumptions like this because "they presuppose an audience that's thinking, that's anticipating, that's involved in the stories they're being told. And if you

expect that, you're more likely to get that" (*Jane in Progress*, 23 May 2006). We're meant to laugh at Andy when he asks in the midst of combat if his assailant really found the client to be sexy. Moreover, the B-storyline involves Simon (played by Tony Hale, formerly of *Arrested Development*) relentlessly hitting on Andy's black secretary. The awfulness of his *Jungle Fever* jokes and his salacious use of a white and dark chocolate cookie, combined with her overt hostility, firmly make him the butt of this runner. It is difficult to say whether the "funny" is that everyone is so warped in their perception of the obese client's sex appeal or whether it is that Andy is so staid — or both. Perhaps Espenson moves the audience just a bit from bias to tolerance. After all, she's the one who had Clem say of Buffy, "Her skin's so tight, I don't even know how you can look at her" ("Life Serial," 6.5).

(12) Food: Espenson uses food and the rituals that build up around meals to reveal character, which should come as no surprise from a writer who ends every entry of her blog with a description of what she had for lunch. Her first episode for *BtVS* used "Band Candy" to regress the adults to their teen-aged state, allowing viewers to see Joyce desperately strive to be cool, Principal Snyder punk out, and Giles as a hooligan (3.6). Espenson gives viewers insight into why Principal Snyder is a humorless martinet. It makes his groveling for the Mayor's approval understandable and his final defiance at the Graduation Day massacre peculiarly redemptive. Seeing Joyce uncertainly try to hold a pose of knowing cool adds a new dimension to her dependence on parenting tapes to manage Buffy's various crises in the first season. It also explains Joyce's anger and confusion at the destruction of the "normal family" façade during "Becoming" (2.21/22). "Pangs" plays Buffy's mania for crafting a "normal" Thanksgiving dinner for laughs against Willow's disapproval of the holiday's politics (4.8). Still, Spike's appeal for sanctuary would never have the unexpected pathos it achieves without the very symbolic context that Willow decries. Much of the repulsive horror of "Same Time, Same Place" (7.3) comes from the fact that Willow is not only paralyzed and trapped with the Gnarl demon, but that it is peeling off her skin and eating it. In "Conversations with Dead People" (7.7), Dawn's improvised ditty in praise of anchovies establishes her youth prior to the harrowing battle she will have to fight against a spirit claiming to be her dead mother. "Storyteller" (7.16) has a silly scene shot from Andrew's perspective that looks like a soft-core cereal ad. The camp subtext surrounding Andrew rapidly became text in the Summers' kitchen. "First Date" (7.14) twists Buffy's appreciation for fine French cuisine into sexual innuendo, lightly touching on the issues of class brought up in Season Six.

It is no wonder Espenson wound up on *Gilmore Girls*, which features a chef, a diner, and a weekly Friday night formal dinner. In the "Chicken or Beef" episode she co-wrote, there's an extended snark-fest over fourth-grader Donny Pass' prize-winning story, "The Happiest Doughnut," during which the characters speculate about an inappropriate dunking scene. In "The Reigning Lorelai," Richard Gilmore mourns for his dead mother through drinking brandy, a desire for mock turtle soup, and a fast. Extreme amounts of food play a central role in her *Andy Barker, PI* episode, while food rationing motivates the action of "The Passage," her first episode for *Battlestar Galactica*.

(13) **"Loss of Dignity Is Hilarious"**[3]: "Doublemeat Palace" (6.12) is Espenson's most extensive use of food-based horror-comedy to date. Xander eats a burger that he belatedly realizes may be made of human flesh. Espenson manages to play the sounds of the slaughterhouse in the training video for laughs. Buffy's uniform includes a baseball cap featuring the fuzzy head of a yellow cow-chicken. And then there is a *Soylent Green* riff, after Buffy finds a severed finger and begins running amok in the restaurant, "No, you can't have this! It's not beef! ... The Doublemeat Medley is people! The meat layer is definitely people! Probably not the chickeny part. But who knows?" To which an old lady customer replied, "What about the cherry pie?" This episode's use of comic grotesquery goes way beyond having Lorelai buy Victoria's Secret panties for her grandmother's corpse in "The Reigning Lorelai."

(14) **Jane's Progress**: Yet the grotesque is horrifying in "Doublemeat Palace," too (6.12). When writers describe the theme of the sixth season as "the big Bad is life," they virtually always make some reference to this episode. Espenson was well aware that she was offering tainted comedy:

> Removing dignity is comedic. But the fact that something dignified is made laughable ... well, we all know that that can be tragic, too. The kind of humor I've been talking about is just a few degrees skewed from poignancy, a point well understood by anyone who's ever had the misfortune to get very angry while wearing a chipmunk costume. It's funny if you're not the chipmunk, it's terrible if you are [*Jane in Progress*, 29 December 2006].

This episode is intentionally degrading. The aesthetic nightmare of the red-striped uniform and absurd hat is magnified when it's on the fashion-conscious Buffy under unflattering neon lights. Buffy's co-workers shuffle listlessly, drone monotonously, and use a "bulb mechanism" to clear grease fat from their ears. She has sex with Spike by a dumpster. All of the positive food associations built up through scenes at the Bronze curdle in our memories. No wonder McDonald's (a series sponsor) was irate (Pasley, 264).

Having joined *BtVS* as a sitcom writer, Espenson began applying her comedy writing techniques to other genres. "Doublemeat Palace" (6.12) was her first successful foray into horror. She got rewritten extensively in her second *BtVS* script, "Gingerbread" (3.11), which she co-wrote with Thania St. John. "I included too many jokes about dead children," she wrote. "At that time, I was going on the principle that anything can be punched up.... Too much joking. Not enough genuine horror" (McDuffee). Given the episode's genuine excellence, Espenson was perhaps being a bit hard on herself. She says she learned how to write "the scene that rips your heart out" by watching Marti Noxon. That took about two years.

The final scene between Buffy and April in "I Was Made to Love You" (5.15) is her first successful tragic climax. Buffy helplessly watches April the robot girlfriend "die" just moments before she walks in on her mother's own dead body. Buffy tries to assuage April's pain and confusion at the cruel abandonment of her maker, Warren, with the kind of comforting lies that nobody will be able to offer her. April twice questions the premises that create her programmed certainty and optimism. April wonders what the meaning of her existence was if she can't love her maker. She fears being lost in the darkness only she can see due to her waning power supply. Buffy promises to stay by April's side as she dies, while Buffy's mother dies alone. Espenson's skill at adding depth and complexity to secondary characters makes the death of a slapstick robot enemy poignant. Espenson returns to the dramatic use of an outdated code in ennobling a character's death in *Battlestar Galactica*'s "The Passage." Rather than April's romantic self-sacrifice, Kat knowingly embraces a code of heroic self-sacrifice rather than romantic self-sacrifice that need not apply to her. Bringing such characters center stage is a central part of her artistic vision. Espenson says, "I feel that even in real life, a lot of people see certain people in their lives as fringe characters, as people who don't live lives as real and complex as their own. I personally enjoy those moments of reveal that show there's a person there. I wish I had the power to do it in real life as well as in a script" (Jozic).

It is in "Afterlife" (6.3) that Espenson adapts her comic writing techniques to writing a fully tragic episode for the first time.[4] When Buffy asks how long she was dead in "Afterlife," Spike immediately responds that it was a "hundred forty-seven days yesterday" (6.3). The precision in his language, normally used by Espenson to pun or to indicate Anya's character, here illustrates the sincerity of Spike's grief. In a later scene, Espenson uses off-the-nose dialogue ending in a blurt to maximize Spike's vulnerability when he says to Buffy, "Uh ... I do remember what I said. The promise. To protect her. If I had done that ... even if I didn't make it ... you wouldn't have had to jump. But I want you to know I did save you. Not when it counted, of course, but ... after that.... I'd see it all again ... do something different.... Every night I save you" ("Afterlife," 6.3). The truth always indicated by the blurt at the end of such dialogue is Spike's survivor's guilt. This is a moment where Espenson, like Buffy, treats the monster like a man. Espenson sometimes cites this scene as the best that she's written, saying,

> I was very fortunate on that, because usually those moments like that are all Joss. I've commented before that if anyone ever compliments a line from an episode, it's a Joss line. That scene was just like I wrote it in the first draft. Marti said, this is great, this is a great scene.... [S]he really loved that scene and I was very fortunate that it stayed how I wrote it. I surprised myself a little with that, ["Jane Espenson: Succubus Club"].

That kind of expression of vulnerability gives characters power in Espenson's scripts. In the *Battlestar Galactica* episode she co-wrote with Anne Cofell, "Dirty Hands," Chief Petty Officer Galen Tyrol can effectively negotiate for his union with President Laura Roslin only after he helplessly asks her if his son can expect nothing more than his lifestyle.

Espenson's *Battlestar Galactica* episode, "The Passage," uses a comic moment to intensify the tension. Colonel Saul Tigh is briefing Admiral William Adama on the effects of severe food rationing on the colonists. To Admiral Adama's question, "I hear they're still eating paper. Is that true?" Colonel Tigh replies, 'No. Paper shortage." After a short pause, a slight smile forms involuntarily on Tigh's face first, followed by a long helpless laugh from them both. Laughing breathlessly, Adama responds, "Not a good sign." Espenson is not afraid to relieve the episode's tension with a joke; she uses "crickets" here; she can build the suspense back up again. Reminding the audience of the essential humanity of tough protagonists only raises the stakes in the long run; as it did on *BtVS*, the comic and the deadly serious build off one another and the distinctions between comedic and dramatic characters begin to collapse. That is an important step towards creating characters that evolve into being more than fictions even as they remain fictional.

Jane Espenson is a highly analytical writer. Her blog catalogs her writing techniques for plotting, joke construction, and characterization and allows her to articulate the artistic values implicit in her creative work. Her work inside and outside the Buffyverse demonstrates the kind of consistency that makes the term Espensode mean something very particular, while still retaining the kind of diversity that permits a large body of work. An Epsensode is marked by the use of inventive word play, a preference for observational comedy over the situational, imprecise and overly precise dialogue, reflexive references, empathic humor and a keen interest in secondary characters — and food is more likely than not to serve an important narrative function. Some later Espensodes can be genuinely emotionally demanding, evoking a complex interplay of horror, disgust, pity, understanding, amusement, self-recognition, and sadness.

Taking Jane Espenson seriously as an auteur working within another auteur's series changes how we think about television. It means thinking complexly about who produces meaning in a television series rather than accepting easy answers. On April 15, 2007, Jane Espenson posted advice to prospective screenwriters on her blog that applies equally to television studies scholars: "You're going to need to adjust to thinking about the creative process as something more open."

Notes

1. I would like to second Rhonda Wilcox's observation that there are Scoobie critics. When it comes to Buffy studies, I'm deeply indebted to the patience, faith and good humor of the following: Peg Aloi, Tanya Cochran, Martie Cook, Laura Kessenich, my parents, Tanya Krzywinska, David Lavery, Matthew Pateman, Patricia Pender, Elizabeth Rambo, Kristen Romanelli, Michael Selig, Angela Tsames, and Rhonda Wilcox.
2. For a fine examination of Espenson's investigation of such issues of identity, please take a look at "'Wait 'till You Have an Evil Twin': Jane Espenson's Contributions to Buffy the Vampire Slayer" by my former student, Laura Kessenich, in the most recent issue of Watcher, Jr. at www.watcherjunior.tv.
3. Except when it's not. See the blog entry this came from for more. (Jane Espenson, "29 December 2006")
4. Much of "I Was Made to Love You" prior to the last scenes is broadly comic.

Works Cited

Bratton, Kristy. "Behind the Scenes." *City of Angel*, 26 September 2000. 1 July 2007. http://www.cityofangel.com/behindTheScenes/bts/jane1.html.
Cantwell, Marianne. "Collapsing the Extra/Textual: Passions and Intensities of Knowledge in *Buffy the Vampire Slayer* Online Fan Communities." *Refractory: A Journal of Entertainment Media* 5 (2004). 01 July 2007. http://www.refractory.unimelb.edu.au/journalissues/vol5/cantwell.html.
Espenson, Jane. *Jane in Progress*. 1 July 2007. http://www.janeespenson.com/index.php.
_____. "The Writing Process." *Jane in Progress*. Fall 2002. 1 July 2007. http://www.janeespenson.com/writing_process.php.
"Jane Espenson." BBC chat transcript. *Girls Kick Ass*. August 2006. 1 July 2007. http://litefoot1969.bravepages.com/buffy/features/jane_espenson_bbc.htm.
"Jane Espenson: Succubus Club." Interview transcript. *Jane in Progress*. 5 May 2002. 1 July 2007. http://www.janeespenson.com/sucl.php.

Jozic, Mike. "MEANWHILE Interviews... Buffy Post Mortem." *Meanwhile*.... 9 December 2005. 1 July 2007. http://www.mikejozic.com/buffyweek2.html.

Kaveney, Roz. *Reading the Vampire Slayer: The New, Updated, Unofficial Guide to Buffy and Angel*. 2nd ed. New York: Tauris Parke Paperbacks, 2004.

Kessenich, Laura. "'Wait 'till You Have an Evil Twin': Jane Espenson's Contributions to Buffy the Vampire Slayer." *Watcher Junior* 3. http://www.watcherjunior.tv/03/kessenich.php.

Larbalestier, Justine. "*Buffy*'s Mary Sue Is Jonathan: *Buffy* Acknowledges the Fans." In *Fighting the Forces: What's at Stake in Buffy the Vampire Slayer*, Rhonda V. Wilcox and David Lavery, eds. New York: Rowman & Littlefield, 2002. 227–238.

McDuffee, Keith. "Jane Espenson answers your Battlestar questions — TV Squad." *TV Squad*. 6 December 2006. 1 July 2007. http://www.tvsquad.com/2006/12/06/jane-espenson-answers-your-battlestar-questions/.

Pasley, Jeffrey L. "Old Familiar Vampires: The Politics of the Buffyverse." In *Buffy the Vampire Slayer and Philosophy: Fear and Trembling in Sunnydale*. James B. South, ed. Chicago and La Salle, IL: Open Court, 2003.

"Popgurls.com: Interviews: 20 Questions: 20 Questions with Jane Espenson." *PopGurls.com: Smart. Sassy. Shameless*. 27 June 2007. 1 July 2007. http://www.popgurls.com/article_show.php3?id=618.

South, James B., ed. *Buffy the Vampire Slayer and Philosophy: Fear and Trembling in Sunnydale*. Chicago and La Salle, IL: Open Court, 2003.

Strong, Hercules the. "Herc Chats Up Comedy Genius BUFFY Writer Jane Espenson!!!!" *Ain't It Cool News*. June 2003. 1 July 2007. http://www.aintitcool.com/display.cgi?id=15587.

Wilcox, Rhonda. *Why Buffy Matters: The Art of Buffy the Vampire Slayer*. 1st ed. New York: I.B. Tauris, 2005.

Wilcox, Rhonda V., and David Lavery, eds. *Fighting the Forces: What's at Stake in Buffy the Vampire Slayer*. New York: Rowman & Littlefield, 2002.

Section 2. Characters (Lovers, Fans and Heroes)

Evil, Skanky, and Kinda Gay: Lesbian Images and Issues

Alissa Wilts

"I'm so evil and skanky; and I think I'm kinda gay."
— Willow ("Doppelgangland" 3.16)

When Willow comes face to face with her vampire double in the third season of *Buffy the Vampire Slayer*, her reaction foreshadows future events: she comes out as a lesbian in the fourth season, and goes evil in the sixth. But more than simply revealing buried personality traits, Willow makes a connection between being evil and being a lesbian. Although this negative connotation was likely not intentional on the part of the *BtVS* writers, such an implied connection perpetuates the harmful stereotype of predatory lesbians that has been repeatedly portrayed in film, television, and literature. Despite the fact that *Buffy the Vampire Slayer* was a program founded on the principle of flouting clichés — in particular the one about the helpless blonde girl in the alley who gets attacked by all the monsters — the program's representation of queer characters is not ideal. The Willow-Tara relationship was generally represented in a positive light, but their association with magic and the supernatural is problematic, and it serves to reinforce long-inscribed homophobic assumptions that lesbians are dangerous, transgressive, and mysterious beings outside of normal society. At the end of Season Six, the death of Tara and the emergence of Evil Willow creates a "two-for-one lesbian cliché package" (Booth), conforming, at least in part, to what has been labeled the Dead-Evil Lesbian Cliché, and igniting a debate about the impact of so-called negative representations, and the importance of authorial intentions in the depiction of lesbians and lesbian couples, both in general and specifically concerning Willow and Tara. The introduction of Kennedy in season seven complicates matters further, due both to the fact that she is the only lesbian in the room other than Willow, as well as her construction of lesbian femininity that reinforces the femme standards of beauty upheld by the depiction of lesbians throughout the series.

There is a continuing debate as to what actually defines good and bad representations of lesbians in popular culture, and how we can encourage real portrayals of lesbians in film and television. To encompass the entire lesbian experience in one or two characters is not possible, but it remains important, even as the subject continues to be contested, that we talk about the reasons why potentially harmful stereotypes continue to be perpetuated in the media — even on a groundbreaking show such as *BtVS*. Sherrie A. Inness points out that "since the dominant culture has marginalized lesbians, representations of them ... can constitute the 'reality' of lesbianism for many people, particularly those who have little or no acquaintance with real lesbians" (3). On such an influential and wide-reaching show as *BtVS*, the portrayal of lesbians could make the difference in a viewer's development of his or her attitude toward the gay-lesbian-bisexual-transgender (glbt) community.

A Short History of Lesbian Representation

It is important to be aware of the historical context into which the Willow-Tara relationship was introduced. But the recognition of a history of lesbian representation is only the tip of the theoretical iceberg, and in her essay "The Death of the Author and the Resurrection of the Dyke," Reina Lewis argues, "It is not enough to write lesbian subjects ... into history and literature unless we also question that subjecthood" (21). Recounting a sample of lesbian representations in literature, film, and television does not tell the entire story, but it gives us a place to start in the discussion of the importance and impact of the Willow-Tara relationship.

Literary lesbian characters have been around since the Victorian period for certain, particularly in fin-de-siècle literature, and possibly earlier. Christina Rossetti's poem "Goblin Market," for example, portrays an image of vampiric lesbianism. Lizzie allows the goblins in the market to crush their fruit all over her body, then takes that symbol of male sexual power back to her ailing sister Laura and says, "Eat me, drink me, love me," and "suck my juices" (qtd. in Faderman, 74). The sisters' lesbianism is a temporary indulgence that functions as salvation for Laura, who had started on the path to sexual knowledge that generally ends in death, according to the narrative of the fallen woman in Victorian literature, because she accepted and consumed fruit from the seductive male goblins. Sheridan Le Fanu's 1872 novella, *Carmilla*, draws on the story in Samuel Taylor Coleridge's unfinished poem "Christabel" to tell the tale of a vampire lesbian who seduces innocent young girls. Radclyffe Hall's *The Well of Loneliness* (1928), which has been called the first novel in English on the topic of "sexual inversion," was banned because of its so-called realistic portrayal of lesbian experience, and landed Hall in court answering to an obscenity charge. On top of the real-life drama surrounding the publication of *The Well of Loneliness*, the story itself is bleak and hopeless, as it tells the tale of a tomboy nicknamed Stephen who chooses to die rather than to subject the woman she loves to the oppression of an intolerant society. Less than ten years after Hall's lesbian tale was published, Djuna Barnes came out with *Nightwood* (1937), in which same-sex love between women is described as "insane passion for unmitigated anguish," and the main character says of her lesbianism, "There's something evil in me that loves evil and degradation" (qtd. in Faderman, 297). More recently, lesbian writers like Audre Lorde, Dorothy Allison, and Jeannette Winterson have inscribed their experience of lesbianism into literary history, giving lesbians a personalized, unique voice in the depiction of that experience. But even in today's literary landscape, clichéd lesbian representations still occur frequently. For example, Susan Swan's 1993 novel *The Wives of Bath* perpetuates the crazy lesbian stereotype in both its book form and its 2001 film adaptation, *Lost and Delirious*. In the book, Paulie murders a man, cuts off his genitalia and attaches it to herself in order to prove to the family of her lover that she is a boy; the movie depicts a slightly less gruesome ending, but it still ends in death, after a rejected Paulie goes slowly insane and ends up jumping off a roof.

Moving on to more film representations of lesbians, *Daughters of Darkness* (1970), *Vampyros Lesbos* (1971), and *The Hunger* (1983) continue the tradition of lesbian vampires started by Sheridan Le Fanu's novella, *Carmilla*. *The Fox* (1967), *Personal Best* (1982), *Kissing Jessica Stein* (2001), and *Gigli* (2003) all portray women who "get over the thrill and head back to boystown" ("Tough Love" 5.19). *The Killing of Sister George* (1968) depicts a possessive, insecure, man-threatened, sadistic lesbian who drinks too much, and the film portrays lesbian relationships as short-lived and vulnerable to infidelity. The Shirley MacLaine–Audrey Hepburn vehicle, *The Children's Hour* (1961), presents an accusation of lesbianism as the ultimate way to ruin the lives of two young schoolteachers. Hepburn's character loses out on the potential "perfect life" with the doctor who sought to marry her, and MacLaine's character ends up hanging herself when she finally does confess her abiding love for her friend. In *Basic Instinct* (1992), Sharon Stone's character and her lover are murderers, and the jealous girlfriend goes crazy and ends up dead; plus, Stone ends the movie by foregoing murder in favor of having all kinds of graphic heterosexual sex with Michael Douglas. *Heavenly Creatures* (1994) is based on a horrifying true crime story in which two girls murder one of their mothers, and their actions are blamed, in part, on their intense and sometimes sexual relationship. Finally, *Mulholland Drive* (2001) ends with one woman arranging the murder of her ex-girlfriend and then killing herself.

Some of the best-known television representations of lesbians before Willow and Tara arrived on the scene include: *Roseanne*'s Nancy, played by Sandra Bernhard, who ends up dating guest-star Tim Curry even after coming out as a lesbian; Angelina Jolie as a drug-addled, doomed fashion model in the TV movie *Gia*; and Ellen Degeneres as the first out lesbian in a sitcom title role, which was cancelled less than a year after the coming-out show amidst rumors that the show had become "too gay."

To summarize the diverse representations that I have listed, we see lesbians who are vampires, drug addicts, murderers or murdered, suicidal or insane, in a phase, deranged, possessive, unfaithful, and certainly never, ever happy. To be a lesbian, according to the aforementioned examples, is to be doomed to unhappiness (like Willow at Season Six's end), death (like Tara) or cancellation (like Ellen).

Negative vs. Positive

Considering this history of lesbian representation, the Willow-Tara relationship was, from its very beginning, "overloaded with expectation far in excess of the expectations audiences have of mainstream images" (Lewis, 28). According to the Children Now 2001 Prime Time Diversity report, released at around the same time we were watching Willow and Tara play out their relationship on *BtVS*, only 2 percent of television characters were queer, 92 percent of which were gay men. That leaves only 0.16 percent of television characters identified as lesbians. Only 3 out of the 7 lesbian characters identified on television at the time were recurring characters — two of which were on *BtVS* (Heintz-Knowles, et al., 19). So as *Buffy*'s lesbians arrived on the scene, they were a welcome rarity for an appreciative lesbian audience, as well as the catalyst of a great deal of discussion about what it means to see lesbians on television, how they should be presented, and whether or not great care should be taken in order to create positive images of lesbians.

As Edwina Bartlem points out in "Coming Out on a Mouth of Hell," the images we see on television are not an exact replica of real-life; however, "fictional representations are still important sites where viewers negotiate personal and cultural concepts of sexuality and subjectivity." The Willow-Tara relationship was not just an image with which real-life lesbians could identify; it was also a lesson for non-lesbian viewers about queer women and their relationships. For the first time, two women were portrayed in a relationship on television with very little emphasis placed on their sexuality. At the beginning of their relationship, the cultural assumption of heterosexuality made it necessary for Willow to deal with coming out to her friends; but after that was done, Willow and Tara were just a fact of life — just another relationship in the Buffyverse, on equal terms with the heterosexual relationships in the series. Their lesbianism was no longer an issue. They were free to exchange terms of endearment, like "baby" and "sweetie" to have occasional spats (just like straight couples), and to be publicly affectionate. In the fifth-season episode "Family," the wiccan lovebirds even share a very public dance in the middle of The Bronze, and no one even bats an eyelash. Their affection for one another, in this case, is portrayed in the context of general society; instead of locating their display in a uniquely queer setting, such as a gay bar, Willow and Tara share their moment out on the dance floor amidst a crowd of heterosexual couples. What message does this convey to the audience? Lesbian love and affection is not a secluded, hidden, or frightening activity; rather, Willow and Tara's relationship is depicted as everyday — in other words, normal.

This brings us back to the necessity of analyzing the subjecthood of lesbian characters, and to the question of the social impact of negative versus positive images. Reina Lewis asserts, "For lesbian readers, the emphasis on positive images limits the sort of writing that is acceptable" (27). June Arnold and Bertha Harris take the notion that positivity can have negative effects even further than Lewis as they "debunk the protective myth surrounding positive images by arguing that in refusing to represent the unpalatable and contradictory elements of lesbianism, writers are disenfranchising lesbians from their own experience" (qtd. in Lewis, 28). But to argue that fighting for positive representations is to ignore the whole of lesbian experience is to disregard the long history of negative representations of lesbians, and to forget the influence that these images have on people with little or no direct knowledge of members of the queer community. As the people of the online forum "The Kitten, The Witches and the Bad Wardrobe" ask in their piece "The Death of Tara, the Fall of Willow and the Dead-Evil Lesbian Cliché FAQ," "We've had enough dead lesbians in the past, is it too much to ask that a show which prides itself on being ground-breaking and cliché-subverting actually keep the lesbian couple alive for once?" (Booth). Tara and Willow's relationship was an important representation precisely because it was, on the whole, a portrayal of two normal young women in love, and the show's acknowledgement of the everyday normalcy of their relationship has an impact on non-queer viewers who may never (to their knowledge) have met a gay, lesbian, bisexual or transgendered person in their life. The Willow-Tara relationship also had an important impact on the development of a positive self-identity among queer and questioning youth. Considering how few lesbian characters there are (if you'll recall, 0.16 percent of television characters at the height of Willow and Tara's run), taking into account the overwhelming prevalence of examples that can be classified as negative portrayals, and considering also that television is a social educational tool, to deny that we are due some positive images of lesbians is to allow society to add even more negative images of lesbians to an already massive pile, and to perpetuate homophobia. In addition, a deluge of negative images may cause feelings of shame and self-loathing among lesbians that see their natural behavior being depicted as evil, obsessive, unnatural, and wrong.

On the other hand, would we in the queer community become complacent without negative images to discuss and combat? Would we, as Reina Lewis suggests, "find comfort in the ease of reading positive images which, rather than motivating them to articulate their experience and rebel against repression, may give a false sense of security and encourage inactivity" (28)? Negative images may serve the purpose of maintaining awareness of discrimination in our society, but at the same time they perpetuate that discrimination. This is not to say that eliminating negative images of lesbians in the media would eliminate homophobia; that would be akin to saying that getting rid of gun violence on television would absolutely reduce the number of gun-related murders. Nothing is a sure bet. But if we wish to strive for equality and the elimination of homophobia in Western society, then portrayals of lesbian relationships in the media like that which was presented in the fourth and fifth seasons of *BtVS* need to become the rule, rather than the exception.

Challenging Stereotypes

The Willow-Tara relationship was, in general, a much more positively presented lesbian relationship than those that preceded them. But as Edwina Bartlem suggests, we must ask, "has the show challenged stereotypical representations of lesbianism, or merely perpetuated them?" How are Willow and Tara similar and different from lesbian characters that came before them? The tradition of queer monsters and vampires "symbolically associate[s] homosexuality with contagion, reinforcing the notion that gay and lesbian people are predatory and are determined to recruit more members" (Bartlem). Willow and Tara were constructed as allies of the hero — moving lesbians in the *BtVS* narrative from their traditional place on the side of evil into the good guys' corner. The development of their relationship does not indicate that Tara made grand overtures to seduce Willow, or to recruit her; instead, the progression of their affection toward one another is chronicled in tender moments, like their conversation in the Season Four episode "Who Are You?" in which they discuss Tara's outsider status, and Willow's desire to have something that is just hers. "I am, you know," Tara says. Willow then asks "What?" and Tara replies, "Yours" ("Who Are You?," 4.16).

Instead of appearing as the corrupting agent who converts Willow to the proverbial dark side (i.e., lesbianism), Tara is a shy stutterer who thinks that Willow is "really cool" ("Who Are You?," 4.16). When threatened by the return of Oz in "New Moon Rising," rather than act like a jealous, possessive girlfriend, Tara tells Willow, "I'll still be here. We'll still be friends," and "You have to be with the person you love." Tara never displays predatory behavior in her advances toward Willow, and their relationship becomes a romance anyway — without the standard stereotype of the lesbian corruptor coming into play.

The development and existence of the Tara-Willow relationship within the *BtVS* narrative subverts a number of lesbian clichés. However, just as no one in real-life is perfect, neither are *Buffy*'s lesbians. While Tara and Willow's portrayal moves away from the trope of the seductive lesbian vampire, the trope of the lesbian witch takes its place. Though the witches' association with magic and the supernatural is a clever way to depict metaphorical lesbian sex on television at a time when homosexuality is still considered controversial enough for a network to debate whether or not to cut one small kiss from one episode, it is a problematic narrative strategy due to the history of Judeo-Christian traditions that have "stigmatized lesbianism and witchcraft as deviant, immoral and evil due to the symbolic threat that they pose to patriarchal power" (Bartlem). *BtVS* is a show that supposedly revels in threatening patriarchal power, so the presence of lesbians in the Scoobies' (the core group of characters dedicated to fighting evil alongside Buffy) inner circle is in itself subversive. But to associate lesbians and lesbianism with witchcraft still leaves them aligned with unstable, otherworldly powers, and "insinuates that lesbian desire and sexuality are anomalies that exist beyond the normal world, beyond representation on mainstream television and beyond the understanding of most viewers" (Bartlem). To relate lesbian sexuality to powers that cannot be understood by general society is to leave room for lesbianism to be interpreted by the *BtVS* audience as something that is unnatural, unfamiliar, scary, and possibly evil.

Up until Season Six though, the association of Tara and Willow's magic exclusively with the forces of good tends to subvert stereotypes. But when the magic is activated as an addictive substance in Season Six, its continuing relationship with lesbianism complicates the narrative meaning of being a lesbian in the Buffyverse and begins the descent into the version of the Dead-Evil Lesbian Cliché that ends the season.

Magic and Manipulation

When Tara sings "I'm Under Your Spell" in "Once More With Feeling" (6.07), we are aware that the meaning is both figurative and literal; Tara is in love with Willow, and also under the memory spell cast to make her forget about their magic-related argument. The double meaning of Tara's song equates lesbian love with magical manipulation.

Magic had already been cleverly and directly connected to lesbianism in a fifth season episode, when Tara's father asserts, "You don't even try to hide it anymore" ("Family," 5.06). Overtly, he was talking about Tara's indulgence in witchcraft, but the undercurrent of "God knows what kind of lifestyle" gives the conversation its lesbian layer; this "subtext ... rapidly becom[es] text" ("Ted," 2.11) in a later scene between Tara and her cousin Beth. So when Tara tells Willow, "You are using too much magic" ("All The Way," 6.06), the implication is that Willow, like Ellen before her, has become "too gay." She has indulged so much in the "wiccan lifestyle" that she becomes a manipulative, selfish, and eventually downright evil lesbian.

Willow's magical-manipulation skills developed at a steady rate for a couple of seasons before "Darth Rosenberg" ("Two To Go," 6.21) appeared.

She demonstrates a clear difference in her approach to vengeance before she comes out as a lesbian. When Willow discovers Oz with Veruca, she makes a decision to cast a spell on both of them: "As thou art burning let Oz and Veruca's deceitful hearts be broken.... I conjure thee by the Saracen queen in the name of hell. Let them find no love or solace. Let them find no peace as well.... Let this image seal his fate. Not to love, only hate" ("Wild At Heart," 4.06). Despite her strong words, Willow cannot go through with her evil hex; when she is about to drop Oz's photo into the spell's fire, she aborts the spell. But when her relationship with Tara is threatened by her abuse of magic, Willow has no qualms about manipulating the situation. In "Tabula Rasa" (6.08), she conjures a spell to make Tara forget their recent disagreements about magic, even though she had promised not to use any magic. She does not hesitate to use her power to obsessively control her lesbian relationship, whereas she could not do the same in her heterosexual relationship with Oz. One could argue that this difference is due to the development of her magical addiction; however, since magic and lesbianism are so deeply linked in their presentation on Buffy, her progress toward being a lesbian is a part of her magical progress. Willow felt that she had to manipulate Tara's emotions in order to maintain their relationship. This implies to the audience at home that lesbians are manipulative and obsessive; they can and will use their "unnatural" influence on anyone that will not bend to their will.

Tara connects lesbian love with magic once again at the beginning of her final episode, while lying in bed with Willow, who had forgotten how things had been between them "without the magic." "There was plenty of magic" ("Seeing Red," 6.19), Tara replies, and then proceeds to spend the majority of the episode engaged in the first non-metaphorical sex that the couple was allowed. At the end of the episode, Tara dies a random, horrible death, and I would argue that had she not returned to the magical lesbian embrace of her relationship with Willow, she may have survived.

After Tara's death, Willow pursues vengeance with such vigor that Anya, back to her demon ways, tells the Scoobies that Willow is beyond the need for demonic help — that Willow is seeking to wreak vengeance personally rather than asking for the assistance of a demon. Willow sucks all the magic out of the dark books at the magic shop and pursues Warren until she brutally flays him in the woods. D'Hoffryn applauds her actions as "water cooler vengeance" ("Selfless," 7.05) and says that he was expecting to hear from her, ostensibly about his fourth season offer to become a vengeance demon. As a lesbian who wields powerful skills of magical manipulation, she is more than qualified. The first time that D'Hoffryn tried to recruit Willow was in the episode entitled "Something Blue" (4.09), when Willow accidentally causes her friends to experience some unwanted magical side effects from a spell gone awry. She had wanted to have her will done — to be able to immediately heal her heart from the pain of her recent break-up with Oz. Willow unknowingly takes vengeance on her friends when they don't listen adequately to her pain. However, when she sees the pain that she had involuntarily caused, she stops the spell and reverses at least the physical damage. She feels great regret for her actions, and atones by making dozens of cookies. Hetero Willow places much greater value on her friends' rational input, whereas Dark-Lesbian Willow mocks their reasonable arguments and follows her desire for vengeance to the bitter end. Afterwards, she has no opportunity to take back the killing of Warren Meers (nor any desire to do so), despite regretting her actions much later during her recovery from addiction. Willow indicates that she has remorse for having killed someone, but no one regrets that he is dead. Her atonement in "The Killer in Me" (7.13) is directed at Tara, rather than the person she killed.

Cliché or Not?

Tara's death began the show's representation of a version of the Dead-Evil Lesbian Cliché, which is essentially a variation of the minority cliché. Like the token black guy who is the first to be killed off in an action movie and the Native American villains in old Western films, Tara and Willow end up dead and evil, respectively. And just like the horror flick teenagers who sneak off for some "alone time," Tara's death comes immediately after a scene of heavy sexual flirtation and at the end of an episode spent mostly naked in bed. Whether intentional or not, this association sends a message to the audience: lesbian relationships end in misery and death. Once could say that their intense, sexual expression ultimately destroys them both. Willow's transformation into the season's Big Bad sends the message that lesbian love is so intense and unhealthy that it causes mental instability. And just to add insult to injury, a man gets to save the world from the crazy, grieving lesbian with his yellow crayon story.

Unlike the usual lesbian cliché characters, Tara and Willow were not introduced into the show as villains, nor were they fodder for the weekly monster, killed off to maintain the hetero status quo. This difference in the usual pattern of the Dead-Evil Lesbian Cliché does not mean that the cliché is entirely absent. The fact of the matter is that Tara ends up dead, and Willow goes insane and nearly destroys the world; those outcomes are an integral feature of the Dead-Evil Lesbian Cliché. It's wonderful that Tara and Willow were never characterized as evil, villainous witches (during Tara's lifetime), but that does not mean that their demise isn't part of the long history of death and misery for lesbian characters. Their descent into death and evil lessens many of the positive aspects of their portrayal.

In Season Seven, Willow begins a new relationship with potential Slayer Kennedy. Kennedy arranges for the two of them to be alone, because "foreplay was threatening to turn into twelve-play" ("Touched," 7.16) thanks to the house full of potential Slayers that prevent the couple from having much private time. Willow, nervous about embarking upon a sexual relationship with her new girlfriend, fears that she will lose her grip and fall back into the evil persona that usurped her life subsequent to Tara's death, tells Kennedy, "I should be restrained. I've been controlling myself, and [...] if I lose that control and let myself go, I — I could just go" ("Touched," 7.16). Willow equates the climax of lesbian sex with a loss of control that could potentially bring out Evil Willow again, and that association implies to viewers that being involved in a lesbian sexual relationship may cause someone to go bad.

Can Straight Authors Write Gay Characters?

At this point, I'll stand with Michel Foucault and ask, "What does it matter who is speaking" (Foucault 979) in the representation of the Tara-Willow relationship? While Foucault affirms the death of the author in his essay "What Is An Author?" Reina Lewis points to a writer-author divide that "posits the author as the point of origin constructed for the text by critic and readers, and the writer as the 'real' historical personage who manipulates physical materials to create the text" (Lewis, 19). It is this "real" person — the writer — that interests me where the Tara-Willow relationship is concerned. We write what we know, as the old adage says, and as a result every writer inscribes a part of herself— a bit of the writer's own particular perspective on the world — on the texts that he/she creates. Therefore, it does indeed matter who is speaking when it comes to the portrayal of lesbians and lesbian relationships in the media, and it is worth considering the effect of a writer's (sexual) identity on the text that he creates — including consideration of the stereotypes that one may unwittingly perpetuate thanks to one's lack of awareness or personal investment in avoiding such stereotypes.

With that in mind, how is it possible that a show like *BtVS*, intending to shatter a long-standing cliché, could end up perpetuating a whole other cliché? Queer people are not the majority in our society; from the perspective of sexuality, heterosexuality is the dominant culture. It is commonly estimated that 1 out of 10 people identifies as gay, lesbian, bisexual or transgendered; none of that 10 percent was involved in writing Season Six of *BtVS*. Because Tara and Willow were television's longest-running queer couple, the glbt community's investment in their storyline was intense (Warn, 2). Their relationship was a break from the labeling and the othering of lesbians. Not one of *Buffy*'s writers has been identified are gay, lesbian, or bisexual person, and therefore they had no personal queer experiences to inform their writing decisions (Marti Noxon has a lesbian mother, but that is not the same experience as actually being a lesbian). The writers' heterosexual experience failed to recognize the history of lesbian representation and made it possible for them to unknowingly duplicate the historical images of lesbians that dominate our film, television and literary culture. This heterosexual writer bias equates the lesbian experience with that of the show's straight white characters, and assumes that it's fine to do bad things to the lesbians as long as the straight people suffer too. The problem with that argument is that *Buffy*'s straight characters do not suffer in the same way. At the close of Season Six, if you were a queer character on *BtVS*, your chances of being either dead or evil were 100 percent — death for Larry and Tara, and evil for Andrew and Willow.[1] And while Xander and Anya suffer through "Hell's Bells," they, unlike Willow and Tara, are both still alive and still carry the potential for reconciliation into the seventh season.

In the end, the biased perspective of *Buffy*'s heterosexual writers privileges the straight experience and perpetuates stereotypical images of lesbians, despite their good intentions. On the positive side, Seasons Four and Five present lesbians and their relationships as a normal fact of life. The degeneration of the Tara-Willow relationship into stereotypical models in Season Six has more to with cultural baggage than actual malicious intent. Great strides forward have been made as more and more queer characters are making their way into our entertainment, and the *BtVS* team deserves applause for their contribution to the increased visibility and acceptance of lesbians, though the mortal and nearly apocalyptic resolution of the Tara-Willow relationship falls into cliché models thanks, in part, to the bias of the straight perspective on gay reality.

Kennedy, Femininity, and the Goddess That Saves the World

Season Seven gave us a new version of Willow the lesbian wiccan. She is doing her own penance for her murderous actions at the end of Season Six, and doing her best to control her magic. And then along comes Kennedy.

It's true that a television show has limited space and time to develop the relationships between its cast of characters, but it's very hard to believe that Willow would start a serious relationship with the first lesbian she meets after Tara's death. Willow does not date; she forms a strangely intense bond with the first new woman in her life, without any sort of a realistic dating transition. In fact, she and Kennedy only go on one real date before they are thrust into what is implied to be a deep and lasting relationship. The development of the heterosexual relationships in the series is much more detailed, and we get to know their partners much better than Kennedy, who we're told is a pushy, self-assured, spoiled brat. She is two-dimensional, and, as far as the audience knows, only the second lesbian that Willow has ever met in her life. This implies that a lesbian will latch onto the first woman that comes along, thereby minimizing the validity and depth of lesbian love relationships.

If Kennedy has one thing in common with Tara, it is her feminine image. It is this common image that is perpetuated in all of the lesbian characters that appear on *BtVS*—even the momentary character of Bree, who is magically attracted to Willow at the Bronze, thanks to Amy's intervention ("Smashed," 6.9). All of *Buffy*'s lesbians could "pass" as heterosexual women, as they are conventionally feminine in appearance.

There are two schools of thought on this phenomenon. Lesbian characters that are mostly feminine in appearance, sometimes known as femmes, can be seen as subversive images, as they do not portray stereotypical lesbians—i.e., mannish, deep-voiced, cross-dressing women. As Clare Whatling says of Joan Nestle's analysis of femme lesbian images, "the femme has always been a problem for heterosexuality, since she appears to exhibit all the prerequisites of heterosexual femininity—and thus of heterosexual desirability—whilst exercising a 'deviant' object choice in that her passion is directed towards other women" (Whatling, 64). Portraying lesbian characters that all have long hair, wear make-up, and occasionally wear skirts or dresses makes them more palatable characters to an audience that may or may not view heterosexuality as the norm. They are also rendered fit for the male gaze, as they remain attractive to straight men, because they conform to standards of feminine beauty, and they may appear available (i.e., heterosexual). Portraying lesbians as feminine women that fit into regular society implies that lesbianism is normal, and subverts the idea that lesbians are monstrous Others. However, a truly positive representation of lesbians on television should include a diversity of character types. Just because Kennedy wears a leather jacket and is a bit bossy does not negate her predominately feminine image.

Willow and Kennedy, as in her relationship with Tara, are an island unto themselves — adrift in the sea of heterosexuality with no lesbian community around them at all (there is never any mention of another lesbian friend). Being a part of a group of women is very important, as it reconnects lesbians to womanhood in general, minimizing any perceived threat of the lesbian identity. It is the series finale of *BtVS* that adds this important layer to lesbian characterization in the series. Willow uses her (lesbian) feminine magical powers to distribute the power of the Slayer to all those women that have the potential to possess that power. A lesbian gives women everywhere the power to save the world. Kennedy calls her a goddess, and Willow says, "That was nifty" ("Chosen," 7.22). More than just being nifty, that immense act aligns Willow's magical powers not just with her lesbian identity, but with her membership in a larger group of women in general. She is an equal colleague to all women, and shares her feminine-lesbian-female power with all of them.

Where Do We Go from Here?

Throughout the history of lesbian representation in popular culture, the impatiently waiting lesbian audience has often been disappointed by the overwhelmingly negative images with which they have been presented. Lesbian relationships have often been portrayed as unnatural or doomed, and women who love women denounced for their shameful, evil urges. We have been told again and again in our television shows, films, and literature that the only possible outcome of a lesbian affair is death, despair or a shattering of the moral compass so profound that it will fundamentally alter a woman's mental state. In recent years, we have seen many more positive portrayals of lesbian love as affectionate and normal, part of our society's fabric, rather than a deviant stain on the bastions of womanhood. The troubling negative aspects of Willow and Tara's relationship are, in part, a continuation of historical imagery linking lesbian love to immoral, corrupt behavior. However, *BtVS* also presents the idea that love, both lesbian and heterosexual, is universal in its expression. We see the open affection between Willow and Tara, and that their friends accept their love on a level that is equal to that of their heterosexual couplings. That being said, we are led to believe that lesbians have little or no diversity of appearance, and that they have no community or friends aside from their heterosexual circle. It is important to recognize and discuss the negative aspects of the representation of any marginalized group in society, in order to inform the voice of the writers that create these representations, giving them an idea of the significant impact they can have on their audience. Stereotypical images of lesbians are dominant in our popular culture because they are what the audience understands as reality, and the few images that we see as a step forward in representation, such as the lesbians on *BtVS*, fail to adequately challenge these narrow views. Although *BtVS* provided its audience with an opportunity to see genuine love between women on prime time television, further progress must be made in order to create a more well-rounded construction of lesbians in popular culture. Such progress will encourage a greater understanding of what it really means to be a lesbian.

Notes

1. I realize that Andrew's sexuality is ambiguously portrayed in the series. I could write an entire paper explaining why I think the character is gay.

Works Cited

Bartlem, Edwina. "Coming Out on a Mouth of Hell." *Refractory: A Journal of Entertainment Media* 2 (2003). 16 July 2007. http://www.refractory.unimelb.edu.au/journalissues/vol2/vol2.html.
Booth, Stephen. "The Death of Tara, the Fall of Willow and The Dead/Evil Lesbian Cliché FAQ." 14 March 2005. 16 July 2007. http://www.stephenbooth.org/lesbiancliche.htm.
Faderman, Lillian, ed. *Chloe Plus Olivia: An Anthology of Lesbian Literature from the Seventeenth Century to the Present.* New York: Penguin, 1994.
Foucault, Michel. "What Is An Author?" *The Critical Tradition: Classic Texts and Contemporary Trends.* New York: St. Martin's Press, 1989. 978–88.
Heintz-Knowles, Katharine E., et al. *Fall Colors: Prime Time Diversity Report 2000–2001.* Oakland: Children Now, 2001.
Inness, Sherrie A. *The Lesbian Menace: Ideology, Identity, and the Representation of Lesbian Life.* Amherst: University of Massachusetts Press, 1997.
Lewis, Reina. "The Death of the Author and the Resurrection of the Dyke." *New Les-

bian Criticism: Literary and Cultural Readings. New York: Columbia University Press, 1992. 17–32.

Warn, Sarah. "How 'Buffy' Changed the World of Lesbians on Television." AfterEllen. com. 6 June 2003. http://www.afterellen.com/TV/buffy-end.html

Whatling, Clare. *Screen Dreams: Fantasising Lesbians in Film.* Manchester: Manchester University Press, 1997.

"It's Complicated ... Because of Tara": History, Identity Politics, and the Straight White Male Author

BRANDY RYAN

> Giles: Yes, it's terribly simple. The good guys are always stalwart and true, the bad guys are easily distinguished by their pointy horns or black hats, and, uh, we always defeat them and save the day. No one ever dies, and everybody lives happily ever after.
> Buffy: Liar.
> —("Lie to Me," 2.7)
>
> Wesley: But you're the Slayer.
> Buffy: Yeah, I'm also a person. You can't just define me by my Slayerness. That's ... somethingism.
> —("Choices," 3.19)

Buffy the Vampire Slayer is a show that consistently and intently pushes back boundaries, each episode offering threads of a complex and extended narrative. It should come as no surprise, then, that *Buffy* developed a positive representation of a monogamous, sexy, and serious lesbian relationship between the characters of Willow and Tara. Nor, perhaps, should it come as a surprise that when Tara was killed at the end of Season Six and Willow went on a dark path of vengeance, *Buffy* looked into the mirror—and the reflection was blurred. The death of Tara, the darkening of Willow, and the rage that almost destroyed the world was difficult to watch when it aired; Stephanie Zacharek rightly draws attention to how this season reveals Whedon's "ear for tragedy." But as the Internet became the battleground for debates about the politics and propriety of Willow's narrative arc, I was struck by a very different reaction to this story. The anger went beyond losing a familiar character on a television series; for many viewers, one of the only representations of themselves on television, a loving, monogamous lesbian couple, had been irrevocably and brutally destroyed. It is not my intent here to dismiss any of the deeply personal responses to this story, but instead to consider the ways in which this narrative represents both a culmination of Willow's narrative arc and a story deeply embedded into the tapestry of Whedon's world.

The Willow-Tara narrative of Season Six, as interpreted by Todd R. Ramlow, Robert Black, Hillary Clay, and Jennifer Greenman, becomes a contested site of identity politics and a history of negative representation. Their position argues that the Willow-Tara story of Season Six presents the Evil-Dead Lesbian Cliché and as such negates, or at least damages irreparably, the positive representation of a lesbian couple on network television. The danger here is that by emphasizing the *end* of Willow and Tara's journey, rather that journey as process, we run the risk of falling unwittingly into the position that the cliché perpetuates. If all that Willow and Tara are can be summed up in "evil" and "dead" "lesbians," which these readings suggest the show asks or forces us to perceive, then we submit to the hegemony that denies lesbian characters moral complexity and personal development. My reading of the Willow-Tara arc aligns itself with the context established by the essays of Allyson, Stephanie Zacharek, Andrew Gilstrap, and James South. As I argue against the reading of the Evil-Dead Lesbian Cliché, I consciously construct my own historical narrative of Willow and Tara in the Buffyverse. As Linda Hutcheon and Mario J. Valdés suggest in "Rethinking Literary History — Comparatively," "History's explanatory ... or narrative 'emplotments,' to use Hayden White's term, are never innocent or without consequences" (5). This view of historical narrative reveals that both readings of the Season Six narrative revolve around the loss of innocence and the confrontation of consequences.

It is fitting that from the first episode the issue of consequences takes a primary position. This is a season which had many viewers asking, as Elizabeth Rambo notes in her Yeatsian essay on Season Six, "What's wrong?" Buffy is torn from heaven through the grave and enters a violent sexual relationship with the soulless Spike, hating herself for using him; Xander puts a stop to his wedding with Anya at the altar, and Anya becomes a vengeance demon (again); Willow becomes addicted to magic, using it as a means to set things right in her relationship with Tara, and Tara breaks up with her; Giles decides that the time has come for Buffy to stand on her own, and leaves; Dawn, struggling with what seems perpetual abandonment, becomes a petty thief. As each character tries to play his or her part, each struggles — sometimes overcoming the battle and sometimes losing to it. For Willow and Tara in particular, the only queer couple on the show, the path winds around and trips them; just when they make it back to each other, Tara is shot and killed by a stray bullet meant for Buffy. Willow's recovery from magical addiction comes to a screeching halt as she invokes the spirit of Osiris and demands that Tara be resurrected. When this fails, Willow hunts down Tara's killer, tortures and skins him, then continues her vengeance by seeking his accomplices and trying to end the world. Going with the concept "Life is the Big Bad," the writers of *Buffy* create ambivalent stories for each of their characters, exploring the darkest and most frightening aspects not of external villains, but of the Scooby gang itself. This is *Buffy* at its best: exploring how people deal with loss, struggle with weakness, and attempt to fight their internal darkness. So what went wrong?

According to the members of *The Kitten, the Witches, and the Bad Wardrobe*, a Web site devoted to Willow and Tara, how we read the portrayal of Willow and Tara changed when two and a half years of the first positive and long-term lesbian relationship ended in death and darkness. *The Kitten*'s FAQ argues that the Willow-Tara arc of Season Six engages the "Evil-Dead Lesbian Cliché":

> a version of the basic "dead/evil minority cliché" in which minority characters are introduced into a storyline in order to be killed or play the villain ... [that] all lesbians and, specifically lesbian couples, can never find happiness and always meet tragic ends. One of the most repeated scenarios is that one lesbian dies horribly and her lover goes crazy, killing others or herself [1].

The Kitten board goes on to create a history of the films and television shows where this cliché has played out: *The Children's Hour* (1961), *Walk on the Wild Side* (1962), *Young Man with a Horn* (1950), *The Fox* (1968), *Basic Instinct* (1992), *Heavenly Creatures* (1994), *Lost and Delirious* (2001), *High Art* (1998), *Mulholland Drive* (2001), *24, All My Children, Babylon 5, Dark Angel, ER, Law & Order, Millennium, Northern Exposure, NYPD Blue, The Practice, Quantum Leap,* and *Xena: Warrior Princess*.[1] This list indicates not only that the cliché exists, but also that it has been repeated over the course of fifty years. The underlying dissent in *The Kitten*'s application of this historical narrative is twofold: some readers claim that *Buffy*'s tendency to wreak emotional havoc on its characters ought not to include its queer characters — under-representation means a lack of other queer characters to replace them — while others take issue with the nature of the death and vengeance in this particular example, which, because of its parallels to historical precedents, reinforces a reading of the text as "lesbian = bad."

But as Willow tells us in "Life Serial," "Social phenomena don't have unproblematic objective existences. They have to be interpreted and given meanings by those who encounter them" (6.5). Both sides of this "social phenomen[on]," those who read the Evil-Dead Lesbian Cliché as the narrative result of Season Six, and those who read the season as a result of narrative development that extends beyond any one character or identity, present ideologies that mirror the original conflict: they place storylines and characters in an historical narrative (whether external, as with the cliché, or internal, within the show's context) and ask us to read them in a certain way. They privilege their narrative over others and attempt to assert authority and legitimacy for this narrative in light of addressing a political or creative issue. Whedon himself picks up on this idea of legitimacy: he refers to Season Six as "the bastard child that everyone's mean to" ("Buffy 101: Slaying Gets Serious"). The historical narratives, identity politics, and authorial intent all seek legitimacy at the expense of someone else's.

The word cliché comes from the French for a stereotyped block used in printing — its connection to *texts* repeated without difference should not go unnoticed. Cliché's figurative meaning is more familiar: it is a "stereotyped expression ... character, [or] style" (*OED* 2). From cliché, we arrive at the concept of a stereotype, "something continued or constantly repeated *without change*" (*OED* 3, emphasis added). The Evil-Dead Lesbian Cliché, argues that the death of Tara and the fury of Willow continues or repeats without change a strong tradition of negative lesbian representation in popular culture. The readings which discuss the relationship between the cultural cliché and Willow and Tara's story, drawing on the history of queer representation, the complexity of identity politics, and *Buffy's* narrative propensities, are diverse: Todd R. Ramlow writes both " 'I Killed Tara': Desire and Death on *Buffy*" and "Ceci n'est pas une lesbianne"; Andrew Gilstrap responds to Ramlow in "Death and the Single Girl: *Buffy* Grows Up"; Jennifer Greenman addresses the conflation of magic and lesbianism in "Witch Love Spells Death"; Stephanie Zacharek defends the narrative in "Willow, Destroyer of Worlds"; Sarah J. argues that "*Buffy* Not So Great at Slaying Stereotypes of Lesbian Relationships"; Hillary Clay claims "I Know Why Willow Weeps"; Carter Bell takes an objective approach with "Dust to Dust: Death Becomes Them"; Emily Almond takes issue with the larger media culture in "Lesbians, Where Art Thou?"; E.A. Week takes issue with Willow and Tara generally in "An Ode to the Love of Death"; and Robert Black presents a particularly vehement response in "It's Not Homophobia, But That Doesn't Make It Right," "The Message Is, 'Pay Attention to the Message,'" and finally "Secrets and Lies Beyond the Fourth Wall." These essays and articles were all posted on the Internet within a few months of each other, and almost all of them touch (if not focus) on one theme: the Evil-Dead Lesbian Cliché. There lies the history; why should *Buffy* not be considered part of it?[2]

I have not seen all the films or television series that inform the *Kitten* board's historical narrative; I have, however, seen enough of them to know that the Willow-Tara arc *is not* a repetition without change. Sarah Warn, from *AfterEllen.com*, argues that rather than presenting one-dimensional figures in Willow and Tara, *Buffy* "humanized its lesbian characters and didn't fall into the trap of making them too perfect." Stephanie Zacharek goes further: Dark Willow, "far from being a cut-out angry lesbian, is more fleshed out, and more terrifyingly alive, than she has ever been before." *The Kitten* board itself acknowledges that the writers of *Buffy* created a powerful, attractive, and grounded lesbian couple over the two and a half years of Willow and Tara's relationship. Willow has been a major character since the first episode of Buffy, and Tara has been her partner for two and a half seasons. This alone argues that Tara is not a minor character introduced into the storyline in order to be killed, nor is Willow introduced only to play the villain.

Buffy's internal history complicates the history of the Evil-Dead Lesbian Cliché. As the show's title suggests, this is a text in which characters will die; from "Welcome to the Hellmouth" (1.1), where a character who might have been part of the Scooby gang dies, we understand that vampires will not be the only casualties. The cliché provides us with an interesting dilemma: do we read Season Six as its own text, or as part of a larger text that provides the context for much of its story and character development? We cannot address a history of homophobic representation without considering the history of *BtVS* as a whole; the context of this story arc and the show itself influences our reading of Whedon's relationship to the historical misrepresentation of the queer identity group. One of the driving forces of the show lies in its ability to use pain, loss, and suffering as metaphors for larger issues: through intense emotion, Whedon tackles the hell of high school and life beyond it in a refreshingly honest and original way. The death of Jenny Calendar works as an aside to the Buffy-

Angel storyline, although her death is emotionally devastating. The death of Buffy's mother, Joyce, adds to Buffy's struggle to reconcile her destiny, while "The Body" (5.16) arguably offers one of the best representations of grief in the history of television. Tara's death plunges Willow into a spiral of grief and abuse of power, an abuse which has been in the making since Willow first lost herself in magic at the end of Season Two. The senselessness and vulgarity of Tara's death make Willow's path all the more devastating and deepens its moral complexity.

The details of the episode "Seeing Red" (6.19) demonstrate how, rather than consciously or unwittingly falling into a repetition of the cliché, Whedon's narrative actively works against this reading. The episode opens with Willow and Tara in bed, sated, naked, and content. We see them in bed again, later in the episode — also naked, and between a previous session of love-making and one that is clearly about to happen. Twice we see Willow and Tara in their bedroom, exchanging kisses, caresses, and expressions of affection, enjoying each other's company without shame. Towards the end of the episode, Willow and Tara, now fully dressed, discuss Buffy and Xander's confrontation when suddenly and without warning, Tara is shot through the back. The confluence of events here impacts our reading of this scene: Buffy has to have defeated Warren's plan to rob the bank; Buffy and Xander have to have argued and then begun a reconciliation; Warren has to come looking for payback in order for this story to reach its pinnacle. Events in the Buffyverse are intricately (although not necessarily causally) connected, and this scene emphasizes how Tara's death is the consequence of actions beyond her control.

When Rambo reads Season Six, she draws on Yeats's "The Second Coming": "'the centre cannot hold'"— the center being here the powerful reunion of Willow and Tara —"through no fault of her own, 'mere anarchy,' in the form of Warren's wild gunshot, will end Tara's life." The argument presented by Ramlow and the *Kitten* board suggests that Tara's "death is directly associated with the act of lesbian sex," implying that the only events of consequence are those involving Willow and Tara's visual affection. For this episode to have emotional power, viewers must be invested enough in Willow and Tara to grieve when Tara dies. A death directly associated with the act of lesbian sex, however, asks that we do not grieve, since the evil lesbians have been punished for their actions. Focusing on the intense sexuality represented in "Seeing Red" as a punishment for Tara unwittingly works against the power and pathos of her death. Rather than asking questions about the abuse of power and worrying about the consequences of Willow's actions, the cliché asks that we focus *only* on her sexual identity. The history of queer representation and the history of *BtVS* are not merely in conflict; they are antithetical. One history claims that the portrayal of a dead lesbian and her vengeful lover exists to assert and reinforce (consciously or unconsciously) homophobic agendas. The other claims that the portrayal of a dead woman and her vengeful lover constitute one more tragic love story within the text. Each history tries to assert its dominance over the other, yet each falls victim to claiming the other is without validity.[3] Ramlow asks, "How can Whedon not see the direct connection between Willow's story of 'weakness' and historical stereotypes of homosexuality as congenital and/or psychological defect?" Andrew Gilstrap responds, "*Buffy the Vampire Slayer* is about death. It is about losing loved ones and struggling to carry on. It is about finding happiness, or some semblance of it, and having it snatched from you." In the liminal space between "historical stereotypes" and a show "about death," lies the crisis of identity — who are the characters, the audience, and the author?

Buffy's history of pain and torment for its primary characters suggests that rather than positing Willow and Tara as a site of difference to be punished in ways unlike its other characters, this storyline cements their equality. Whedon's own identity group, the straight white male, is constantly and consistently under fire throughout the series. In "Innocence" (2.14), Whedon draws on the cliché of the boyfriend who turns evil after his girlfriend sleeps with him for the first time, but here Angel *literally* becomes a monster: as the soulless Angelus, he kills one of Buffy's friends and Willow's goldfish, invades Buffy's room, and engages in a campaign of psychological warfare that devastates Buffy's emotional stability. As with so many clichés that are overturned throughout the show's history, however, Angel is given back his soul just as Buffy is about to kill him. This narrative forces us to ask questions about action and consequence, power and innocence. Whedon goes even further in the text to signal his awareness of his group's historical guilt towards other ethnicities; in "Becoming (1)" (2.21), Angelus kills the daughter of a Gypsy (Roma) tribe. The tribe curses him, not with death, but with a *soul*: he is cursed with a conscience, to carry the knowledge of his sins. Further, after Angelus returns to his human (ensouled) status, the text denies forgiveness and Buffy kills him. It is only after several hundred years of torture in a hell dimension that Angel is brought back and set again on a redemptive path.[4]

This historical narrative of the straight white male identity group [is necessary to recall, because Whedon evokes it again in "Seeing Red" (6.19) and because it self-reflexively deals with the loss of innocence and consequences. The details of Tara's death are an intrinsic part of how we read this story — details that, for the most part, are left out of arguments based on the Evil-Dead Lesbian Cliché. Tara is shot by Warren, who has already revealed frighteningly misogynistic behavior. Warren creates a sex-bot girlfriend ("I Was Made to Love You," 5.15), because her responses are easily programmed; he also uses mind control on his ex-girlfriend Katrina ("Dead Things," 6.13), turning her into a willing sex toy to be shared with his friends. When Katrina wakes up from the "cerebral dampener," she shifts a reading of the incident from boyish prank to rape. Facing a vocal and angry woman instead of the docile, maid-dressed toy he had anticipated, Warren smashes a bottle on her head, killing her.

Warren's target in "Seeing Red" is not the evil lesbian, but the Slayer, a powerful woman who thwarts his plans and emasculates him one time too many. Whedon sets the dynamics of Tara's death very carefully: we know, as Buffy says in "Flooded," that guns "are never useful" (6.4).[5] We also know that Warren is not one of the good guys, thinking it "cool" that he and his Troika had got away with the murder of Katrina. What happens to Tara *is* cruel and perverse, and it is meant to be, but not because a lesbian is being punished: showdowns are supposed to occur between the Slayer and her foes. The scene in "Seeing Red" is set in the Summers' backyard when Warren enters the act; Tara is not even on stage for this battle, nor is she Buffy's secret weapon, as Willow has been. Tara's death brings about a loss of innocence for all viewers: we expect that the Slayer might die in battle, but not that the consequence would be the death of a character off-scene. Whedon makes Tara's killer an unsympathetic misogynist, one whom we are in no way meant to read as anything other than the potential of human evil. A reading based on the Evil-Dead Lesbian Cliché asks that we read into Warren either the conscious or unconscious presence of *Buffy's* writers — a presence that would undercut everything that has come before.

The journey Willow and Tara take in Season Six through the dark woods is so compelling a story because as characters *and* as a couple, they are strong and complex enough to merit this tragedy. Ramlow argues that Willow and Tara's representation over two and a half years lends itself to a reading of the text as lesbian = bad, and that the series' use of magic in the sixth season provides ample support for a negative reading of the arc:

> Throughout the double-episode season finale, Willow repeatedly refers to herself as a "junkie." But to what is she addicted? The power of witchcraft or lesbian sex? Well, both, considering how *BVS* has gone to such lengths for the past three seasons to code Willow and Tara's spell-casting as queer sexuality ["'I Killed Tara'"].

Ramlow contends that the conflation of magic and sexuality in "Who Are You?" (4.16) reflects insidiously on Willow's addiction to magic in Season Six. If spells are used to signal the subtext of a lesbian relationship, then an addiction to spells must somehow connect to this earlier signification. It is impossible not to remember the beginning of Willow and Tara's relationship as lovers: they work magic, complete with heavy breathing and heaving chests that culminate when Willow falls onto a pillow and arches with orgasmic delight. Ramlow sees in this code "*BtVS*'s reluctance to show much intimacy between the two lovers," and suggests that "Whedon's skittishness about being too explicit around Willow and Tara's love life" is its cause ("'I Killed Tara,'" pars. 5, 6) . Whedon deals openly with accusations of this kind, arguing that network censorship necessitates a code for the early stages of Willow and Tara's love story, but that it allows him to portray something more powerful than anything we've seen before:

> Are we forced to cut things between Willow and Tara? Well, there are things the network will not allow us to show.... Restrictions are often a writer's best friend — they force him to be CREATIVE. The spell scene in 16 was on one level a sex scene, on another level not. It was (barely) subtle compared to smoochin' and rompin.' The blowing out of the candle was lovely and poetical.... Look at Buffy and Riley. All their sheeted shenanegins leave most people cold compared to the tension between Willow and Tara... [*The Bronze*].

Angel and Buffy do not explicitly have sex onscreen until a flashback much later, and Xander and Anya's first time is also played off-screen. As for the Buffy-Riley episode that revolved around the two of them in bed, "Where the Wild Things Are" (4.18) has appeared on more "Worst Buffy Episode" lists than nearly any other episode. The "skittishness" Ramlow accuses Whedon of having towards his lesbian couple is not without precedent — sometimes we do not need to see the actual act for it to have impact, and sometimes the explicit act (e.g., Buffy and Riley in "Where the Wild Things Are") is far less intriguing and enticing than what we do not see. The connection between magic as addictive and Willow extends beyond the symbolic connection of Willow's sexuality and her lesbianism.

The source of some of this interpretive dilemma lies in following the writers' discussion of magic as metaphor. Ramlow is not the only critic to associate magic with lesbian sex as a stable metaphor; E.A. Week, Robert Black, and Edwina Bartlem also read the use of magic in Willow's arc as an extension of the code of magic used in the early stages of Willow and Tara's relationship. This reading neatly lines up magic, lesbianism, addiction, death, and darkness in a row. But as another social phenomenon that requires interpretation, magic on the show can be read as a fluid symbol rather than as a stable metaphor for lesbian sexuality. A symbol, as "something that is itself and also stands for something else," includes a "permanent objective value, independent of the meanings that it may suggest" (Harmon and Holman, 507). Reading magic as a symbol rather than a metaphor allows it to retain the dangers of the power it literally and inherently possesses, extrinsic to the lesbian sexuality it is evoked to represent in the early stages of Willow and Tara's relationship. Magic is always magic in *Buffy*; its connection to Willow and Tara's relationship is only one aspect of its presence in the series. Edwina Bartlem contends, "Witchcraft and magic are therefore unstable signifiers that constantly change in the Buffyverse, but they nearly always represent signs of female deviance" ("Coming Out on a Mouth of Hell"). Perhaps the most memorable moments are (one thinks of Amy's three-year tenure as a rat), but in actual fact, the show divides its use of magic, as well as its positive and negative representations, evenly between both male and female practitioners.[6]

The episode in question distances itself from magic's former association: as Willow and Tara lie naked in bed together in "Seeing Red," Willow says, "I forgot how could good this could feel. Us, together, without the magic" (6.19). Gilstrap also reminds us that much of the magic we see Willow doing is devoid of sexual symbolism: he points to "her reliance on magic to manage daily life — to wash dishes, turn on lights" (par. 10). The first explicit representation of lesbian sex on the show is consciously depicted without the coyness of the earlier symbolism: this is two women in love and finally back together after a season of strife, lounging naked in bed. Consider, too, that when the writers give Willow another "magically-inclined friend" ("Smashed," 6.9), she (Amy) is written as a straight character, reinforcing the distinction between magic as addiction and magic as lesbian sexuality.[7] And, as Tanya Krzywinska argues in her essay on magic and witchcraft in *Buffy*,

> When Angelus kills Jenny, it is Willow who steps into the role of witch.... This development allows witchcraft and its powers to be explored through a central, familiar character. As both Willow and Jenny are set up as benevolent and more "ordinary" than the preternaturally strong Buffy, witchcraft gets freed from many of the traditional trappings of transgression and salaciousness [187–88].

Reading magic as a symbol, associated with a "benevolent and ... ordinary" character like Willow, permits us to read it fluidly, against the more fixed metaphoric association Ramlow argues for in both lesbian sexuality and addiction. The most potent evidence against a metaphoric causality between lesbianism, magic, and addiction, however, lies with Tara herself: if magic and lesbianism cannot be separated for these characters, then Tara's break-up with Willow is tantamount to telling her that she is being too gay. Tara's problem with Willow lies far more in the terrain of power and its abuse than it does in magic in itself.[8]

Buffy has always found its greatest strength in stories of power and complexity. While in the first season, the delineation between good and evil — human and demon — seemed well-founded, it took only seven episodes for the first gray area (the ensouled vampire Angel) to appear in an otherwise black and white landscape. Since that point, the only clear examples of black and white are the costumes often worn to complicate the characters' actions.[9] The narrative arc of Season Six presents another color for contemplation — red. The episode that depicts Tara's death and the start of Willow's dark journey is aptly named: "Seeing Red." This title alludes to the splatter of blood on Willow's shirt after Tara is shot, refers to Willow's eyes, flashing red as she roars at Osiris, who has refused to bring Tara back, and it is also the nickname Rack has for her, suggesting that "Seeing Red" refers to a new way of *seeing Willow*, or a way of seeing a new Willow.

The narrative arc at work here draws together not only the writers' penchant for being, as Allyson aptly describes it, "Kings of Pain"; it also relies on the strength of Willow and Tara as characters in the Buffyverse. For Willow, this story is about power: in the season opener, "Becoming, pt. 1," we see Willow atop a crypt, directing the Scooby gang's vamp slaying telepathically (6.1). Willow truly is "boss of us" ("Bargaining, pt. 1) before Buffy is brought back, but this is a progression rather than a new development. In "The Gift," the finale of Season Five, Buffy tells Willow, "You're the strongest person here. You know that right? ... You're the only person that's ever hurt Glory. At all" (5.22). Part of Willow's ability to hurt Glory lies in her magical ability, doubtless, but there is also an aspect of involvement here: like Buffy, Willow's "emotions give [her] power" ("What's My Line II," 2.10). The power of Willow's love for Tara and what she will do to someone who has hurt Tara enables her to weaken a god, and that occurs after Tara has been injured (albeit with a potentially permanent mental injury), not killed. In Season Six, we see Willow act against the forces of nature in her spell to bring Buffy back, something Giles finds nearly incongruous with her character: "Of everyone here ... you were the one I trusted most to respect the forces of nature" ("Flooded," 6.3). We also see her act against what we understand as *her* nature when, sitting in a pastoral landscape and wearing a white blouse, she kills a young deer to acquire its blood for the spell. As James South notes in his essay on Willow and irrationality, the reaction about Willow's darkness took the following form:

We don't recognize Willow in these episodes." I think that response is only half right. It is half right, because our ordinary notion of Willow is one in which Willow would never do the sorts of things she did. It is incomplete as a response, though, because it assumes that we could ever fully understand Willow, that there are no dark currents in her, that we could ever construct a coherent and consistent narrative for Willow. There have always been dark currents in Willow, but she has always managed to swerve when they emerged, to cover them over [145].

Willow cannot "swerve" or "cover over" her grief when Tara dies, nor should she. There are "dark currents" in Willow, and in the tradition of Giles after Jenny's death, Willow reacts instinctively, drawing on the power she had abandoned.[10] We see both Willow's power and capacity for darkness at the end of Season Five and the beginning of Season Six, even though we are still able to hold to our "ordinary notion of Willow." But as Dark Willow will say in "Two to Go," "Willow doesn't live here any more" (6.21).

South argues, "At the end of the sixth season, Willow is the one core character from the series who has not yet found her place in the world. She is still struggling to define who she is" (134). The fear Willow carries with her and one part of the force that drives her to rely so heavily on magic, is the "fear that, deep down, she hasn't changed at all; that beneath all the layers of social roles she has assumed, she is still the nerdy schoolgirl that she was when the show first started" (South, 134). The first time Willow loses herself in magic is "Becoming, pt. 2," where in doing the Restoration spell that will re-ensoul Angel, she stops being Willow — frail, quivering voice speaking an unfamiliar language — and becomes the spirit of the gypsy woman who first cursed the vampire. She snaps her head, up and down, and firmly gripping the sides of a lap tray, speaks in an altered voice in fluent Latin. The visual and oral cues here signal that the Willow who has her "resolve face" on several minutes earlier has been overtaken by something powerful and magical. We see a similar take-over in "Afterlife" (6.3) when Willow and Tara do a spell — Willow stops chanting, drops Tara's hand and, head straight up, is lost in the magic. There is little here that can be read as lesbian subtext. This is magic as magic, connecting to its inherent power and danger.

If Willow's path figured power and danger as early as the second season, then Tara's path is presented as the antithesis to this, going back to Season Five, when she tells Dawn in "Forever" that "witches can't be allowed to alter the fabric of life for selfish reasons" (5.17). I follow Rambo's reading of Tara as the falconer: Tara becomes "the voice of wisdom and strength ... [who] could be trusted to take care of Dawn, make pancakes, use magic responsibly, make the hard decisions — no matter how painful to herself and her loved ones — and show compassion to the lost." We should also remember that on more than one occasion, Tara is Willow's anchor — from their first spell together in "Hush" (4.10) to the argument with Anya about Willow's decision not to use magic in "Older and Far Away" (6.14), Tara supports, helps, and defends Willow and her responsible use of magic. Tara is also the one person Buffy turns to about her involvement with Spike, and when confronted with the seemingly impossible idea — Buffy and Spike sleeping together — Tara neither judges, nor intervenes, simply and gently stroking Buffy's hair as she breaks down. Willow and Tara are greater than the sum of their parts: these are hybrid characters that defy any attempt to place them in a single reading. Their place in the Buffyverse is earned, and the pain they encounter in Season Six means that they have become powerful enough to suffer as heroes.

Hillary Clay, however, argues, "Anything that happens to Willow and Tara is necessarily excluded from equal treatment because they are the only lesbian couple of its kind on television" ("I Know Why Willow Weeps"). But as one of the epigraphs to this article indicates, the show resists singular or permanent labels: Buffy's response to Wesley's comment that she is the Slayer argues for a broader reading of character and identity, "I'm also a person. You can't just define me by my Slayerness. That's ... somethingism" ("Choices," 3.19). Their lesbian identity is absolutely a part of *who* Willow and Tara are, but it is not *what* they are.[11] Denying them equal treatment means saying that they are different from the straight characters on the show — and this undoes the huge amount of work Whedon and his writers have undertaken to make Willow and Tara fully fleshed-out characters. Whedon himself says,

> I knew some people would be angry with me for destroying the only gay couple on the show, but the idea that I COULDN'T kill Tara because she was gay is as offensive to me as the idea that I DID kill her because she was gay. Willow's story was not about being gay. It was about weakness, addiction, loss ... the way life hits you in the gut right when you think you're back on your feet [*The Bronze*, May 22, 2002].

Critics have often taken Buffy's writers to task for not going far enough to balance harmful clichés (race, feminism, and masculinity are only three of these justified concerns), but Whedon never presents himself as representing The World: instead, he creates *a* world that occasionally parallels our world. Jennifer Greenman writes perhaps the most balanced critique of the Evil-Dead Lesbian Cliché, acknowledging the conflict between external and internal histories:

> I respect Whedon for staying true to his vision even if I don't agree with it. I respect him for pushing the envelope with the networks to open the way for better portrayals of gay love. I even applaud aspects of this story for its sheer audacity and ability to make my jaw drop at every turn. Part of me is sad that I can't

see this story the way Whedon must have intended it, where all the characters really are treated the same in death and in life. Because I don't live in Joss Whedon's world [3].

We *don't* live in Joss Whedon's world. And that's why it's complicated. The consequences of the historical narrative presented by critics who apply the Evil-Dead Lesbian Cliché are dire for Willow and Tara because it focuses on one reading of the end of Season Six to the exclusion of much that came before. Tara's death is deeply saddening, and Willow's fury is powerful beyond words. Whedon writes as though a negative history of evil and dead lesbians does not line the blissful shores of pop culture that he plays upon, but the fact is that it does. For the purposes of representing the world as it exists in his creative vision, he might chant under his breath, "Let Lethe's Bramble do its chore. Purge their minds of memories grim, of pains from recent slights and sins" ("Tabula Rasa," 6.8). The final defense for Whedon, which attempts to mimic a blank slate, is to claim artistic right — the one refuge where writers can create new worlds, even if they look uncomfortably like the one in which we live. In "Selfless" (7.5), Buffy and Xander fight over the ethics and desirability of killing Anya, Xander's recent ex-fiancée and even more recent vengeance demon. Xander argues that Anya's identity as part of the gang ought to exclude her from Buffy's human = live, demon = die mode of slaying. Their dialogue also functions as a response to the criticism of Season Six's narrative. To Xander's comment, "This is different," Buffy responds, "It is always different! It's always complicated, and at some point, someone has to draw the line, and that is always going to be me. You get down on me for cutting myself off, but in the end, the Slayer is always cut off. ... Human rules don't apply. There's only me. I am the law."[12] Buffy's invocation of "the law" as part of her identity is frightening; a friend's response to my suggestion of this subtext commented on Whedon as "fascist" in this particular light. Yet, Buffy and Whedon are the law in their worlds of Sunnydale and the text. Each has the power, and each must struggle to use that power according to their view of the world they inhabit. Histories and identity politics in *Buffy* reflect in important ways the moral ambiguity and ethical ambivalence the characters themselves often face. Whedon creates a world where death can devastate anyone, and where happiness, because of its elusiveness, becomes incredibly precious. Every character in Whedon's text offers complex hybrids, different shades and textures of strength and weakness, desire and fear. To limit a character to one identity trait is analogous to claiming that human nature can be reduced to one aspect of its diversity, and that falls dangerously close to the discrimination Whedon fights against with every character he writes. He fights a battle for queer representation, but he does it his way — without a conscious or intentional allusion to history and politics. At the end, however, we go right back to the beginning: "It's not about right. It's not about wrong. It's about power: who's got it and who knows how to use it" ("Lessons," 7.1).

Notes

1. The FAQ presents a fuller explanation of how each text complies with the cliché: http://pub106.ezboard.com/fthekittenthewitchesandthebadwardrobe36671frm1.showMessage?topicID=910.topic.
2. Since 2002, when Season Six aired its polarizing finale, a number of articles have presented both a more general narrative reading of the internal darknesses that haunt the show's characters and a more particular examination of the show's queer politics. The articles that came out in 2002, however, represent the majority view of both sides, so I refer largely to them as being a part of the political debate about the issue.
3. Whedon denies knowledge of the cliché, while using his usual sardonic humor: "Two things: I actually wasn't aware of the dead/evil lesbian cliché. I wasn't aware of the 'add a young girl in the fifth season' cliché either. I think I don't get out much." (The Bronze, May 22, 2002)
4. A colleague brought up the highly suggestive idea that evil — as an absolute, joyful, sociopathic frame of being — is reserved for non-humans in the Buffyverse. Humans (and other ensouled creatures) are capable of being rehabilitated or redeemed: they might be temporarily bad, but are never permanently evil. Anya, Angel, and Spike are all, at times, on Buffy's to be killed list, but the moment they are either human, ensouled, or bechipped they are, like Faith, Willow, and Andrew, in need of non-lethal punishment and rehabilitation. As Erma Petrova suggests in "'You cannot run from your darkness.' / 'Who says I'm running?': Buffy and the Ownership of Evil," the "measure of good and evil in Buffy is choice." In other words, "being good is defined as having the ability to choose evil and yet not choose it." To be evil, then, by Petrova's formulation, demands the absence of a choice to be good. Further, and perhaps more problematically, the status of a dead body in the Buffyverse reveals much about its moral condition: the death of evil, demons, is always flashy, goopy, or punctuated by dust or fire. The death of a person, a human, however, is typically quiet: the corpse is visible, static, dead (Joyce, Buffy, Tara, Allan, Jonathan, Anya). Whedon codes the behavior of the corpse so that we can tell at a glance whether or not the life (or unlife) was evil. In both "Seeing Red" and "Villains," he returns us on several occasions to the corpse of Tara — almost as much as "The Body" returns us to the corpse of Joyce.
5. It is worth noting further that the season begins with an eerie harbinger of Warren's gun: Razor, the head demon in "Bargaining I and II," uses a gun to set off the bikers as they quarter the Buffybot.
6. Briefly, the characters we see practicing magic (by gender) are: Catherine (Amy's mom), the Gypsy woman in Romania, Jenny Calendar, Amy, Anya, Kathy (Buffy's college roommate), Tara, Glory (albeit a god), Dawn, Willow, Halfrek (Anya's vengeance demon friend), and the coven in England that empowers Giles. The men are: Giles, the Zookeeper from "The Pack," priests (both those who deal with Molloch and those who create Dawn's human form), Ethan Rayne, Angel, the Mayor, frat boys, Jack the bartender, Jonathan, Oz, Warren, Andrew, Rack.
7. We also we find out in Season Seven that Amy went through her own addiction and

downward spiral. She may not try to destroy the world, but she does seek revenge on Willow in the form of a "penance malediction."

8. Jes Battis suggests that while magic is often coded through female characters, "Willow is not intentionally accessing a grand, feminine, spiritus mundi. Unlike Tara, who holds intricate and reverent knowledge of the variegated mythologies which underpin the show's pseudo–Gardnerian type of magic, Willow's relationship with her power is visceral and emotional. Magic brings her closer to Tara, and closer to what she believes is an authentic identity. It becomes for her ... a unity of sexual and elemental power that is every bit as primal as the Slayer's strength" (36).

9. A great example of this is the Season Seven episode "Help," where the real Buffy and Spike's hallucination of Buffy appear in opposing outfits of black and white.

10. In "Doppelgangland," Willow confronts her evil self and, horrified, says, "That's me as a vampire? I'm so evil ... and skanky. And I think I'm kind of gay" (3.16). This comes perilously close to falling in line with the Evil-Dead Lesbian Cliché, as Willow's vampire self is undeniably evil and gay, but only if we omit good Willow's personality from the equation. What we see in vampire Willow, the power and potential for evil as well as her attraction to women, is only part of Willow as a whole: she is also, as Battis notes, a "shy academic; computer expert; budding witch [and] ... ingénue" (26). This evil Willow, too, has no connection to magic; her lack of morality comes directly from the lack of a soul.

11. So too does Buffy respond to Riley when he discovers her secret identity, bluntly asking her, "What are you?" After a brief exchange, she poses her own question, "Who are you?" Note that Riley's militaristic attitude places the question as "What are you?" while Buffy's more organic attitude locates the question with a pronoun denoting human quality.

12. Buffy is also the one who insists Willow has to be stopped before she kills Warren. Xander and Dawn are both, at least initially, okay with Willow's vengeance. Buffy notes here, as she had with Faith in season three, that they "can't control the universe," and that there "are limits to what we can do. There should be" ("Villains," 6.20). As much as Buffy cuts herself off from her friends in order to fulfill what she sees as her duty (and nowhere else is this more clear than in the last half of Season Seven), she always does so with a strong sense of where the line is drawn between what she is permitted, by her powers and by her humanity, to do.

Works Cited

Allyson. "Bring It On, Baby: Kings of Pain." *Scoop Me!* 2 December 2002. http://www.scoopme.com/tv/articles/default.asp?article_id=71381.

Battis, Jes. "'She's Not All Grown Yet': Willow as Hybrid, Hero, and Middle Child." *Blood Relations: Chosen Families in Buffy the Vampire Slayer and Angel.* Jefferson, NC: McFarland, 2005.

Bell, Carter. "Dust to Dust: Death Becomes Them." *Scoop Me!* 8 July 2002. http://www.scoopme.com/tv/articles/default.asp?article_id=67668.

Bercovitch, Sacvan. "The Problem of Ideology in American Literary History." *Critical Inquiry* 12 (1986): 631–53.

Bianculli, David. "Joss Whedon." *Fresh Air Online.* May 9 2000. 3 December 2002. http://discover.npr.org/freshair/day_fa.jhtml?display=day&todayDate=May/9/2000.

Black, Robert A. "It's Not Homophobia, but That Doesn't Make It Right: Creative Freedom, Responsibility, and the Death of Tara." *The Other Side.* 31 July 2002. http://www.xtreme-gaming.com/theotherside/homophobia.html.

_____. "The Message Is, 'Pay Attention to the Message': More Thoughts on the Craft of Writing and the Death of Tara." http://www.xtreme-gaming.com/theotherside/the message.html.

_____. "Secrets and Lies Beyond the Fourth Wall: The Part of Tara's Death Mutant Enemy Won't Discuss." http://www.xtreme-gaming.com/theotherside/tarasdeath.html.

The Bronze VIP Board Posting Archives. James T. Hsiao. http://www.cise.ufl.edu/~hsiao/media/tv/buffy/bronze/.

Buffy the Vampire Slayer. Joss Whedon. 1997–2003.
"Bargaining (1 & 2)," 6.1–2. Marti Noxon. 2 October 2001.
"Becoming (1)," 3.21. Joss Whedon. 12 May 1998.
"Choices," 3.19. David Fury. 4 May 1999.
"Doomed," 4.11. Fury, Jane Espenson, and Noxon. 18 January 2000.
"Doppelgangland," 3.16. Whedon. 23 February 1989.
"Flooded," 6.4. Espenson and Douglas Petrie. 16 October 2001.
"Grave," 6.22. Fury. 21 May 2001.
"Hell's Bells," 6.16. Rebecca Rand Kirshner. 5 March 2001.
"Help," 7.4. Kirshner. 15 October 2002.
"Innocence," 2.14. Whedon. 20 January 1998.
"Lessons," 7.1. Whedon. 24 September 2002.
"Lie to Me," 2.7. Whedon. 3 November 1997.
"Life Serial," 6.5. Fury and Espenson. 23 October 2001.
"New Moon Rising," 4.19. Noxon. 2 May 2000.
"Seeing Red," 6.19. Steven DeKnight. 7 May 2002.
"Selfless," 7.5. Drew Goddard. 22 October 2002.
"Smashed," 6.9. Drew Z. Greenberg. 20 November 2001.
"Tabula Rasa," 6.8. Rand Kirshner. 13 November 2001.
"The Body," 5.16. Whedon. 27 February 2001.
"The Wish," 3.9. Noxon. 8 December 1998.
"Two to Go," 6.21. Petrie. 21 May 2001.
"Villians," 6.20. Noxon. 14 May 2001.
"Who Are You?" 4.16. Whedon. 29 February 2000. *BtVS* Episode Guides and Transcripts. http://www.buffy-vs-angel.com/guide.shtml.

Clay, Hillary. "I Know Why Willow Weeps." *The Other Side.* 31 July 2002. http://www.xtreme-gaming.com/theotherside/hillary.html.

Friedman, Susan Stanford. "Making History: Reflections on Feminism, Narrative, and Desire." In *Feminism Beside Itself,* D. Elam and R. Wiegman, eds. New York: Routledge, 1995. 11–53.

Gilstrap, Andrew. "Death and the Single Girl: Buffy Grows Up." *Pop Matters.* 17 July 2002. http://www.popmatters.com/tv/review/b/buffy-the-vampire-slayer3.shtml.

Greenman, Jennifer. "Witch Love Spells Death." *Sacramento News & Review.* 23 June 2002. http://www.newsreview.com/issues/sacto/2002-06-06/arts.asp?Print=1.

J., Sara. "Buffy Not So Great at Slaying Stereotypes of Lesbian Relationships." AfterEllen.com. 1 August 2002. http://www.afterellen.com/TV/Tara.html.

"The Lesbian Cliché FAQ." The Kitten, the Witches, and the Bad Wardrobe. 9 June 2002. http://pub106.ezboard.com/fthekittenthewitchesandthebadwardrobe36671frm1.showMessage?topicID=910.topic.

Petrova, Erma. "'You Cannot Run from Your Darkness.' / 'Who Says I'm Running?': Buffy and the Ownership of Evil." *Refractory 2* (2003). http://www.refractory/unimelb.edu.au/journalissues/vol2/ermapetrova.html.

Rambo, Elizabeth. "Yeats's Entropic Gyre and Season Six of Buffy the Vampire Slayer." Forthcoming in *Blood, Text and Fears: Reading Around Buffy the Vampire Slayer.* Proceedings of the first international conference on *Buffy the Vampire Slayer.* University of East Anglia, Norwich. 18–20 October 2002.

Ramlow, Todd R. "'I Killed Tara: Desire and Death on Buffy." *Pop Matters.* 23 June 2002. http://www.popmatters.com/tv/reviews/b/buffy-the-vampire-slayer2.shtml.

_____. "Ceci n'est pas une lesbianne." *Pop Matters.* 23 June 2002. http://www.popmatters.com/tv/reviews/b/buffy-the-vampire-slayer4.shtml.

Robinson, Tasha. "Joss Whedon." 5 September 2001. The Onion. 05 December 2002. http://www.theonionavclub.com/avclub3731/avfeature_3731.html.

South, James B. "'My God, It's Like a Greek Tragedy': Willow Rosenberg and Human Irrationality." In *Buffy the Vampire Slayer and Philosophy: Fear and Trembling in Sunnydale*, Chicago: Open Court, 2003. 131–145.

Valdés, Mario J., and Linda Hutcheon. "Rethinking Literary History-Comparatively." *American Council of Learned Societies Occasional Paper* 36 (1995): 1–13.

Wanda. "Watch with Wanda." *E! Online.* 26 July 2002. 2 December 2002. http://www.eonline.com/Gossip/Wanda/Archive2002/020726c.html.

Week, E.A. "An Ode to the Death of Love." *Scifidimensions.* 2 August 2002. http://www.scifidimensions.com/Aug02/deathoflove.htm.

Whedon, Joss. "Joss at the Bronze. 24 March 2000." "Official Quotes on the Willow/Tara Storyline." Buffyguide.com. 30 June 2002. http://www.buffyguide.com/extras/josswt.shtml.

White, Hayden. "The Value of Narrative in the Representation of Reality." *Critical Inquiry* 7.1 (1980): 5–27.

Zacharek, Stephanie. "Willow, Destroyer of Worlds." Salon.com. 25 May 2002. http://www.salon.com/ent/tv/feature/2002/05/22/buffy/print.html.

The Candide of Sunnydale: Andrew Wells as Satire of Pop Culture and Marketing Trends

IRA SHULL AND ANNE SHULL

"Tell me, my dear Pangloss ... when you were hanged, dissected, cruelly beaten and forced to row in a galley, did you still think that everything was for the best in this world?"
— Voltaire, *Candide*

"Everything's shifting around. I feel like we're in Hellraiser. I hate Pinhead."
— Andrew, "Conversations with Dead People" (7.7)

Andrew Wells is a marketer's dream. Young but socially inept, seemingly affluent yet unsophisticated, blond-haired but nerdy, he is well-versed in some of the most popular fantasy and science fiction entertainments of the last forty years: James Bond, *Star Trek*, and the *Star Wars* trilogy, and many others. He is not just a fan of these entertainments, but a member of the target audience for them — the 18–34-year-old male advertising demographic, which is precisely who they are made for and marketed to. As such, Andrew is a prime candidate for the selling of happiness, fulfillment and self-esteem to replace dissatisfaction and insecurity.

If the overriding goal of marketing is persuasion, think of Andrew as a case study for success; he generally lives in an idealized fantasy zone of heroes and anti-heroes pieced together from science fiction, comic books, and other pop culture institutions. In Andrew's mind there is no difference between James Bond and Dr. No, Darth Vader and Obi-wan Kenobi;

they are all part of iconic fantasy worlds imagined by other people, and therefore, cool. Since Andrew is a youth, no longer in high school but still not fully formed as an adult, he is susceptible to manipulation by dark forces, both demonic and market-share driven.

Andrew may largely function as comic relief during Seasons Six and Seven of *BtVS*, but the evolution of his character contains satirical commentary by the show's writers on how products are pitched to certain audiences, along with the dangers of critical thinking skills being ignored, under-developed, or dialed down. Ultimately, Andrew may be seen as a modern-day Candide, Voltaire's 18th century adolescent torn between optimism and pessimism the way Andrew is torn between both good and evil and individual thought vs. mindless following.

A minor character introduced midway through "Flooded" (6.4) in Season Six, Andrew at first appears one-dimensional and distinctly unthreatening. He's a member of "the Trio"—the self-proclaimed "super villains" who have joined forces to take over Sunnydale—and he is part sci-fi dork, part southern California adolescent stereotype. Unlike the two other members, Warren Mears and Jonathan Levinson, Andrew is unknown to us or to the members of Buffy's Scooby gang. His personality is an amalgam of catch words ("dude") and pop culture references ("What are you, some kind of ... Jedi?" [6.4]). He is essentially a blank slate, the younger brother of a one-time villain named Tucker Wells who sent devil dogs to attack the prom at Sunnydale High (3.20). (In a funny bit of sibling rivalry, Andrew is credited with having sent flying demon monkeys to attack the school play, though the event happened off-screen and the concept was likely stolen from his brother. It is writers Doug Petrie's and Jane Espenson's way of establishing Andrew's ironic limitations as a villain—he's so unformed he can't even think of a good evil idea of his own.)

In trying to emerge from his brother's nefarious shadow during his first appearances in Season Six, Andrew can be seen as a kind of sci-fi fop. Whether he is painting the Death Star from *Star Wars* on the side of the Trio's van or offering a spirited defense of Timothy Dalton's unpopular portrayal of James Bond ("Timothy Dalton should get an Oscar and beat Sean Connery over the head with it!") in "Life Serial" (6.5), it is clear that he lives vicariously through fantasy entertainments and is desensitized to both the violence and moral choices they sometimes offer. He has no depth, no capacity for reflection, and no understanding of what true villainy really entails.

Andrew's character arc becomes more complex later in Season Six and throughout Season Seven. He follows Warren into increasingly dark criminal activity, from abetting the murder of Warren's ex-girlfriend Katrina — his first confrontation with real as opposed to staged violence — to stabbing his best friend Jonathan at the behest of ancient evil the First, which takes Warren's form and functions as a devil on Andrew's shoulder. Like Candide, the character is a kind of naive apprentice, always looking for someone or some philosophy to follow. In Andrew's case, he seems to seek a role model (such as Warren, and later Spike) who will enable him to live out his own fantasies of being a romantic hero or, more frequently, an anti-hero. He then gladly acts out these roles in rote fashion, reciting clichés that mimic the responses of classic villains. For example, during the jet pack scene in "Seeing Red" (6.19), Andrew tells Buffy, "Well played, Slayer! This round to you. But the game is far from over." He then, of course, crashes.

This trend of enabling young men's fantasies of heroic power is not exclusive to *BtVS*. Indeed, it is a linchpin of modern advertising and influences the selling of everything from cars to beer to videogames and Hollywood blockbusters. However, in a time when the equating of male purchasing power with sexual attraction and virility has never been more transparent (witness advertising for Viagra and Cialis), it is interesting to note how Andrew's and Jonathan's desirous comments about women seem utterly false and automated, as if they are parroting what they think they should want ("free cable porn," "chicks, chicks, chicks" [6.4]) as opposed to what they actually do want. Andrew seems far happier playing with his prized *Star Wars* action figures (such as Boba Fett) during Season Six than he does fantasizing about any woman. (This is humorously underscored in "Two to Go" [6.21], when Xander asks him, "You've never had any tiny bit of sex, have you?")

Some have speculated about Andrew's sexual orientation, and whether he is intentionally closeted. Yet if anything, the question of sexual orientation seems more appropriate to pop culture villains of the past than it does to Andrew. During the 1950s and 1960s, many villains who today seem to have gay subtexts (Lex Luthor, the Joker, Dr. Zachary Smith from *Lost in Space*) were not allowed to be overtly gay on television. Whether their repression contributed to their villainy is an open question, but it was nonetheless part of who their characters were and made their blend of villainy distinctive. As such, the mystery of Andrew's orientation could be a nod on the writers' part to this historical reality as opposed to a full-fledged embrace of Andrew's homosexuality. During Season Seven, when Andrew is one of the few males living in a house full of nubile potential slayers, he becomes almost effeminate and fey — neutered of evil and of the grandiose pretensions of super villainy he fostered the previous year. Unlike the villains he admires, who never change, Andrew begins to develop a character arc. While he has been beaten down by Buffy and Willow during this time and has chosen a somewhat self-serving path to redemption, the character he begins to most closely identify with is Spike, a classic anti-hero emboldened with the kind of male confidence and bravado to which Andrew is attracted.

Andrew's initial inability to distinguish between good and evil also manifests itself in his denial of responsibility for his own actions. Because he is easily led (first by Warren, then Jonathan, and later Buffy), he is unable to see himself as complicit in Katrina's death or his own stabbing of Jonathan. His constant refrain is, "I didn't do anything; he [Warren or Jonathan] made me." It's a pure, child-like response, consistent with his character and fantasy world approach. There is no individual responsibility in Andrew's mind, just a series of warped rationalizations. As Buffy admonishes him in Season Seven's "Storyteller" (7.16), "You make everything into a story so no one's responsible for anything because they're just following a script." Indeed, in this episode we see just how strong Andrew's fantasy life and capacity for denial are through his distorted re-tellings of events from past episodes, with Andrew's role drastically altered to place him in the position of strong and decisive leader.

"Storyteller" also offers a revealing glimpse into Andrew's psyche because it shows him living out a different kind of fantasy — that of a detached journalist using a video camera to document the lives of the Slayer and her friends. As an example of one of the most effective contemporary satirical formats, the mockumentary, the early sequences in this episode feature Andrew talking directly into his camera and attempting to interview reluctant others in the household. They are wonderfully sly additions to the genre.

The sharp humor and repartee in "Storyteller" turn to pathos, however, when Andrew is forced to admit into his camera that he killed Jonathan and was aware of his actions. He turns off the camera and turns over a new leaf. By the end of Season Seven he has been transformed from mock heroic to actual hero, admitting to Anya in "End of Days" (7.21), "I'd like to finish out as one of those lame humans trying to do what's right." In a sense, the line also sets the stage for Andrew's transformation from geek caricature to suave adult during Season Five of *Angel*.

If, as Joseph Addison observed, satire should "pass over a single foe to charge whole armies" (Kiley and Shuttleworth, 479), then the overall contribution of Andrew to *BtVS* seems clear. Aside from his character motivations, one of the reasons Andrew lives to end of Season Seven and beyond (while the other members of the Trio do not) is the opportunity he affords the writers to make clever observations about marketing and media trends. Whether or not Andrew typifies a *BtVS* or UPN viewer, he certainly behaves in the sort of Pavlovian fashion that advertisers hope for from 18–34-year-old males.

"Can't I have a cool, refreshing Zima?" he asks when Buffy and Spike pressure him for information in "Storyteller" (7.16). "Mr. Giles, Faith stole the last meatball-and-mozzarella-flavored Hot Pocket out of the freezer" he whines in "Empty Places" (7.19). "See, it's not the Hot Pocket itself — even though it did have that new and improved thicker tomato sauce." Because modern advertising is about branding and building positive associations between products and customers, Andrew's dialogue can be viewed as a kind of ironic exaggeration — he responds so genuinely to these products (which he presumably likes) that their selling points are branded into his mind.

This type of satirical, post-modern conceit also allows the writers to (seemingly) insert their own opinions apart from Andrew's while maintaining the character's consistency. "I'm bored," Andrew mutters to himself in "Showtime" (7.11). "[Star Wars] Episode I bored." Then there's this comment about actor Matthew Broderick: "I miss 'Ferris' Matthew. 'Broadway' Matthew — I find him cold" ("Villains," 6.20). His repeated references to Timothy Dalton as the best James Bond are both funny and fascinating, since they reveal Hollywood knowledge about the Bond franchise, including an insider reference to the film's producers, Albert R. Broccoli and his daughter Barbara, that Andrew seems unlikely to have come up with on his own. From "Showtime": "You know, Timothy Dalton never got his props 'cause he came in at the end of the old regime, but he had it goin' on. He went rogue with the Broccolis. They were just treading water, stylistically." We don't worry about where this aside comes from (nor do the other characters), because part of Andrew's charm is his penchant for babbling and non sequiturs, even if we're aware of the writer (in this case, David Fury) speaking through him. It's also an example of marketing that failed with the general public but clicked with Andrew.

If we think of the writers' intent behind Andrew's character then as part cultural satire, part representation of adolescent gullibility (as Buffy says about him in "Potential" (7.12), "He's not evil, but when he gets close to it, he picks up its flavor like a mushroom"), then the parallels with *Candide* become interesting. Voltaire stated in the article on "Ignorance" in his *Philosophical Dictionary*, "Through a quarter of my lifetime I was absolutely ignorant of the reasons for everything I saw and heard and felt, and was merely a parrot prompted by other parrots" (Maurois, 7). This observation about the writer's youth certainly informs the portrayal of Candide, and in a sense, Andrew, who is constantly parroting ad copy and movie lines instead of forging his own identity.

Candide is described on the opening page of the novel as "a youth endowed by nature with the gentlest of characters. His soul was revealed in his face. He combined rather sound judgment with great simplicity of mind" (Voltaire, 17). Because he does not think critically and his self-image is undefined, Candide stubbornly clings to his mentor Dr. Pangloss' philosophy of optimism amidst the atrocities he witnesses: "If Pangloss hadn't been hanged ... he'd give us good advice" (Voltaire, 37).

Andrew also engages in a stubborn optimism, at times denying both his own evil actions, and the existence of true evil and betrayal in the world. He holds out false hope that Warren will rescue Jonathan and him from jail: "Warren never abandoned us ... this is like, his test" ("Villains," 6.20). Implausibly, he also believes the urgings of the First (in the guise of Warren) that by killing Jonathan and opening the Seal of Danthalzar to the Hellmouth, the Trio members will "live as gods" in some utopian paradise. Even after stabbing Jonathan (in a similar fashion to Candide's stabbing of the Baron, the brother of his beloved), Andrew believes that his friend is in "a place of joy and peace" ("Bring on the Night," 7.10). Because neither Candide nor Andrew can reckon with the nature of evil, they are susceptible to unscrupulous forces including their own instincts. They commit murder, and are manipulated at various times — Candide by a Dutch ship captain and a judge who rob him, as well as by an impostor pretending to be his true love — and Andrew by the First.

Whereas Candide embarks on an episodic series of journeys that continually result in his pummeling, Andrew's episodes in *BtVS* also function as a kind of journey that strips away his innocence. In the end both characters choose their own middle ground — Candide by "cultivating our garden," or limiting his activity to the small task that seems to be within his power (Maurois, 8), and Andrew by accepting that life isn't an idealized movie; although he will probably die in the apocalyptic battle with the First, he can play a small, positive part in the outcome.

We have seen how Andrew, as an unformed youth hoping to live out his fantasies, is always searching for a leader who will enable him to play a glamorized role. In his early super villain days with the Trio, Andrew follows and idolizes Warren in a similar manner to how Candide initially idolizes Dr. Pangloss. But the leader who Andrew latches onto most interestingly, perhaps, is Spike, who functions for him the way the scholar Martin functions for Candide in the second half of the novel. Whereas Martin introduces Candide to a caustic world view based on his observations of human nature ("'But for what purpose was the earth formed?' asked Candide. 'To drive us mad,' said Martin" [Voltaire, 80]), Spike's unique blend of misanthropy and James Dean-type cool inspires Andrew to begin dressing in a long leather coat at one point as he walks down the street.

Once Andrew is captured and becomes the Scoobies' "guestage," as he refers to himself ("Get It Done," 7.15), he is still floundering about in search of someone to emulate, although a semblance of conscience and individual thought begins to seep into his fantasy world. At first his interest in joining the Scooby gang seems characteristically childlike, although his discomfort with his own evil actions begins to influence his thinking. (As he coyly asks Xander in "Bring on the Night" (7.10), "So, how long have you followed Buffy? She seems like a good leader. Her hair is shiny. Does she make you stab things?")

Candide, on the other hand, listens to Martin because of the suffering that he and Martin have endured: "'But there is *some* good in the world,' replied Candide. 'Perhaps so,' said Martin, 'but I haven't seen it'" (Voltaire, 78). The old philosopher and the leather jacketed vampire are both callous and cynical, and yet they resonate with Candide and Andrew, respectively (at least initially) because of their resoluteness. Candide has no choice but to consider darker philosophies in the wake of what he's seen and experienced, while Andrew comes to see himself like Spike, as "a man with a burden, a man with a dark past" ("Storyteller"), on a mission of redemption. Unlike others who have manipulated Andrew, Spike's suffering (like Martin's) is genuine and his attempt at atonement is sincere.

Before long, Andrew begins to learn that joining the good guys will require sacrifice and pain. He is forced to take on increasingly risky activities (wearing a wire to get information on Jonathan/The First; confronting his own past evils to close the Seal of Danthalzar; preparing for the final apocalyptic battle with The First) and to ultimately trade in his idealized fantasy world for harsh realities. As Buffy lectures him in "Storyteller": "This isn't some story where good triumphs because good triumphs. Good people are going to die! Girls. Maybe me. Probably you." This mirrors Candide's recognition about the nature of the world that occurs under Martin's influence: "What kind of a world is this....What demon exercises his power everywhere?" (Voltaire, 92). Once Andrew accepts his fate, however, he is better able to stand up to those who might try to influence him (such as when Jonathan/The First unsuccessfully tries to get him to kill the potential slayers), just as Candide, while not exactly disowning Pangloss' contrived optimism at the end of the novel, asserts his own world view: "'Well said,' replied Candide, 'but we must cultivate our garden'" (Voltaire, 120).

Some might argue that it is questionable to draw parallels between an 18th century literary character and a 21st century television character whose ironic and post-modern world is completely self-referential. But one of the great pleasures of *BtVS* is its omnipresent subtext; whether the series writers even paused to consider *Candide* when they created Andrew is irrelevant. While it seems that Andrew cannot exist without his catalog of movie and product references, many products do not exist (for long) unless they are embraced by their target audience. Since advertisers count on the fact that 18–34-year-old males buy things but don't generally make informed decisions, the constant wooing of this group with advertising and marketing is ripe for satire. Voltaire, as a social critic, wrote *Candide* in response to a cultural trend—the relentless pushing of optimism by the German philosopher Gottfried Wilhelm Liebniz (Maurois, 7)—and the tendency of people to follow blindly and not question what they are told. While it can certainly be argued that marketers feast on this tendency, its dangers have only grown stronger since the end of *BtVS*, given the United States' blind charge into the Iraq war and the subsequent ramifications that continue to unfold.

The fact that both Andrew and Candide become so memorable and share so many apparent similarities is less a testament to their writers' intentions and more to organic nature of characters, who can sometimes take on a life of their own apart from their texts. While *BtVS* and *Candide* were created at different times and under wholly different circumstances, both share common instincts: to skewer the status quo, and to remind us of the world's capacity to harden innocents, through experience and adversity, into adults who accept their limitations and take responsibility for themselves.

Works Cited

Kiley, Frederick, and J.M. Shuttleworth, eds. *Satire from Aesop to Buchwald.* Indianapolis: Bobbs-Merrill, 1971.
Maurois, Andre. "The Sage of Ferney: An Appreciation." In Voltaire, *Candide.* New York: Bantam, 1959. 7–8.
Voltaire (Francois-Marie Arouet). *Candide* New York: Bantam, 1959. 17–120.

Section 3. Story
(Flesh, Style and Purpose)

Buffy *and the Death of Style*

MICHAEL ADAMS

Oscar Wilde wrote, "Form, which is the birth of passion, is the death of pain," privileging style over substance (399). For five seasons, Buffy and her confederates are nothing if not stylish, especially in their creative, clever, and playful use of the English language. They adopt, adapt, and coin slayer jargon, from the term *Slayer* itself to *Scooby Gang* and its derivative forms, like *Scoobies, Scoobs,* and *the Gang*. They speak in slayer slang replete with ellipsis, clipping, affixation, and functional shifts, all of the stuff described and recorded in *Slayer Slang: A Buffy the Vampire Slayer Lexicon*.[1] And they are prone to sarcasm, punning, and other rhetorical fun. Their hip language and unrelenting humor function simultaneously as weapon, emotional defense, and social currency: they are manifestations of control but also the means to it; they are manifestations of friendship but also essential ingredients in the group's identity. How do we know that Robin Wood is a Scoob? Consider this dialogue from "Storyteller" (7.16): "[Buffy:] 'It's like, all the Hellmouth's energy trying to escape from that one little spot and it's getting all ...' [Wood:] 'Focusy.' [Buffy:] 'Careful — starting to speak like me now.'"

After her resurrection in Season Six, however, style no longer answers Buffy's metaphysical and spiritual needs and, as they shed adolescence, neither does it answer the needs of her friends. The season's pivotal episode, "Once More, with Feeling" (6.7), is both the apotheosis of slayer style and an example of style out of control. In "Once More, with Feeling, we encounter the limits of style: we don't need songs, but something to sing about, and the song that doesn't have something meaningful behind it, that consists of Hamlet's "words, words, words," however clever or innovative, but nothing more, is art for art's sake. Form isn't the death of pain — content is. Or, perhaps content ignites passions, but nothing, neither style nor the purpose or understanding it clothes, can slay the pain inherent in living. As Spike points out, " Life's not a song. / Life isn't bliss. / Life is just this: it's living"(6.7). And one lives regardless of the pain that mingles with every joy, the failure that attends every success. Whereas style can help one manage responsibility, pain, and frustration, nothing manages any of them as finally as simple acceptance.

One might take Seasons Six and Seven as a quest for content or meaning; certainly, slayer slang and slayer style are less consistently persuasive than in previous seasons. Content, then, may be the death of style. Newly earnest, the show may have lost some of its zing, as substance ascends over style; but I admire *Buffy the Vampire Slayer* partly because it is truthful in ways that television usually isn't. We lament the demise of style, but the show's revised priorities effectively, if somewhat depressingly, imitate coming of age in America. There is an awakening, and the show argues, I think, that there is unexpected power in accepting life for what it is, and for locating one's purpose in it, rather than deflecting it in style. We are all accomplished at such deflection, one reason for the show's appeal. But we also recognize its limits. We all hope to be at least as focusy as the Hellmouth and the inveterate danger it represents.

By now, to say that verbal style is central to *Buffy the Vampire Slayer* is a commonplace. As I asked and answered in *Slayer Slang*,

> What does it mean for American English that the world's protector, its thoroughly contemporary American savior, is a rapid-fire quipster, a hip teen who knows the language of her place and time, but who, by virtue of her role as Slayer, however hesitantly accepted, is necessarily an unacknowledged hero, an essentially normal person whose destiny casts her out of the mainstream, whose status paradoxically erases her status in the conventional world? Buffy needs slang, as a means of shrugging off millennial expectations, as a weapon, and as an expression of personality officially denied her by her role: in a sense, she is slang, as are those who associate with her [Adams, 3].

Karen Overbey and Lahney Preston-Matto, in their excellent contribution to *Fighting the Forces,* "Staking in Tongues: Speech Act as Weapon in *Buffy,*" most eloquently agree:

> Buffy is able to survive longer than the other Slayers because she is embedded in language and because she embodies language. It is a very particular language, with its own vernacular, but it behaves like all languages in that it creates, it compiles, it translates, it follows well-attested rules, it draws on shared knowledge, and it must be wielded with precision, in order to be effective..... Any Slayer can brandish a weapon, but for Buffy the Vampire Slayer, the tongue is as pointed as the stake [83–84].

As Buffy would say, her verbal style, and that of her associates, is entirely pointy. So, Jana Riess observes,

> We see the importance of Buffy's humor most clearly when we witness how her strength seems to be depleted without it.... "Sarcasm accomplishes nothing," Willow admonishes Giles in "Pangs" [4.8] as they try to figure out why Xander is exhibiting symptoms of a mystical syphilis. Giles counters that sarcasm is actually "sort of an end in itself." But in terms of the Buffyverse, they're both wrong: sarcasm accomplishes something vital, and it's not just an end in itself [43, 41].

In other words, already in Season Four, the Scooby Gang has begun to address the tension between mission and style, and it's not least interesting that the proponent of style, in this case, is the somewhat stuffy Watcher, and the advocate of seriousness, of attention to the facts as they are, a teenage member of the Gang. The apparent reversal of roles is eloquent enough to represent the truth.

Riess further argues, "Because Buffy's humor comes from her confidence and belief in herself, it's not surprising that the sixth season is probably the series' most humorless" (45). This constitutes a shrewd reading of the series, yet I take it as more suggestive than conclusive. First, while less humory, Season Six is rife with slayer slang. Play with language is significant even at the ultimate point, when Xander reminds veiny Willow of her crayon-breaky origins. Second, though Buffy comes to crisis in "Empty Places" (7.19), she is nothing but confident in Season Seven; but the last season isn't notably humorous, and, in it, wordplay is also depleted. In other words, the more confident Buffy becomes, the more she fixes herself to a purpose, the more she feels conviction, the less she indulges in the verbal style that has characterized her throughout her teen years. It isn't that Apocalypse invites seriousness — it hasn't before. The change occurs, not in the circumstances, but in Buffy's response to them; and, as usual, her response is reflected in the verbal responses of others.

In any event, none of us was wrong to claim, as we did, that verbal style is a fundamental attribute of the Slayer's life and work, and attribute of the lives and work of those who fight alongside her. We just didn't realize that the terms of engagement would change fundamentally after Buffy's resurrection, and that the balance of verbal style and metaphysical purpose would shift in favor of the latter, in favor of clear-sighted adulthood. Most of us should find this validating, however much we might wish otherwise, because we are adults now, even if we weren't when we watched *Buffy* on the WB, UPN, FX, or Fox.

Season Six is, indeed, the apex of the series' arc. Typically, the apex in the Buffyverse is deflating. Buffy has sacrificed herself instead of Dawn, only to be recalled by Willow, wrested and from Heaven and returned to the mortal coil without a clear purpose, *sans raison d'etre*. She doesn't really develop a sense of purpose until Season Seven, but Season Six explores the terms on which she might engage, and "Once More, with Feeling" is the episode in which purpose and style definitively clash. Consider, for instance, Buffy's opening song, "Going Through the Motions," replete with rhyme, internal rhyme, feminine endings — the style is hyperactive, but the song's message is metaphysical, an inquiry into the nexus of action, feeling, and justification.[2] After all, where does one draw the line between defense and productive action? As Marti Noxon so eloquently sings, in "The Parking Ticket," "It isn't right; it isn't fair. / I think I've paid more than my share." Her ditty contains the gist of the episode and also that of the entire series: pretty songs, and this one is awfully pretty, don't erase traffic or any other violations. Dream on.

"Once More, with Feeling" proposes that style is vicious. As a musical, it has more style than can easily be accounted for on television. There are rhymes, and oblique feminine rhymes. There are outright, verbal metaphors, of the kind that song invites, but that television dialogue resists, as in Tara's "Under your spell": "Surging like the sea ... I break with every swell ... Spread beneath my willow tree."

One central message of "Once More, with Feeling" is that style lies. "Where there's life, there's hope" — no, there isn't, and throughout Season Six Buffy herself demonstrates the opposite, unless, interestingly, this claim is performative, an essay on hope. "Every day's a gift" — well, no, it isn't, not if your friends have wrested you from a peaceful afterlife, as Buffy makes dissonantly plain later in the episode.[3] "Wishes can come true" — well, they may, just as Dawn's wishes are coming true in the episode. "Whistle while you work" / ... /To be like other girls / To fit in this glittering world." The music at this point is as complicated as Whedon gets, and it's not bad. It's very expressive, but the obliqueness is unmistakable, and style is the vehicle for skepticism: none of this is true; none of this is right. The message is, "Get over it."

Of course, as in all great art, style and message in "Once More, with Feeling," while distinguishable, are inseparable. It's a ballsy and very successful episode, and we are more likely impressed with its style than with its argument. But we have to remember that our inclination to be so impressed is part of the point. It's better to be outside the episode than within it, and irony pays out its usual dividends.[4] The dissonance of Spike's "Life's not a song" passage affects the audience at home more than the immediate audience, Buffy, who seems not to be listening.[5] And when

Sweet sings, "Why'd you run away? / Don't you like my style?," he's not speaking only to Dawn; Sweet's style is the honey that traps us, the tacky unintended consequences of apparently carefree song and dance.

In "Once More, with Feeling," everyone sings and everyone dances. But everyone is ultimately immolated in style. You can sing along, but you'd better not. The episode explains all that comes after it: there may not be any metaphors or rhymes, but the stuff that follows the musical episode is the stuff reality is made on. The seventh season makes clear that every aesthetic hope is dashed by reality — to what other purpose could we put Spike's utter humiliation in "Lies My Parents Told Me" (7.17)? Poetry is subordinate to, well, everything. And style, as in the self-conscious introduction of one's natural parent into one's vampire family, is likely a reversal. But as Spike learns from comparing his situation with Robin Wood's, the issue is not what the vamped parent says, but what the pre-vamped parent would mean. Substance matters more than style, and Spike remembers substance in "Lies My Parents Told Me," though his catharsis is triggered by a folk song.

So, Buffy insists, "Don't give me songs / Give me something to sing about." Eventually, as she focuses on The First and the series' ultimate battle, she finds the purpose for which she longs in Season Six. But the story does not answer her plea immediately. There were, of course, practical reasons for Whedon and his team to attenuate the plot, but there is also intellectual value in complicating it, in exploring the notion of purposeful action. As contrast to what comes in Season Seven, the writers considered three instances of purpose presumed, but somehow gone awry.

The first and, to my mind, most poignant of these is Anya's pursuit of the meaningful in marrying Xander. Anya frequently complains about the aimlessness of human activity. After having spent a millennium or so focused utterly on revenge (in a flashback in "Selfless" (7.5), Halfrek marvels that Anyanka is all work, no play), she struggles to find meaning as a human. Jilted, she becomes a demon again, only to discover that it no longer satisfies her, and she willingly surrenders to humanity and its greatest cruelty, death, in "Selfless." As she says to Xander in that episode, "My whole life, I've just kinda clung to whatever came along.... What if I'm really nobody?" Being somebody requires choice and purposeful action; choice and purposeful action require a rationale. In Season Six, she had adopted love and marriage as her rationale, though we may not have realized how much she felt fulfilled by the prospect of marriage until "Selfless," in Season Seven, when, skewered to a fraternity house wall, she (and we) flash back to her lovely, moving, and substantial song, the one cut from "Once More, with Feeling" and helpfully inserted later just to underscore human pursuit of meaning, mission, purpose, matter, substance, or whatever you want to call it.

The Troika, Buffy's comically evil "nemesises" are another example of purposefulness, but they are self-involved, somewhat lazy, and prone to random acts of violence, so their purpose is finally unfulfilled (or, one might say, in Andrew, "absorbed" into Buffy's ultimate mission)—they are the comic subplot that mirrors Anya's tragic one. And, of course, they provoke Willow into frightening focus—no longer a dabbler in "magicks," nor a "rank amateur," as Giles accuses after she resurrects Buffy at the beginning of Season Six, she embodies in a newly preeminent way what at least some demons and such like have embodied all along, the purposefulness of evil bent on nothing less than the destruction of the world. All of this goes to show that purpose, or mission, or a sense of meaning does not equal justification. Only the good purpose is something to sing about, and even then, as in Anya's case, the song is sometimes misplaced, and style hardly answers the situation. After all of this, however, after "Once More, with Feeling" and these preliminary, almost typological representations of mission and purpose, Season Seven is poised to take the sense of mission a little further.

As Buffy clarifies in "Storyteller" (7.16), not only for the Scooby Gang, the expanding army of potentials, and various hangers on, but also for the audience, as they begin to grasp Season Seven's thematic arc, "The mission is what matters." The spare, unstylish dictum departs considerably from Buffy's versified angst in "Once More, with Feeling," how once "brave" and "righteous," she's "wavering," how she can't see what she is but "just wants to be alive," not just living, though that's what, unless style kills her, she'll go on doing. In the end, it isn't enough to be alive; by its nature, to be alive is to be insecure. When confronting evil, especially the First Evil, the Slayer (or Slayers) provide limited, perhaps largely symbolic protection for those living insecurely in a surprisingly dangerous world. For five seasons, Buffy's bravery and righteousness had been expressed in slangy style; until she was called back from Heaven, she had been the embodiment of Castiglione's *sprezzatura*, simultaneously performing verbal gymnastics and fighting demons without much evidence of effort, without breaking a sweat. Having wavered spiritually, she has turned from style to mission; she is no longer worried, in her erstwhile adolescent way, of letting others see her effort. Finally, the antagonist, the First Evil, is too dangerous to worry about saving face.

I suspect that, in Season Seven, Buffy's bravery is all the more admirable because she knows fear; earlier, she is sometimes afraid, but youth has saved her from existential fear, something Watchers bring to their primeval relationship with Slayers. Buffy leaves her indestructible phase behind in Season Five. She sounds like her old self at the outset of "Once More, with Feeling": "Well, I'm not exactly quaking in my stylish yet affordable boots, but there's definitely something unnatural going on." None of her innocent, exuberant, apocalyptic sacrifice is recoverable in Season Six, however; she realizes this in the course of "Once More, with Feeling" and works towards a new Slayer morality, one that corresponds to her resurrected psychology. A new psychology motivates a new morality; both together motivate a new style.

Season Seven is not bereft of style, of course, but the terms of style have changed radically, and the importance of style as an instrument of self-fashioning has diminished as the importance of purpose or mission has increased. Buffy is still clever, if rueful. Consider the following two classic Buffyisms from "Lessons" (7.1.). First, when Principal Wood refers to her school record as "kind of a checkered past," Buffy responds, "More like a plaid, kind of a clan tartan of badness, really." In a conversation with Xander, she says, "My sister's about to go to the same high school that tried to kill me for three years…. So peachy with a side of keen, that would be me." It may be significant that these quips come early in the season and that Buffy quippage is less and less frequent as the season proceeds. It may be significant that Buffy is no longer singing "What can't we face if we're together?" (however half-heartedly), no longer asserting, as she has so many times previously, "We'll deal."

It may also be significant that the cleverest wordplay and outright funniest lines are given to characters other than Buffy, indeed, other than the extended Scooby Gang. In "Get It Done" (7.15), Buffy explains to Robin Wood that "Andrew is our … actually, he's our hostage," to which Andrew replies, "I like to think of myself more as guestage," a wonderful play on the word-formative pattern, since the Middle English meanings of *host* (from Old French) are "one who receives or entertains" and "guest" so that *hostage* and *guestage* are etymological synonyms, even if, because *host* and *guest* are semantically converse terms now, most in the television audience would be unaware of the fact. *Guestage* sounds too much like *baggage* and *luggage*, so that Andrew has put himself in his place, so to speak. Of course, though Andrew is not a member of the Gang when he says this, he is a Scooby wannabe, and has achieved quasi–Scooby status by the end of the season; if for no other reason, he is, inexplicably when one remembers Anya, among those who survive. The prize for funniest line must go to

D'Hoffryn, who surveys the frat house carnage in "Selfless" (7.5) with the withering, "It's like somebody slaughtered an Abercrombie and Fitch catalogue." Andrew is worried about saving or, more precisely, about creating face; D'Hoffryn's sense of purpose is well-established and, anyway, he is outside the central conflict — whereas Andrew still needs style, D'Hoffryn is immune to it.

When it comes to lexical innovation, so obviously important to the rest of the series, Season Seven is relatively flat. Given the tendency of earlier seasons to derive new forms from the old (consider the twenty-two pages of *Slayer Slang* devoted to *slay, Slayer*, and derivative forms), it seems fair to say that Slayer jargon develops minimally in Season Seven. In "Conversations with Dead People" (7.7), Buffy reintroduces herself to her old schoolmate, the newly vamped Webs, with, "I'm the Slayer. It's sort of a thing," while in "Potential" (7.12), Dawn rattles on about "slayage biz," deflated reiterations of jargon familiar to all since the first episode. In Season Seven, we are reintroduced to *The First* (*The First Evil* from "Amends" [3.10]) and its minions, the *Bringers* (also appearing in "Amends"). *Bringers* is linguistically clever, a metathesized innovative clipping of *harbinger*, we discover.[6] We become very familiar with the word: as Buffy asserts in "Potential" (7.12), Sunnydale "is lousy with Bringers" throughout the season. Indeed, *Potential* "up and coming Slayer" is itself a new item of jargon. Though *ubervamp* had some life in the larger Buffyverse (and *uber-* had been used to form many items of slayer slang), it is new to the show in Season Seven, as is *neandervamp* ("Showtime" [7.11]); Webs threatens to *vampify* his college girlfriend, so that they will always be together, but Buffy resists the derivation, pointing out that the proper term is *sire*. Otherwise, it's the usual suspects: *Chosen One, dust, Hellmouth, Old Ones, stake, undead,* and *Watcher* most prominent among them.

Season Seven slang isn't much more exciting. There are the usual phrasal verbs (*freak out, pissed off*) and their clipped alternants (*deal, figure, freak, mess, show, stress*); shifts from adjective to noun (*the crazy* [dating at least from "Enemies" (3.17)], *the random*, and *the talky* [for which, hypothetically, the adjective *talky* was formed first]); plenty of *no big* and *my bad*; an inevitable *wiggins*, "with extra wig" ("Beneath You" [7.2]); the suffix-*age* had mostly run its course by Season Five, so *guestage* is a reminiscent form, all the more pleasing and plausible in its isolation; Dawn suggests that everyone "Check out 00-Xander," which would be cleverer had Cordelia not applied the adjective *007* to Xander in "The Prom" (3.20).

By contrast with —*age*, the suffix-*y* is still productive, and some of the new forms are clever enough, as they push the envelope pretty far from the-*y* of standard English: Kennedy's *new agey* ("Showtime" [7.11]), Willow's *casual dressy* ("For someone who's sick, you look surprisingly robust and casual dressy," from "The Killer in Me" [7.13]), Buffy's *Firsty* ("So, when I kicked its ass, the whole Firsty circus decided to back off for a while," from "Potential" [7.12]), Xander's *swoony and crushy* ("It's the jacket. It's true, something about the big letter on the chest makes girls get all swoony and crushy," from the off-arc "Him" [7.6]), Faith's *repenty* ("Not if you're all repenty—takes the fun out of it," from "Dirty Girls" [7.18]), Buffy's *stay togetheriness* (what her parents weren't good at, she tells Webs, in "Conversations with Dead People" [7.7]), and especially her *'splainy* (from "Chosen" [7.22], a pop-cultural allusion to Ricky Ricardo's, "Lucy, you got some splainin' to do" and-*y* suffixation packed into six phonemes) all come to mind.

Many of the other-*y* suffixed forms are lexical reprises we could do without: *angsty*, from "Help" (7.4), already had a life in slayer slang; *broody*, from "Him" (7.6), had occurred in "Buffy vs. Dracula" (5.1); and *researchy* (from "First Date" [7.14]); Xander's *contracty goodness* in "Lessons" (7.1) too obviously depends on Cordelia's infamous *salty goodness*; incredibly, *Hellmouthy* (used in several episodes) is new in Season Seven, but even the most enthusiastic fan wouldn't hear it as new; getting all *bouncy* ("Chosen" [7.22]), *thrusty* ("Him" [7.6]), or *wriggly* ("End of Days" [7.21]) are hardly inspired euphemisms for having sex. When Willow worries in "Beneath You" (7.2) that she might revert to her "*veiny* and homicidal" self, we know somehow that the days of *yellow crayon-breaky-y* suffixation are gone.

By Season Seven, slang and other manifestations of verbal style no longer consistently serve their original purposes; the frequency of slang per episode declines, and, since slang is supposed to be somewhat racy and rebellious, the degree of slanginess per item has declined, too—it's all too familiar. Throughout the first six seasons of her eponymous television show, Buffy was the exemplary practitioner of new word formation; in Season Seven, she is the source of focus, not of new words. Or perhaps focus is the new style: nightly *slayage*, even occasional world *saveage*, prompts demon-baiting *quippage*; the mission, on the other hand, demands plain style, a style of transparency and no distractions.

For those less focused, the style is not particularly appealing or persuasive, as we know from the reaction of the Gang and Potentials to Buffy's Henry the Fifth speeches, declaimed while a faux William Walton score plays in the background. Kids these days don't read Shakespeare much and never listen to Walton; even if she's adopted the right style for the mission, it's the wrong style for her audience. Anya, of course, notices that this new stylistic tendency isn't merely rhetorical or restricted to the Summers' dining room; rather, it indicates a new Buffy altogether, so in "Selfless" (7.5) she taunts her, "C'mon, Buffy, don't you have a clever retort for me?" She doesn't.

The rules governing discourse and action have changed. In Season Seven, in fact, from "Once More, with Feeling" forward, Buffy acts individually and the social basis for slayer slang thus changes: slang is all about who's in, who's out, and why; it marks group identity and makes group identity. As Anne Billson suggests of Season Seven, "After six seasons of being supported by the Scooby Gang, Buffy finally has to go it alone and reassert her individuality" (127), even though, as Jana Riess argues, the series is, until Season Seven, devoted to "the power of friendship" (54) faith in which, she notes, is conveyed by "What can't we face if we're together?" a choral number from "Once More, with Feeling" (64).[7]

The tension between individual and social commitments pulses through Season Seven; in this, the show reflects Joss Whedon's metaphysical and moral preoccupations. As Len Schiff explains in *The Sondheim Review*, Stephen Sondheim's musicals were central to Whedon's aesthetic development; they clearly influenced "Once More, with Feeling," and Sondheim's preoccupations, insofar as they underlay Whedon's preoccupations, directed the series' thematic arc from the musical episode through the final season. Schiff reports that "One of *Follies'* numbers, 'The Road You Didn't Take,' posed a particular challenge to young Whedon: 'the notion that every choice you make means that other possibilities are eliminated forever — as a kid, I found that terrifying. As an adult, I still find it scary'" (34). And who doesn't? Yet Buffy has taken her road and isn't looking back. Let the Scooby Gang and the Potentials hold council after council to assess the relative desirability of various roads. Buffy has learned to face the challenges inherent in adult engagement with the world.

The First represents many things, among them pure evil and the catalyst of purpose, the focus of action. She/He/It is all spirit, so in order to do mischief is forced to adopt many forms. Obviously, the evil is in the spirit, not its embodiment, but evil is persuasive according to the style in which it presents her/him/itself. Paradoxically, then, there's nothing to slay; all you can dispatch is The First's current fashion statement, an attempt (as when she takes on Eve's form in "Showtime" [7.11]) to fit in with a group long enough to dissuade it from following the Slayer's chosen road. Fundamentally, the First Evil has no style of its own; in order to accomplish anything, however, it is all style. Caleb, too, is a great stylist, and one suspects that evil and style, then, are more closely related than you hoped in your youth, when, like Tara and Willow, you sang and danced in meadows, along the banks of a river, in bed. One thing is certain: if Buffy defeats The First, she'll be ready for The Next.

After six seasons of high style and stylistic exuberance, we are finally asked, in Season Seven, to put style in its place. For Whedon, the most stylish of television *auteurs*, the show identifies metaphysical and moral truths that supersede style at its most persuasive, say, in "Once More, with Feeling." But those truths aren't always imperative. At the end of the musical, the Scooby Gang asks in Chorus, "Where do we go from here?" At the end of the final episode, Dawn asks, "Yeah, Buffy, what do we do now?" Buffy is literally at the end of the road she did take, and she smiles: first thing, they're all off to the mall; with The First out of the way, Buffy has nothing to sing about — she can sing for the Hellmouth of it. Form, which is the birth of passion, is the death of pain, after all.

Notes

1. Information about particular lexical items from the Buffyverse treated in this book is included here without citation since the information can be found in the glossary, which is organized alphabetically.

2. Wilcox emphasizes this stylishness in *Why Buffy Matters*: "Allusions (verbal, visual, musical) to the worlds of literature, film, television, and music play through the episode. From Dickens to Disney, from Simon and Garfunkel to Sondheim, 'Once More, with Feeling' is a constant dance of reference" (192); she quotes Michael Dunne as writing, "'Once More, with Feeling's 'self-conscious separation of "natural" diegesis and "unnatural" musical production numbers would seem to fulfill Bertolt Brecht's program for denaturalizing art'" (196). Albright also focuses on the relationship of irony and style: "Yet despite the self-consciousness that this is not normal behavior, even in Sunnydale, there is an intriguing tension between the elaborately stylized and choreographed conventions of the musical, the sense that this is not real or normal, and the subjects of their songs" (¶11).

3. As Billson puts it, "But then dying is easy and living is hard, as Buffy finds out to her cost. It's not unheard of for dead heroes to be resurrected, but they rarely linger long on this earthly plane, and certainly not to engage in real life on a daily basis" (114).

4. Pateman points to "the astonishing timing of the arrival of the fire trucks into the shot on the word 'fire' during the song 'Walk Through the Fire,'" (233, n29) which is about as ironically self-conscious as it gets; on the other hand, he notes that "Conversations with Dead People" (7.7) is "the only [episode] that uses the technique of superscripting the date and time of the action. The date and time ("November 12, 2002; 8:01 P.M." are exactly synchronous with the date and time of the episode's first airing in America. A technique that is a clear sign of the show's constructedness is attempting to force a direct equivalence between its world and the world of the viewer" (203), that is, to collapse irony (by means of a potentially ironic device) rather than glorify it, ostensibly another way of gauging the difference between the apotheosis of style in Season Six and its death in Season Seven. See also Albright, ¶4 and ¶9.

5. Stafford asks a question along similar lines: "Also, why doesn't Buffy hear anything

Giles says in his heartfelt song? She's working out in the same room, and he's singing a few feet away from her" (333). Perhaps, the episode argues, style inhibits communication.

6. Metathesis, for those not familiar with it, is the arbitrary reversal of sounds within the structure of a word; by means of this process, Old English *bridde* became Modern English *bird*, Old English *thridde* became Modern English *third*, etc. In this case, the metathesis would have to occur before the clipping, as English phonotaxis does not allow the cluster /rb/ at the onset of a syllable — there can be no **rbinger* from *Harbinger*, so the hypothetical process of change in this case would be *Harbinger* > **Habringer* > *Bringer*.

7. See Riess, pp. 53–64 for an excellent discussion of the importance of friendship and group identity to Buffy's (and *Buffy*'s) success. As Billson notes, Buffy's assertion of individuality and individual responsibility is at the core of Season Seven (127); a tart, insightful comment on the Scooby Gang's ultimate groupiness comes later in the book (132).

Works Cited

Adams, Michael. *Slayer Slang: A Buffy the Vampire Slayer Lexicon*. New York: Oxford University Press, 2003.

Albright, Richard S. "'[B]reakaway pop hit or ... book number?': 'Once More, with Feeling' and Genre." *Slayage: The Online International Journal of Buffy Studies* 5.1 (2005).

Billson, Anne. *Buffy the Vampire Slayer: A Critical Reading of the Series*. London: BFI, 2005.

Overbey, Karen Eileen, and Lahney Preston-Matto. "Staking in Tongues: Speech Act as Weapon in *Buffy*." In *Fighting the Forces: What's at Stake in Buffy the Vampire Slayer*. Rhonda V. Wilcox and David Lavery, eds. Lanham, MD: Rowman & Littlefield, 2002. 73–84.

Pateman, Matthew. *The Aesthetics of Culture in Buffy the Vampire Slayer*. Jefferson, NC: McFarland, 2006.

Riess, Jana. *What Would Buffy Do?: The Vampire Slayer as Spiritual Guide*. San Francisco: Jossey-Bass, 2004.

Schiff, Len. "Joss Whedon: Absolute Admiration for Sondheim." *The Sondheim Review* 11.4 (2005): 34–35.

Stafford, Nikki. *Bite Me!: An Unofficial Guide to the World of Buffy the Vampire Slayer*. 2nd ed. Toronto: ECW Press, 2002.

Wilcox, Rhonda. *Why Buffy Matters: The Art of Buffy the Vampire Slayer*. London: I. B. Tauris, 2005.

Wilde, Oscar. *The Artist as Critic*. Richard Ellmann, ed. New York: Random House, 1969.

"Set on This Earth Like a Bubble": Word as Flesh in the Dark Seasons[1]

RHONDA V. WILCOX

From the first chapter of John, in the Bible: "In the beginning was the Word.... And the Word was made flesh."
—(John 1.1, 1.14)

From the first episode of the last season of Buffy, spoken by the First Evil in the form of Buffy's first nemesis, The Master: "[We're going] right back to the beginning—not the bang—not the word—the true beginning."
—("Lessons," 7.1)[2]

And in the words of a demon to Buffy after her return from the dead: "You're the one who's barely here—set on this earth like a bubble."
—("After Life," 6.3)

Over the years, *Buffy the Vampire Slayer* has often been criticized for its presentation of a lead character who is strongly attractive within conventionally accepted standards (Pender, 36–38, 42–43). But the *Buffy* series never stopped surprising its viewers, and my favorite moment of the opening two-parter for Season Six was a vivid view of the rotted, decayed corpse of our heroine. How did we get from the bouncy hair and push-up bras of Season One to the undone flesh of Season Six? The journey has been a gradual one: a head wound on her eighteenth birthday ("Helpless," 3.12); a stake in the gut from a random vamp when she's nineteen ("Fool for Love," 5.7); when she's twenty, the dead body of her mother—and Buffy's body slumped in the hospital waiting room; then, a few months later, her own death. And Buffy does not travel alone. In Season Six, her best friend, Willow, becomes physically and morally monstrous; in Season Seven, their friend Xander is physically damaged when he loses an eye. These are characters with whom most viewers identify. Instead of the invincible heroic flesh of youth, they have all become vulnerable in one fashion or another. Carol Senf speaks of how *Dracula* focuses on the "similarity between Good and Evil" (421). In the last two seasons of *Buffy*, we see the similarity of the heroic and the monstrous. Buffy sees her own flesh as monstrous, while Willow becomes monstrous by detaching herself from the flesh. For the past several centuries, much of the western world has identified the flesh with both wickedness and woman — Eve, the temptress who gives in to the snake and offers Adam the bite.[3] But as *Buffy* proceeds, it demonstrates ever more clearly the necessity of the joining of flesh and spirit, even if that joining is painful. The last two seasons of *Buffy*, the dark seasons, show its protagonists — Buffy, Willow, and Spike in particular — coming to terms with their own existence as creatures of both spirit and flesh.

One of the most powerfully attractive elements of *Buffy* is the balance between the conceptual and the incarnate. From the first season, viewers have enjoyed the series' use of metaphor and heightened language. We know that we are helping to make the meaning when we engage the metaphor. *Buffy* is created by storytellers and full of characters who are storytellers, or word-wielders, in some way or another. The last two seasons deal in part with finding the balance between the word and the flesh, the conceptual and the incarnate. Buffy's final enemy, the First, is completely noncorporeal; and it hides a story that comes from *before* the time of the biblical Word.

So: The Word, the Flesh, and the Slayer — how do they work together? At the end of the fifth season of the series, Buffy sacrifices her life to save the world. As Bowman, Holder, and I, among others, have discussed, her action can be seen as part of the pattern of the hero, Campbell's monomyth. It can also be seen as in part suicidal, as Marti Noxon points out; in "Fool for Love" (5.7), Spike, who has killed two Slayers, tells Buffy that every Slayer has a deathwish. Now, at the beginning of Season Six, she is brought back from death by her friends Xander, Anya, Tara, and — leading the others — Willow. Secretly, Willow kills a fawn, with her own hands, to provide blood for the spell to bring Buffy back — "vino di madre," wine of the mother, she calls it. (She recites Hebrew words to the Father-God in taking it.) Giles later tells her she has opened herself up to all sorts of dark forces by casting this spell — and we see the opening quite literally: as Willow speaks the spell, kneeling at Buffy's grave with the others, she is surrounded by blood-red light, and her arms are slashed by invisible forces. These words damage the flesh. Immediately thereafter we see a snake emerge from her mouth. The spell's words entailed acceptance of the snake. The image of the snake will return in the last episode of the season, when once-gentle Willow plans to destroy the world. Imminent world-destruction is an ironic eventual result of these actions to bring back Buffy, who saved the world. A lot. The snake is traditionally seen as phallic, and the woman's acceptance of the snake as a sign of her sin; it might even be seen as Willow's endorsement of the patriarchal story of the fallen woman — a bad sign for an intellectual lesbian such as Willow.

It is at this point that we see the image of the rotting Buffy reincarnating in her coffin. Her friends, believing the spell has failed, have left the graveside, chased by demons who have followed the Buffybot — a robot which they had been using to convince the demons that the Slayer is still alive. Because her friends have left, Buffy emerges from her grave alone, one hand clawing through the dirt. She reads her own tombstone with horrid realization. She wanders, dazed, through a landscape she mistakes for hell. The demons, realizing the deception of the Buffybot, have taken over the town. Foucault begins his *Discipline and Punish* with the ancient physical horror of a detailed description of a man being drawn and quartered (3–6). Buffy is not drawn and quartered herself, but she views the event as it happens to her simulacrum: she watches the demons draw and quarter the Buffybot, who calls to Buffy as her robot body is destroyed. Buffy thus witnesses a violent variation on her own physical dissolution. One is organic and the other is mechanical, but the effect of both is that viewers are extensively confronted with Buffy's destroyed body as she returns from death.

It is only right, then, that Buffy's ability to re-inhabit her own body will take long months, or years, of struggle. "To feel" refers not only to the physical, but also to the emotional; so, too, when we are "touched" (cf. the episode of that title). In the proceeding months *Buffy* shows us the difficulty of reintegrating the two, of living, as the sixth season musical episode says, "Once More, with Feeling" (6.7). The visual representation of Buffy's dead body is an extreme example of Memento Mori. The fact that she is walking around in a body that was once dead aligns her with the monsters; and in the seventh season episode "Conversations with Dead People" (7.7), she declares, "I behaved like a monster."

In "After Life" (6.3), the third hour of the sixth season, Spike recognizes their kinship when he looks at the bloody hand with which Buffy "clawed her way out of her coffin. Done it myself." In the fourth season episode "Primeval" (4.21), the original Scooby gang — Giles, Xander, Willow, and Buffy — mystically join, representing Spirit, Mind, Heart and Manus — the Hand. Buffy is the Hand, the only physical element of the four, and her hand serves repeatedly as a synecdochic representation of herself.[4] So it is significant when Spike damages his own hand as he contemplates her suffering, or when he gently holds hers and offers to try to heal them. When her sister, Dawn, who has found her just after her return, leads her down the stairs of their home to confront Spike for the first postmortem time, Buffy fumbles with her shirt, buttoning it. It is the first sign she has shown of consciousness of her own body; she does it in awareness of Spike's presence, and it foreshadows her long, fiercely physical affair with him. As she later says to Tara, "The only time I feel anything is when," and she pauses, unable to put into *words* the fact of their physical connection. (She later refuses to name their relationship, not even willing to call it a "thing," in the episode "Dead Things" [6.13]). She has entered into an affair with him in the belief that she may have returned from the dead less than human. Though she repeatedly tells him she is not demonic, she nonetheless asks Tara to research Willow's spell, and is unable to accept Tara's declaration that she is "the same Buffy." Buffy *wants* to see her body as monstrous in order to justify her connection to Spike and her own violent sexual predilections — both of which help her feel. As Judith Halberstam says, "Monsters ... confirm that evil resides only in specific bodies and particular psyches. Monstrosity as the bodily manifestation of evil makes evil into a local effect" (162). This series sets about undermining that localization of evil. Buffy's self-condemnation follows a long tradition which represents the sexually desirous female as monstrous (see, e.g., Diehl). Buffy is different in that she will, eventually, get over the either-or, virgin-whore, human-monster dichotomy.

For the time being, however, seeing herself as monstrous allows her to engage in sexual pleasure, and allows many viewers pleasure as well. Spike and Buffy begin their lovemaking as sequel to a fight: Spike hits her to demonstrate that the computer chip preventing him from harming humans no longer works on her. Buffy herself initiates the affair; we hear her unzipping Spike's pants shortly before the sound drops away and we hear the music of their passion (music which Whedon chose). Buffy struggles with the idea of herself as monstrous while she immerses herself in the passion of the physical. It is a necessary counterbalance to the lack of emotional feeling she experiences upon her return. Again, in "After Life" (6.3), on her first night back among the living, she is confronted by a demon which was created as a side-effect of Willow's spell. Willow's description of the demon might equally apply to Buffy: "Its consciousness is here but its body is caught in the ether between existing and not existing." It can live in this world if it kills Buffy, so it attempts to demoralize her as it fights her — and like many dark creatures in the Buffyverse, it does so by speaking truth: "You're the one who's barely here — set on this earth like a bubble. You won't even disturb the air when you go." These are devastating words spoken to someone who is, in one way, the survivor of a suicide attempt. It is part of Buffy's heroism that she does not give in to the death wish. And it is all the more clear why she needs to reclaim the physical. It is to Spike she turns at the end of this episode, beginning her recovery by speaking her misery, at least to him.

Willow, like Spike, enables Buffy to fight — though she does so here as part of a pattern that leads Willow to a darker and darker place. The demon of "After Life" is at first, like the First, noncorporeal; it is, as Willow and Tara later say, a "Child of Words" — of the spell that retrieved Buffy. If Buffy is investing in the flesh, Willow is consumed by words — magic words. At first, Willow and Tara chant together, casting a spell on the demon so that, as Xander says, Buffy can "kick its fully embodied ass." But the spell concludes with Willow's dropping Tara's hands (recall the hand motif).[5] Her eyes black with magic, Willow alone speaks the one word "Solid" that makes the demon flesh. Throughout the series Willow has fearfully desired control — planning to use a de-lusting spell on Xander, applying a spell to have her will done after Oz leaves her; but in Season Six she repeatedly distances herself further and further from feeling — both physical feeling and truly connected emotion. Willow's nickname, of course, is Will, and her words contain her will, binding the world in her speech-acts. Her ability to control the physical and the solid with her mind and spirit leads her to feel a greater and greater distance from the physical; rather than feeling herself connected to the world, she sees herself as able to manipulate it as a possession. This relationship to the physical world is yet another attitude often associated with the traditionally patriarchal — dominion over the earth. (Cf. Buffy's dream of Riley and Adam and their plan for world domination in "Restless," 4.22). As Season Six proceeds, Buffy immerses herself in the physical while Willow, exerting control over it, distances herself from it.

Willow and Tara quarrel over Will's cavalier attitude; in "All the Way" (6.6), for instance, Willow proposes to search for the missing Dawn by transposing everyone else in a nightclub to another dimension for a fraction of a second. She recklessly disregards the potential physical harm and assumes nothing can go wrong, in spite of the fact that things *do* sometimes go wrong with her spells. It is only Tara's anger that interrupts her.

The title of the episode, "All the Way," of course has a sexual referent, and it most obviously relates to Dawn's Halloween encounter with a teenage vampire. But there are other sexual elements to the story, introducing a painful trope that recurs through *Buffy*'s two dark seasons. Sexual encounters can be seen as quintessential representations of relationship. It is sadly significant that there are at least four attempted rapes in *Buffy*'s last two seasons, one of which may have been completed. Many viewers have discussed Spike's attempted rape of Buffy (See Ch. 2 of *Why Buffy Matters*); there is also Warren, Jonathan, and Andrew's attempted rape of Katrina ("Dead Things," 6.13); there is the attempted spiritual rape of Buffy by the Shadow Men in "Get It Done" (7.15); and there is the conclusion of "All the Way." The last scene of this episode shows Tara and Willow preparing to go to bed together, Tara vehemently angry at Willow. Willow, a flower of forgetfulness in her hand, whispers the one word "Forget," a magic spell to wipe Tara's mind of the argument. For me, no scene in the series is more chilling than this moment. When she later realizes what has happened, Tara tells Willow that she has "violated" her mind — the more dangerously because of the mental damage Tara endured at Glory's hands. And it is not her mind only. "All the Way" is the episode in which Xander and Anya announce their engagement — a development which clearly stuns Willow, who in contrast is having trouble with her relationship. She wants a fantasy world of no-problem relations which bend to her will (cf. Warren's robot). By controlling Tara's mind, Willow also controls her body. The formerly angry Tara snuggles in bed with Willow, and her playful conversation suggests they may be about to have sex. In effect, horrible though it is to say, Willow rapes Tara.

It is not surprising, then, that Tara feels she must leave Willow, or that the series later makes a very clear parallel between Willow and Warren, who leads the trio in magically clouding the mind of his former girlfriend Katrina, with the intent to have sex with her. The nerd trio talk and play so long that the spell wears off just as Warren is about to have Katrina perform oral sex. She angrily confronts the three of them: "This is not some fantasy. It's not a game, you freaks. It's rape!" Warren's magic is not as strong as Willow's, and Katrina avoids the sexual possession of her body. (In that sense it seems she may be more fortunate than Tara.) But when Katrina threatens to send him to jail Warren kills her — the ultimate possession of another's body.

Unlike Warren, Willow can still respect some body boundaries. She has unhappily gotten to the point where she uses magic because "It took me away from myself" ("Wrecked," 6.10). But when the magic causes physical harm to Dawn, she completely stops. Later she will learn to reintegrate the magical and the physical, but for now she gives precedence to the basic humble needs of the body. She is no longer the woman who can speak a few words and shift dimensions. Willow's focus on the physical eventually brings Willow and the physically grounded Tara back together.

Tara and Willow first mutually recognize their choice to be together sexually in the fourth season, at the end of "New Moon Rising" (4.19). The moon goddess is Artemis, a huntress who lives without a man. At the beginning of the sixth-season episode "Seeing Red" (6.19), Willow and Tara are in bed together after lengthy make-up sex, and Willow asks, "When did morning happen?" "After the moon went down," Tara answers, foreshadowing the end. The misogynist Warren, shooting at Buffy, recklessly flings his gun around and unwittingly kills Tara. This kind of man hurts women even when he has no particular intent to do so, and his phallic weapon is only too appropriate. There have been many descriptions of, and many reactions to, the anguish of Tara's death. Its physicality is flung in Willow's face — literally, as Tara's blood splashes on her — vino di madre of another sort, the fulfillment of the blood sacrifice Willow began for the sake of Buffy's return. Willow sees blood, sees red, sees anger — and another of her nicknames is Red. She shakes the face of the gods when she shouts magic words demanding Tara's return, but she is repulsed, since Tara's death, unlike Buffy's, was an action born in the physical world. When Willow realizes she has lost Tara, she *has* lost the world: Tara's name means earth (her last name, Maclay, reiterates the point), and Willow has been rooted in Tara, the earth mother.

Her reaction *shows* her rejecting body for mind, rejecting flesh for word. Having lived for months within the physical, she now furiously rejects that world. She rushes to the Magic Box, with its store of powerful books. Visibly pulling their words into her body, she becomes Dark Willow, the witch of words. Her eyes and hair turn from their usual color to *inky* black. Small dark veins can be seen (more and more noticeably) on her forehead and around the edges of her face: the subtle monstrosity of *this* body suggests its emphasis on the mind. While Willow's third-season vampire alter ego Vamp Willow retains her red hair and clearly enjoys various pleasures of the flesh, Dark Willow lives in a cold fury. She takes Buffy and Xander with her on her way to revenge, as far as they will go. When they will go no further, she finds Warren alone. When she catches him, she stitches his mouth together so that she speaks and he has no words. She slowly, magically presses a bullet into his flesh so that he can know what Tara felt. When she does allow him to speak once more, her reaction to the emptiness of his pleading results in another of the series' most chilling moments. From Dark Willow's mouth comes Vamp Willow's characteristic phrase, "Bored now": and Willow in an instant flays Warren alive. Tara's murderer is made more than naked, his skinless flesh exposed.

This flesh is something in which Willow now sees no value. When Dawn later confronts her, Willow considers changing Dawn back from a flesh-and-blood girl to the magical ball of energy she once was — and Willow does not even register this as a loss. When Giles doses her with the help of a coven of witches, she is touched with positive magic, the magic of connection; as she says, "I'm connected to everyone." But her reaction is to want to put us all out of our misery, to destroy the suffering human flesh of the earth. Flesh hurts, so she wants to make it stop; and she has the magic words to do so. She can construct her own reality (and ours, too).

Willow is brought back not by Buffy but by her oldest friend, Xander. As she plans to destroy the world, she raises a buried temple with the figure of a naked woman (Proserpexa) entwined with a snake; the location is Kingman's Bluff. Despite the gender of the figure on the temple, Willow is following the king-based patriarchal style of controlling, rather than living with, the world. This view accepts the entwining of naked woman and evil. She sends out crackling waves of power towards the snaky image, but Xander throws his body in the way. He is marked, now, almost as she was marked at the season's opening. Later, everyone agrees that he saved the world with his words ("Same Time, Same Place," 7.3). But it works because he is willing to sacrifice his body, too: he tells her that she should kill him before she kills anyone else. His words express genuine acceptance of her, and his body lives out that acceptance as he takes her magical blows. Claiming his role as a carpenter, he very literally turns the other cheek. And I will note that in the seven years of *Buffy*, the word "Christ" is uttered as an exclamation only once — by Xander, when he learns of Tara's death and realizes Willow's unhealthy silence about it.)[6] Rather than using words to communicate her sadness, she uses them to conquer her enemy. It is because Xander unifies word and flesh that he succeeds. He not only speaks to Willow; he hugs her.

In the following year, it will take Willow a long struggle to achieve that kind of integration of body and spirit (and for his part, Xander does not manage to maintain it). She trains in England with the coven, and feels the connectedness of the world, but fears to use her magic. Sometimes it operates in spite of her: in the episode of her return to Sunnydale, she fears to face her friends, and so she unwittingly makes them not be in the same place at the same time ("Same Time, Same Place," 7.3). It is not simply that they cannot see each other; they cannot touch each other, either. The problem results in her entrapment by Gnarl, a demon which flays its victims alive and, singing a happy little song, eats their skin. The Scoobies find flayed victims and, remembering Willow's past, fear she is responsible. The balancing of the scales is only too clear when we see Gnarl slowly strip a sliver of skin from paralyzed Willow's belly — and, in one of the most grotesque of the series' scenes, he eats it. Strip after strip, he consumes her. The scene is also vaguely and horridly sexual as he crouches, naked, over her helpless body. It might be considered the Dark Seasons' fifth rape scene. Having violated Tara, Willow endures her own version of rape. She has flayed another human being, and now she is herself partly flayed. She is tearfully happy to find that she can touch her friends once again after the spell, and the episode ends with Buffy and Willow holding hands, sharing their strength for Will's recovery.

As for Buffy, she immerses herself in the flesh that Willow comes to disregard. But, like Willow, she is finding a way of escaping herself. When Willow tells Buffy that magic has been an escape for her, Buffy answers, "I get that, more than you..." — *know*, one assumes; and the audience knows Buffy is referring to her sexual encounters with Spike. Buffy and Spike are shadow figures for each other, and their parallels and mirrorings do much to account for their mutual attraction, for their pleasure of the flesh (see Ch. 5, *Why Buffy*). I for one enjoyed the idea of a female protagonist taking such pleasure (see Burr). But Buffy, at this point in her journey, does not trust the flesh; and, as she bluntly tells him, she does not trust Spike ("Dead Things," 6.13). The morning after their literally shattering first sex together, she tells him, "Last night was the end of this freak show" ("Wrecked," 6.10). Attentive viewers may recall that when her first love, Angel, broke up with Buffy in Season Three, he called their relationship a "freak show" ("The Prom," 3.20). Buffy has been wounded in her relationships in the past, so it is hardly surprising that, whenever Spike attempts to connect with her, she rebuffs him. "What did you think was going to happen? We were going to read the newspaper together?" she asks scornfully. Sharing words — a ridiculous idea. Here and elsewhere (e.g. "Gone," 6.11), when Spike is rejected in his attempts to communicate with her, he makes her respond physically, sexually, instead — since that is all she will allow him. She can only accept wordless flesh. When Spike returns to Sunnydale in the seventh season after he has regained his soul, it is not surprising that, in his maddened state, he asks her, "Am I flesh to you?" ("Beneath You," 7.2). She has tried to convince herself that he has been nothing more to her; and this is what has made him monstrous to her.

Through the first half dozen episodes of season six, after her return from the dead and during the time when she is aligning herself with him in monstrosity, Spike never appears in vamp face. In "Once More, with Feeling," (6.7) he vamps out briefly, but his back is to her. In "Tabula Rasa," (6.8) the episode before the one in which they first make love, the main characters all suffer magical amnesia, and Buffy and Spike are already becoming close before she sees him vamp out. Her angry disappointment carries over when she regains her memory, as she first rejects then passionately kisses him. It might be said that Buffy brings out the human side of Spike, while Spike brings out the monstrous side of Buffy. Like Willow, the two of them are certainly liminal characters, as we hear right before they make love: While they throw punches at each other, laughing, Spike mocks her: "Poor little lost girl — she doesn't fit in anywhere — she's got no one to love," and she answers, "Me? Lost? Look at you, you idiot — Poor Spikey — can't be a human — can't be a vampire — where the hell do you fit in?" In fact, by the end of the series, the majority of the central characters are liminal, and that in terms of the monstrosity of their bodies, as well: they are liminally monstrous. As Halberstam says, "The monster, of course, marks the distance between the perverse and the supposedly disciplined sexuality of a reader" (13) or a viewer; and when Buffy and Spike first make love, viewers are not sure of the status of Buffy's body. We know that the chip in Spike's head prevents him from harming humans, but no longer prevents him from harming Buffy; we know that she, like a vampire, has preternatural strength, monstrous strength, and that they use this strength in their lovemaking can be seen in its aftermath: "When did the building fall down?" Buffy asks on the morning after. But we do not see Spike making love to Buffy in vamp face. His invisible monstrosity, however, allows us to imagine her as invisibly monstrous, too. And when we do learn, from Tara, that it is not Buffy's body which is monstrous, we watch Buffy's misery as she realizes that she has crossed over another kind of line.

It might be tempting to say that Buffy's rejection of Spike, her rejection of monstrosity, is a rejection of sexuality, but the series is not so simple as that. When Buffy breaks off their affair, Spike almost rapes her in a horrid attempt to reassert their physical connection, hoping she will "let yourself love me." While their first violent lovemaking is surrounded by poignant, wordless song, there is no music in the harsh light of the attempted rape; and Spike's face is completely human. This monstrosity is a human act. And Spike, recognizing his own monstrosity, is driven, afterwards, to search for his soul.

When Spike returns, he and Buffy are in some ways more similar than ever, for he has regained his soul, yet he still has some elements of the monster. As for Buffy, in the fifteenth episode of the last season, we learn that, as many of us had suspected, Slayers *are* part demon. In the fourth-season closing episode, the all-dream "Restless," the patriarchally named Adam implies that they both get power from demonic sources. Now, in "Get It Done" (7.15), Buffy enters a place of testing where she meets the Shadow Men — a magical three African men from an ancient past. In that past, the first Slayer was made by being infused with the nature of a demon — "violated," as Buffy says. Now they offer to make Buffy *more* demonic: in fact, they chain her to the rocks like some desert Andromeda. "This is how it was then. How it must be now. This is all there is," they say, as dark, demonic energy swirls around the struggling Buffy's hips. The scene is clearly another of the dark seasons' attempted rapes, a spiritual rape this time (though in a sense all these attempted rapes are both spiritual and physical). But Buffy breaks free of her chains and fights off the demonic energy, rejecting the control of the Shadow Men. One of them carries a staff, a phallic, hierarchical symbol, and to stop their power she breaks it, saying, "I knew it — it's always the staff." In this same episode, she has goaded Spike to re-connect with his own monstrosity and power — "What I want is the Spike that's dangerous," she tells him. He subsequently re-emerges as a powerful warrior for their side, vamping out to battle successfully the demon that must be conquered in order to return Buffy to this dimension. Here Buffy is not troubled by, indeed she seeks, the wild, masculine power of Spike, the maverick (cf. Heinecken, 121). What she rejects is the hierarchical male power structure as represented by the Shadow Men who, we learn, were the forefathers of the highly patriarchal Watchers' Council who have controlled Slayers over the centuries.

Buffy, by fighting off the demonic energy the Shadow Men try to force on her, has chosen to remain in her liminal state rather than to become more fully demonic. But this episode does confirm that her power is rooted in the demonic; as noted in "Buffy vs. Dracula" (5.1), it is rooted in what is normally seen as monstrous. The big bad, or major villain, for the last season, is a power called the First Evil or just the First. It is that which initiates *all* evil, and it is completely noncorporeal; in that sense it is not a monster, not an inhabitant of monstrous flesh. It is able to appear in the shape of people who have died — including Buffy and Spike, among others. Its first lieutenant is a misogynist ex-preacher called Caleb, who considers all potential Slayers "Dirty Girls"; as in the traditional patriarchal story, flesh is foul, and women, in Caleb's words, "were born dirty."

His is a worldview, however, which is rehearsed only to be rejected; and it is rejected in more than one form. One of the most vividly monstrous bodies in the seventh season appears in "Lies My Parents Told Me" (7.17). The episode focuses on the relationship between Robin Wood and his mother the Vampire Slayer, and Spike and his mother. The authors changed the title from "Lies My Mother Told Me" because the episode also explores the relationship between Buffy and her father-figure, Giles (DVD episode commentary). When Drusilla sires William, turning him into the vampire who is to be Spike, he in turn bites his terminally ill mother to turn her. "Lies," the episode before "Dirty Girls" (7.18), depicts the rejection of the mother in a grossly Oedipal scene, acknowledged as such by the writers. The mother who was so happy to listen to William's bad poetry is now a vampire, taken over by a demon (as the *Buffy* mythology explains vampirism). This mother wants nothing more than to escape Spike, and she says she has wished to leave "ever since the day you first slithered from me like a parasite"— she turns them both into monsters with her words. And she taunts him about the woman he loves: "Think you'll be able to touch her without feeling me? All you've ever wanted was to be back *inside*. You finally got your wish, didn't you? Sank your teeth into me in an eternal kiss?" These memories Spike has repressed for over a century. Now the First is using the song his mother sang him to trigger Spike as a killer in spite of his inhibiting chip and his ensouled choice not to kill. The old folk song itself, with its lines "Oh, don't deceive me / oh never leave me / How could you use a poor maiden so?" refers to sexual desertion, a desertion alluded to by the vampire version of Spike's mother. Her name is never given in the episode, but the writers in the DVD commentary point out that it was Anne — Buffy's middle name. The writers also note that they chose an actress who they believed looked like an older version of Buffy actress Sarah Michelle Gellar. Whether or not viewers were aware of these similarities, I noted another. I have elsewhere discussed the imagery of light as pain in this series, primarily as it applies to Buffy and Spike. Spike is a vampire who seeks the light; in "Fool for Love" (5.7), in the poetry we hear his human version William making, he is looking for words that mean light; Dru, when she turns him, offers him something "effulgent" (in telepathic response to his desire), and when he sees Buffy as most beautiful, he calls her "glowing"— in the sixth season episode

"Hell's Bells" (6.16), for example, and in the seventh season in "Same Time, Same Place" (7.3). Now in "Lies My Parents Told Me," before his mother is in vamp face but after she is turned, released from her illness, he tells her she is "glowing." For me, that was the moment to know that, in this series as full of foils as *Hamlet*, we were seeing here another version of Buffy. Something of the monstrosity of the way Buffy has treated him can be seen in this version of his mother-lover. It is monstrous because it denies feeling and recognizes only flesh.

This version of the mother-lover is fully monstrous and fully hideous. It is the liminally monstrous characters who can be of the flesh without being consumed by it. So now, in the seventh season, the ensouled Spike is able to confront this long-buried memory, which led to murder, and know that, whatever demon words were spoken, the love between him and his mother was real. And he will eventually be able to make Buffy see that the relationship between him and her is also more than a monstrous connection of flesh alone.

In "Conversations with Dead People" (7.7), the series shows the complexity of interweaving the word and the flesh. This episode is one of only two which are labeled with a title, and it starts out with the broadcast date and then the time on the screen — simultaneously claiming existence in our reality and calling attention to itself as a human-named creation. The episode starts with a song, performed diegetically by musicians at the Bronze; the words were co-written by Whedon, and they call attention to the theme of aloneness (which pervades the dark seasons) and to the relationship between Buffy and Spike. We see first Buffy patrolling, and then Spike, in the past the possessor of the "wolf grin," as this phrase is heard. Ironically, given the title, Spike speaks not a single word in the episode; and there *is* something he is not telling. The episode (credited to Espenson and Goddard) has four interweaving segments, one of which was written, uncredited, by Whedon: this is the conversation between Buffy and Holden Webster, the new vampire, former schoolmate, psychology intern who analyzes Buffy's relationships, particularly her relationships with men. By the end of the episode she has acknowledged aloud that Spike did love her. And it is at this moment of openness that she and we learn that Spike has been killing again.

Throughout the episode, we have caught glimpses of his being with an attractive young blonde — one of his many Buffy substitutes. At the end of the episode, we learn from Holden Webster that it is Spike who sired him, days before. Buffy, who has sponsored Spike's freedom, is also responsible for the young psychologist's birth as a vampire; in effect, she is the mother for Spike's siring. And as the song returns, at the end of the episode, we see intercut the shot of Buffy killing the vampire childe just after we see Spike in perhaps the most physically monstrous face he ever wears. He drops the bitten blonde and, bloody-mouthed, licks his lips. As the image disappears, we see Buffy and then we hear the last word of the song: "alone." Buffy has not understood herself, but just as she begins to, she learns she has not understood Spike, either. Later we learn that in yet another of their similarities, he has not understood himself; neither of them is given to self-examination. It is only after he confronts the memories of his vampiric mother's lies (in "Lies My Parents Told Me") that he stops being controlled by the monstrous uses of the flesh. By the end of the series he lives *with* monstrosity; his demon side makes him one of their most powerful warriors and fits him for heroic self-sacrifice.

Shortly after "Conversations with Dead People," one of the most poignant moments of the season represents the value of the physical. It comes exactly halfway through the season. Spike and the others have now realized he has, under the influence of the First Evil, been killing again, and he tells Buffy she should kill him. But she tells him she knows that he has truly changed (and, in the Buffyverse, change is the hallmark of humanity); she tells him she believes in him. Immediately thereafter, he is kidnapped by agents of the First. Through day after day of torture, he is able to hold on by recalling her words. The First adds to the torment by appearing to him in the guise of Buffy. When Buffy herself is finally able to rescue him, Spike does not know at first that it *is* Buffy, and he feebly attempts to defy this "figment." It is when his hand touches Buffy's shoulder, flesh to flesh, that he knows this is not his incorporeal enemy, but someone he can lean on. Buffy's faint smile, as she accepts his touch, shows the meaning the moment has for her as well.

There are other such moments of the significance of the physical: Willow and Buffy holding hands as Willow heals; the spell-breaking kiss between Willow and Kennedy; and Willow and Xander in the hospital after his wounding come to mind. Elizabeth Rambo points out that there is a season-long motif of the touch of hand to face, seen with various characters. But the idea is most obviously depicted in "Touched" (7.20), when most of the major characters are shown taking physical comfort with another—sexual in the case of Willow and Kennedy, Xander and Anya, the second Slayer Faith and Robin Wood; and nonsexual in the case of Buffy and Spike. The noncorporeal First says, "I envy them."

The fleshless First, in fact, represents a remarkable reversal of traditional patterns identifying the flesh with wickedness. And Buffy's defeat of the First shows a different way in which she liberates herself and those who align themselves with her.[7] The chief agent of the First, Caleb, represents a dark version of the teachings of the church fathers, who rejected the "Dirty Girls" and their connection to the flesh; his is the word which has constructed much of western society's view of women and men, too, for that matter. And some would go farther on the word's control of the flesh: as Judith Butler says, "According to Lacan, the paternal law structures all linguistic signification ... and so becomes a universal organizing principle of culture itself" (79). Playdon argues that *Buffy* actually expresses pre-historic, pre-patriarchal mythic patterns. I would point out that one of the faces the First Evil repeatedly takes is that of Eve, a murdered potential Slayer; and of course the name recalls the name of the biblical first mother who, giving in to the snake's seductive temptation, condemned us all by the weakness of her flesh. This view of the world corresponds to the "Dirty Girls" theory of ex-preacher Caleb. But it should be noted that the First *falsely* takes the place of the true Eve, just as one might say that the traditional interpretation of the Genesis story misrepresents the true place of woman. In "Empty Places" (7.19), Spike and Andrew reconnoiter an ancient church, and a robed churchman shows them what seems to be an image of Mary (cf. Duricy). The honoring of the Virgin Mary is commonly viewed as a veiled continuation of ancient goddess worship. The churchman tells them of the frightening visit of Caleb, and says, pointing to the image of Mary, "Behind this he revealed something even we didn't know was here." Most churchmen certainly do not know everything that is behind the veneration of Mary; but here Spike and Andrew find an "ancient inscription." Reporting back to Buffy, Spike lifts her spirits when she is at her lowest; this is the night they spend together, touching, closer than they have ever been. The next day she uses the clue to find the female-forged weapon, the Scythe, and the last female Guardian, one of those who hid the weapon from the Watchers' Council and their predecessors. "I'm as real as you are," she says; she is ancient flesh and blood. And though the Guardian is cut down by Caleb (as the old religions were taken down by patriarchal ones), still the Guardian helps move Buffy one step closer to finding the way to resist the noncorporeal First Evil.

How can she resist? By turning from stereotypical solo heroics to power sharing. Buffy's plan is for Willow to use the power of the scythe to share her strength with all potential Slayers. For this to happen, Willow must be willing to risk fully using her power, fully being herself— something many an intellectual woman fears. For this to happen, women have to be willing to accept something of what's called the demon within;

those who can have the potential to be Slayers — have the potential to be leaders. The "Dirty Girls" will rule the world; the sisters of Eve can inherit the earth. And for this to happen, someone who has been demonized — someone like Anya or Spike — has to be willing to die for humankind.

In the miracle play of this myth, all of these things do happen. The characters rewrite the words to the ancient patriarchal story, and they accept the side of themselves that rejoices in the flesh. Whedon has commented that he felt that, with the time of the series running out, he had to present the story in shorthand, in compressed form ("Chosen" commentary). Ironically the series itself, towards the end, sometimes leans more towards idea than embodiment, more towards the word than the flesh. But I would like to focus on some moments that do, I think, succeed in conveying the delicate balance of spirit and body.

In the last battle of Sunnydale, set in the high school, Willow — Buffy's Will — acts physically and symbolically upstairs while Buffy, Spike, and the other champions battle demons below, uniting the conscious and the subconscious. And Willow, like Spike, glows with light. In fact, at one point his shaft of light breaks into her chamber (see ch. 6, *Why Buffy*). Willow is the woman who has tried to control the world and almost killed it, and herself. Her final spell, she says, will entail a "total loss of control." But now she allows herself to access her own power and more; and the result is not just world-changing strength shared with the women around her, but the joy, the pleasure of her own body. As the light of the spell fades, she tips over with a happy little postcoital, "That was nifty." And at this point, the positive identification of magic with sexuality, made much earlier in the series, has returned.

While Willow glows above, Spike burns below. Spike — who once was only flesh to Buffy — is now willing to give up his body. "I can feel it, Buffy," he tells her. "What?" she asks. "My soul — it's really there. Kind of stings." He is joining flesh and spirit, and now Buffy finally does say the words "I love you"; he gets the words only when he is about to lose the world of the flesh. Buffy and Spike bookend the dark seasons with their deaths. But of course it is *because* he is willing to die, to give up his body, that the ever-reticent Buffy is moved to speak the words. It could be seen as an endorsement of spirit over flesh except for one telling sign: when Buffy and Spike clasp hands, flames rise from their fingers in a visual representation of the passion still between them. Buffy leaves, and Spike laughs as his body burns away in a climactic explosion; "I want to see how it ends," he says.

Buffy ends with a question: "What do we do now?" The same openness can be found on the matter of spirit and body, word and flesh, in a brief scene in the final episode added by Whedon at the last minute. For three (the magic number) nights, Buffy and Spike stay together — the night of "Touched" (7.20), when Spike helps Buffy regain her confidence; the night when Buffy has the idea of how to hold off the First, how *not* to be alone, as she stays with Spike in her basement; and the night before the final battle. In a brief, *wordless* scene, Buffy and Spike look at each other across the basement where they have slept together. My first thought was, "This is an invitation to fanfic"; and indeed, in the commentary Whedon says that he wants viewers to freely imagine Buffy and Spike's time together. "If people believe that on their last night together they made love, great. If they believe that on their last night together they talked all night, great." Both flesh and word are available to them now. And Whedon adds, "It's almost the most important shot in the show — because it really shows the *mystery* of their relationship."

There is always a mystery in the way we try to frame a mental shape to the experience of the physical; in the way we try to give word to the flesh. *Buffy* attempts to encompass both transcendence and immanence. The heroes of *Buffy* engage us in part because they stand on the edge of monstrosity. But to the degree that the monstrous represents the limitation, danger, and pleasure of dwelling in one's own flesh, they come to accept it. They do not tell the old story that the flesh is the source of sin, though they do know that it can be the source of pain. To dwell truly in one's flesh means to know the risk of its loss, and the spirit bears this knowledge. We are all set on this earth like a bubble; and that is both the horror and the beauty of it.

Notes

1. Thanks to Lisa Yaszek, organizer of the Monstrous Bodies Symposium (Georgia Tech, Atlanta, March 29–April 1, 2005), where the first version of this chapter was presented.
2. "Bang" here can refer both to the Big Bang scientific theory of the creation of the universe and the slang term meaning coitus, i.e. the procreative flesh act.
3. See, e.g., Barbara Johnson.
4. Consider her use of her hand to destroy Adam in "Primeval," or the demon at the end of "Normal Again," when she must choose once more to bind herself to the experience of this world.
5. In one of the series' most touching moments, Willow requests that Tara read her palm and asks, "What do you see?" With charming focus on the physical present, Tara answers, "Willow hand."
6. On Xander as a Christ figure, see Stevenson 69, 101–02, 242–3, 257. As indicated in

various discussion lists, many Buffy viewers immediately recognized the Christ imagery. Though Whedon is an atheist, he invokes religious tropes.

7. While much of the series repudiates certain standard interpretations of Christianity, it also might be said to align itself with liberation theology, the theology of the Christ who overturns the tables of the moneylenders and shares the wine with the wedding party. The story of Jesus is, after all, a story of incarnation.

Works Cited

Bowman, Laurel. "Buffy the Vampire Slayer: The Greek Hero Revisited." Homepage (2002). 12 October 2002. http://web.uvic.ca/~lbowman/buffy/buffythehero.html.
Burr, Vivien. "Ambiguity and Sexuality in the Buffyverse: A Sartrean Analysis." *Sexualities* 6.3-4 (2003): 343-60.
Butler, Judith. *Gender Trouble: Feminism and the Subversion of Identity*. London: Routledge, 1990.
Diehl, Laura. "Why Drusilla's More Interesting Than Buffy." *Slayage: The Online International Journal of Buffy Studies* 4.1-2 (October 2004). http://slayageonline.com.
Duricy, Michael. "Marian Symbols in Buffy the Vampire Slayer." Paper presented at the Slayage Conference on *Buffy the Vampire Slayer*. Nashville, TN, May 28-30, 2004.
Foucault, Michel. *Discipline and Punish: The Birth of the Prison*. Translated by Alan Sheridan. New York: Pantheon, 1977.
Halberstam, Judith. *Skin Shows: Gothic Horror and the Technology of Monsters*. Durham, NC: Duke University Press, 1995.
Heinecken, Dawn. *The Warrior Women of Television*. New York: Peter Lang, 2003.
Holder, Nancy. "Slayers of the Lost Arc." *Seven Seasons of Buffy: Science Fiction and Fantasy Writers Discuss Their Favorite Television Show*. Glenn Yeffeth, ed. Dallas: Benbella, 2003. 195-205.
Johnson, Barbara. "My Monster/My Self." Diacritics 12 (1982): 462-70. Reprinted in *Mary Shelley, Frankenstein: The 1818 Text, Contexts, Nineteenth-Century Responses, Criticism*. J. Paul Hunter, ed. A Norton Critical Edition. New York: Norton, 1996. 241-251.
Kaveney, Roz, ed. "'She Saved the World. A Lot': An Introduction to the Themes and Structures of Buffy and Angel." In *Reading the Vampire Slayer: An Unofficial Critical Companion to Buffy and Angel*. Rev. ed. London: Tauris, 2004. 1-82.
Pender, Patricia. "'I'm Buffy and You're ... History': The Postmodern Politics of Buffy." *Fighting the Forces: What's at Stake in Buffy the Vampire Slayer*. Rhonda V. Wilcox and David Lavery, eds. Lanham, MD: Rowman, 2002. 35-44.
Playdon, Zoe-Jane. "'What You Are, What's to Come': Feminisms, Citizenship, and the Divine." In *Reading the Vampire Slayer: An Unofficial Critical Companion to Buffy and Angel*. Roz Kaveney, ed. Rev. ed. London: Tauris, 2004. 156-194.
Rambo, Elizabeth. "'Lessons' for Season Seven of Buffy the Vampire Slayer." *Slayage: The Online International Journal of Buffy Studies* 3.3-4 (April 2004). http://slayageonline.com.
Senf, Carol A. "Dracula: The Unseen Face in the Mirror." In *Dracula: An Authoritative Text, Contexts, Reviews, and Reactions; Dramatic and Film Variations; Criticism*.

Nina Auerbach and David J. Skal, eds. A Norton Critical Edition. New York: Norton, 1996. 421–431.
Stevenson, Gregory. *Televised Morality: The Case of Buffy the Vampire Slayer*. Dallas: Hamilton, 2003.
Wilcox, Rhonda. *Why Buffy Matters: The Art of Buffy the Vampire Slayer*. London: Tauris, 2005.

Bodies and Narrative in Crisis: Figures of Rupture and Chaos in Seasons Six and Seven

GREGORY ERICKSON AND JENNIFER LEMBERG

"From Beneath You It Devours"

The first five seasons of *Buffy the Vampire Slayer* were organized around certain assumed ideas: the metaphor of adolescence as hell, the battle of good versus evil, and season-long arcs ending with the definitive defeat of a different big bad. In the final two seasons of the show — the dark seasons, the UPN years, post–Buffy's death, and post–9/11— these defining elements of the show were abandoned, subverted, and blown to hell as good and bad characters traded places, evil became a fluid concept, metaphors dissolved and shifted, and faithful and thoughtful viewers were forced to react to what many saw as annoying, boring, confusing, disgusting, inconsistent, and incoherent structuring elements and plot developments. *Buffy* was always subtly subversive; the final two seasons, however, were constantly disruptive, upsetting the progress of storyline and character while drawing attention to these disruptions, forcing viewers to reconsider the narrative consistency of the show.

The final seasons challenge metaphysical assumptions about time, continuity, and narrative and cut to the heart of our contemporary anxieties about the stability of those long-held assumptions, creating tension between a desire for coherence and an unsettling awareness of destabilizing figures of rupture. Elements of inconsistency, insanity, and violation serve as (de)structuring devices and push us to question received ideas of structure and reception — questions which may have been part of the thematic structure of the first five seasons, but which now become part of the viewing experience. By looking at the disturbing idea of heaven, the multi-layered themes of rape and violation, the uncanny, ironic, and confusing nature of the villains, and the subversive presence of chaos that underlies the final two seasons, we will illustrate the tension produced when viewers' dependence on particular tropes to hold a series together is challenged by devices pointing to the impossibility of such unity. Like the images of torn and decaying bodies that threaten our ideas about the stability of the self, these images of rupture compel viewers to face the impossibility of coherence that is a defining feature of the last two seasons and of our postmodern world.

"Where Did I Go?"

From the shocking scenes of Willow violently stabbing a struggling fawn and vomiting up a snake, to Buffy's waking up in her coffin, the first episode of Season Six ("Bargaining" parts 1 and 2) announces in a multitude of ways that *BtVS* will be different from what it was in the past. We are in a different world — one where Buffy and her friends will suffer and inflict extreme violence and terror — and these extreme experiences are often expressed and negotiated through the idea of the body. Seasons Six and Seven develop the idea of the body as cultural text, rewriting it through acts of (re)appropriation, misappropriation, passing, imitation, doubling, and resignification. In a short sequence near the end of the second hour, for example, we see Buffy as a rotted corpse, we see a body torn into pieces, and we watch a demon threaten violent, flesh-tearing rape. Decaying bodies, torn limbs, and ripped vaginas are just a few of the ways that Seasons Six and Seven use the body as a site and metaphor of rupture, insecurity, and destabilization.

Therefore it is not surprising that the most striking scene of rupture in this episode requires us to witness a body destroyed. Midway through the episode, a dazed Buffy, having clawed her way out of her grave, wanders through Sunnydale, while a gang of demon bikers prepares to destroy the Buffybot, a robot replica of Buffy that her friends have been using to keep the demon-vampire world ignorant of her death. The bikers form a circle around the robot, each bike attached by a chain to its body, while the human Buffy, still disoriented, drifts unobserved onto the scene. In celebration of his triumph, Razor, the leader of the gang, points a gun in the air (the rare and always startling appearance of a gun on *BtVS* indicates another radical direction this season will take), announcing: "This here's a momentous occasion. The beginning of a new era." They are performing, he declares, "a symbolic act to commemorate a new order ... all in one quick really *really* violent fell swoop." The gun fires as the two Buffys recognize each other. The Buffybot calls out an unheard "Buffy!," the real Buffy screams "No!," her first word since emerging from the grave, and the bikes roar off in different directions, tearing the body of the Buffybot into pieces before Buffy's eyes.

The symbolic, metaphoric, and structural importance of this scene is evident on several fronts. Razor's heralding of a "new era" evokes *BtVS*'s move to a new network, while Buffy's watching herself being ripped violently apart proclaims the emergence of a darker, more violent series. Buffy's destroyed body is a metaphor for the dark and fragmented Season Six, encapsulating questions about how she will react to her own death, whether she will be able to put herself back together, and if she can accept and move beyond the death and violence that define her renewed existence as a Slayer. The doubling of Buffy with the Buffybot is emblematic of the splitting which Buffy will experience in multiple spheres and across the season, including the division between her sexual relations with Spike and the front she presents to her friends, and the psychic confusion she will suffer at the hands of the Trio. Further, Buffy's body itself will become a site of questioning. Her liminal status between living and dying forms a location at which ideas about life-death, human-not human, heaven-hell, here-not here are negotiated throughout Season Six. The scene also presents a larger project for Seasons Six and Seven, which use the idea of the body as a space to question ideas of fragmentation, unity, and continuity, and to explore what it is that makes us human. Our ideas of solidity and of certainty reside in the fragile security that we know who we are, and that we know the limits and boundaries of our own skin, and from the pieces of the Buffybot, to Buffy's "No!," to later scenes of violation, flaying, and torture, Seasons Six and Seven continually investigate this sense of certainty through challenges to the idea of bodily integrity.

When Dawn picks her way through the broken body parts, the robot suddenly opens its eyes wide and asks, "Where did I go?" Dawn slowly realizes that the question refers to the "real" Buffy, but it also resonates on a deeper level. The robot's final, "Where did I go?" along with the first sentence Buffy asks Dawn, "Is this Hell?" form the framing questions of Seasons Six and Seven, seasons that will be defined and characterized by questions. Buffy's existential questions, from "Where did I go?" and "Is this Hell?" which develop into "why am I here?" and "what is my purpose?" as well as the frequently asked, "What did you do?" go unanswered, and are instead established as unanswerable. Willow's spell, Razor's words, and the broken robot are all violent figures of rupture — figures that explore and enact a breaking away from the expected, safe, and predictable into territory that destabilizes the ground of understanding. By the end of Season Six, the Hellmouth is no longer just beneath Sunnydale, it is beneath viewers of the show as well.

By Season Seven, although Buffy appears to have put herself back together, her most common answer to difficult questions will be only a repeated, "I don't know." If Season Six offered a more violent and fragmented vision, then Season Seven challenges expectations through disruptions to the expected linear viewing experience. Although critics such as Elizabeth Rambo and James South have argued persuasively for the "philosophical consistency" of Season Seven (South) and its "remarkable coherence" (Rambo, 32), the arc of the entire series can also be seen as a move from coherence to incoherence, order to chaos. The final two seasons are about constructing new identities and new modes of organizing information — constructions that will question (although not abandon) concepts of linearity, duality, and causality. From Buffy's heaven, which shouldn't exist, to the shocking theme of rape, to evil characters that make little narrative or logical sense, both Seasons Six and Seven remove the grounds of certainty from which standard views of understanding narrative depend, moving instead towards a network of fragmentation and chaos.

"Things That Are Not": Negative Spaces of Instability

The violence required for bringing Buffy back to life, her terror when it happens, and the force of her later revelation that she believes herself to have been ripped out of heaven establish her return as an important rupture within Season Six. Buffy shares her feelings about it with Spike:

I was happy.... At peace.... And I was warm and I was loved and I was finished. Complete. I don't understand about theology or dimensions, or any of it really, but I think I was in heaven ["After Life," 6.3].

This heaven seems far removed from the Christian ideal, and more like a state of absence or nothingness: Buffy was happy because she was *not*. Furthermore, her concept of heaven as a negative space is thematically interwoven with her questioning of herself as human. Her conception of heavenly existence is strongly connected to other, more negative (and less angelic) states of being in which she is no longer present, and Buffy's absent presence in Season Six continually challenges the ontology of being and not being. If she was not really here when she existed as the Buffybot, her return, in her original, human form cannot guarantee her presence. In Season Five, Dawn profoundly said of Spike, "Chip—soul—same dif"; now, in Season Six, she cuddles with the Buffybot, only to later tell the human Buffy, "You're not really here anyway" ("Dead Things," 6.13). Buffy strikingly embodies the final line of John Donne's "A Nocturnal Upon St. Lucy's Day": "I am re-begot / Of absence, darkness, death; things that are not." What really is the difference between the Buffybot and the Buffy-*not*? Buffy's idea of her heavenly state is a form of negative theology, as she describes a divine experience by what it *is not*: "no pain, no doubt." Though encouraged to understand Sunnydale as hell, we are uneasy at the idea of heaven as a blissful non-existence: it is too final, too totally unimaginable.

If we are unable to comprehend or fully accept the radical non-being that constituted Buffy in heaven, we are equally unsettled when we witness her, and the show's narrative itself, unraveling in "Normal Again" (6.17), where Buffy's hallucination that she is in an asylum offers another means of escape. Located at an uneasy place in the middle of Season Six, the episode shows Buffy expressing the desire to leave her life that drove her suicide attempt in the musical episode, and that she experiences throughout the season. After Buffy has ultimately rejected the institution and chosen the reality of Sunnydale, the doctor looks into her eyes and says, "I'm afraid we lost her." This surprising final moment invites troubling interpretations: unless the institution is somehow real, it makes no linear or literal sense. While few viewers could accept that the show would employ the "it was all a dream," cliché, the other alternative, that the writers would willingly allow uncertainty as to which reality Buffy occupies, is also disquieting. The scene and its links to Buffy's idea of heaven present irresolvable challenges to the moral or narrative continuity of the season. Buffy's doctor insists that her "fantasy world" of slayers and vampires is coming apart—Dawn's arrival caused "inconsistencies," and the grand monsters have become "three pathetic little men"—a meta-critical and postmodern comment on the discontinuities of the show itself in Season Six. "Normal Again" forces viewers to acknowledge fictionality, to see the cracks in the narrative—to be aware of an imperfect text.

Dead Things

At the beginning of Season Six, the dismembered Buffybot, its remains left in the street and never properly disposed of, foreshadows the human Buffy's traumatized condition upon her return, which will be fragmented, lost, difficult to piece together. Where Buffy's sojourn in heaven is beyond our knowledge, her reentry into Sunnydale is a psychic trauma with profound and continuing impact, echoed in further traumas that image rupture for viewers of the series. Thus, the splitting and splintering of Buffy's (robot) body and (human) psyche prepares us for what comes later, repeated in many facets of Buffy's existence and in the series as a whole.

The literal line between life and death that Buffy crosses at the will of her friends suggests an important metaphorical boundary between wholeness and disintegration. By depicting her return as a traumatic event, the show attaches a conceptual vocabulary to an unimaginable experience. Psychological trauma represents a rupture or a complete break from the past (post-traumatic stress disorder was initially defined by the American Psychiatric Association as being caused by something "outside the range of usual human experience" [qtd. in Herman, 33]), and it offers an appropriate framework within which to understand Buffy's having survived an event outside of established (slayer) boundaries, both in terms of the questionable ethics of Willow's act of magic in accomplishing it and the destabilizing effects of Buffy's idea of heaven. It is not Buffy's death that makes her "detached" ("Normal Again," 6.17), or "dead inside" ("Dead Things," 6.13), but the trauma of being pulled from another dimension and then left alone underground.

If Buffy's friends ruptured boundaries between dimensions by returning her to life, her crawling out of her grave alone establishes a trope through which this act of violation can be understood. The intentions and methods of Buffy's friends may be questioned (in Season Seven, we learn that their act created "unstable disruptions" that allowed for the rising of The First, therefore indirectly resulting in multiple deaths), but that they leave her alone in the ground, in frightening, darkened scenes that take us into the claustrophobic space occupied by a Buffy who does not yet know what has happened, irrefutably offers viewers an image of trauma. In this way, the series layers a moment of trauma over Buffy's unknowable, indescribable experience that she believes was heaven. If heaven, or death, was beyond description, then leaving the grave — something understood only by vampires — is a shameful, highly embodied trauma. Buffy conceals her sense of woundedness, but when she finally tells of her belief that she was torn out of heaven, the disclosure opens up the idea not only that her friends have wrenched her from a peaceful state of non-being, but also that they have violated her by bringing her back.

Buffy's feelings after returning from death reflect the sense of some trauma survivors that they have "outlived" themselves and lead a "posthumous" life (Brison, 8–9). Their sentiments reveal the feeling that their true self has died at the site of the trauma, fragmenting their identity. Having herself survived being raped and left for dead, philosopher Susan Brison writes: "The line between life and death, once so clear and sustaining, now seemed carelessly drawn and easily erased. For the first several months after my attack, I led a spectral existence, not quite sure whether I had died and the world went on without me, or whether I was alive but in a totally alien world" (9). Brison's statements shed light onto the uncertainty of Buffy's posthumous state: death may have offered Buffy a welcome respite from her calling, but being brought back to life through an act of violation prevents her from ever feeling complete, or even completely alive. Forced to live, she will continually wonder if she is dead.

If Buffy's task in Season Six will be to recover an integrated sense of self, she first experiences increasing fragmentation, especially through her sexual involvement with Spike. Buffy and Spike's relationship will lead to the most extreme example of sexual violation, an important figure of rupture throughout Season Six. But the idea of violation will often be signified through literal and metaphorical threats of rape, as suggested from the beginning by Razor's violent, sexualized threats, and by Buffy's discovery in Season Seven that the first Slayer was herself profoundly violated, or, as Buffy puts it, "knocked up by some demon dust" ("Get It Done," 7.15). The primal significance of rape functions in these seasons as a powerful trope evoking fragmentation and disconnection, raising questions about our ability to trust and to harm one another; they are questions that, once introduced, prevent us from existing comfortably within the world of the show.

Rape, like other traumatic events, can "overwhelm the ordinary systems of care that give people a sense of control, connection, and meaning," splintering our relationship to the world around us (Herman, 33). By depicting traumatic events, especially rape, that disrupt the individual's connection to the systems organizing daily life, Seasons Six and Seven represent a departure for *BtVS*. In considering this idea, we may once again turn to the opening episodes of Season Six and the rampaging biker demons. Encountering Buffy's friends, Razor threatens the women with sexual violence, more explicitly than any demon before him. "We're not going to fight you," he tells them, "we're just gonna hold you down and enjoy ourselves for a few hours. You might even live through it except that certain of my boys got some anatomical incompatibilities that tend to tear up little girls" ("Bargaining," 6.2). Although Nikki Stafford echoes many fans when she deems this speech "completely unnecessary" (324), Razor's declaration of a "new era" is literalized in his terrifying threat, which introduces the possibility of violation through rape, threatening the dissolution of bodily integrity as well as feelings of connectedness and unity. While rape may not be "outside the range" of women's experience, as Judith Herman argues (33), it has been nearly unheard of in Sunnydale, so that the uttering of Razor's words constitutes a break with the past.

In the final seasons, the show also establishes connections between the concept of rape and broader themes of violation by pushing us to consider what happens when the assailant is a friend or loved one rather than a demon. As Lorna Jowett points out, more than once during Season Six Willow's actions may be understood in terms of rape (40). Willow's killing of Warren in "Villains," itself an enormous transgression in the taking of human life, is framed in ways that evoke the theme of rape, through her "penetrating his male body with a phallic weapon," the bullet that killed Tara, and her stripping him of his skin, which renders him an anonymous, barely recognizable form (Jowett, 40; Simkin, 26). Ultimately, of course, Willow's return to Sunnydale in Season Seven will be achieved in part through her falling victim to Gnarl, who, straddling her and luxuriating in tearing away her skin, simulates her earlier act of violation. Willow's shifting role as perpetrator and victim in a related series of violations further blurs the line between the human and the non-human, the violated figures of flayed bodies striking but no longer adequate markers of the boundaries between the two.

While Willow's acts of violation are powerfully rendered, nowhere will the theme of rape as violation be dramatized as explicitly as when Spike sexually assaults Buffy ("Seeing Red," 6.19). Where the violent, complex nature of Buffy and Spike's earlier sex scenes confronted us with uncomfortable connections between sex and power, desire and shame, now Spike nearly carries out Razor's terrifying threat. Like Buffy's friends, who assume that she suffers in death, he insists that he knows what she needs, despite her protests. His actions extend his earlier assertion, in 6.18, "Entropy," that what is between them is real, as the rape becomes a highly misguided way to force his reality upon her, to finally fix the meaning of what she is and what she feels. The rape is therefore a violation on multiple levels, an idea that is borne out in the repetition of Spike's language in another scene. As Stevie Simkin observes, when Willow penetrates Warren with the bullet ("Villains," 6.20), she declares her wish for him to feel it, in language that directly echoes Spike's insistence that Buffy feels their connection when he is inside her, and that she will feel it again when he forcibly enters her (26; n.25). The visceral sense of the real penetration is increased by its extreme contrast to the clean and non-graphic staking of vampires that characterizes the show. Accustomed to years of jokes about "Mr. Pointy," viewers of the show are likely to be astonished by these elaborate attempts at penetration and their clearly bodily consequences — not dust but wounds left in their wake.

In these scenes, the repeated language of desperation, vengeance, and desire — for power, for sex, for revenge or restitution — signals Spike and Willow's occupying an in-between space of good and bad, human and not-human. Additionally, in requiring others to feel what *they* believe is real, in other words, by dominating them, the friends who perpetrate these acts of violation will mimic the dizzying disruptions to time and space, blurring of identities, and repetition of events eventually effected by the Trio, and foreshadow the slippage between feeling, truth, reality, and violence that characterizes the actions of the First.

Uncanny Evil

The villains of Seasons Six and Seven serve to break the mold of previous seasons, forcing (often reluctant) viewers to revise their perception of what constitutes evil. The nerds of Season Six and the First Evil of Season Seven challenge viewers by being both too familiar and too impossible. Like Freud's "uncanny," which is defined by the juxtaposition of familiarity and strangeness, the Three are familiar as parodies of the personalities that consume texts like *BtVS*, yet they perform some of the most unbelievable acts, shifting time and realities at will. Similarly, The First is primarily psychological and internal and yet radically different and other, impossible to comprehend in its entirety. The fact that it is possible to describe Willow as the big bad of Season Six and Buffy as the big bad of Season Seven, as many have done, offers further evidence of the slippery construction of evil in the final two seasons. The evil characters should "wear a sign," as a confused Faith says upon her return to a more ambiguous Sunnydale ("Dirty Girls," 7.18).

Much of Buffy's suffering during Season Six is caused by the Trio, the Three or the Troika, whose antics, pathetic at first, grow increasingly dangerous. With Warren in charge of technology, Jonathan working magic, and Andrew summoning demons (channeling figures of disruption from the prehistoric to the postmodern), they seek Buffy's attention even as they wish to defeat her, their interest in her failures and triumphs rivaling that of her friends. Lacking superior physical strength except when they borrow or channel it, their efforts frequently take the form of mind control, and they repeatedly succeed in deepening Buffy's feelings of confusion, isolation, and fragmentation by seeming to bend space and time or to blur the lines between life and death. As the season progresses, the young men focus their inventiveness, but also their rage, on exercising their power in highly sexualized ways.

In a pivotal scene, the Trio accidentally kills Warren's ex-girlfriend, Katrina ("Dead Things," 6.13). While her actual death is a shocking event, the episode is profoundly disturbing from the outset. In an experiment designed to test the "cerebral dampener," Warren goes to a bar, looking for Katrina, who left him when she discovered, earlier, that he had built a sexually submissive robot girlfriend ("I was Made to Love You," 5.15). Warren uses the dampener on Katrina, bringing her back to the clubhouse dressed in a provocative French maid's uniform, and making her behave like one of the sex-toy robots he has created. When Jonathan and Andrew join him in admiring Katrina and wonder when they'll get their turn, Warren promises them, "You play with her all you want, after I'm done with her." Alone with her, Warren tells her first "I love you baby," but then says "get on your knees." Dominating Katrina but willing to share her, Warren becomes a pimp, whose job it is to prepare a woman to service other men (Farrell, 284). His actions are consistent with what Kirby Farrell describes in another context as a "master-slave fantasy," in which, by "breaking the 'slave's'" will, the pimp becomes an executive self commanding other bodies — as in vampirism and the Nazi economy," and through which he establishes a "predatory prosthetic relationship" (284). In making Katrina less than human (as a human incarnation of the robots he made in the past), Warren, too, is transformed.

The Trio's violation of Katrina makes clear that no matter how humorous they may be — we laugh both with and at them, and, recognizing their sci-fi references, we identify with them more than we'd like — they are willing to perform the unthinkable. They are part of the darkness of Season Six, not just comic relief from it. While Season Six seems designed to make us uncomfortable with the boundaries between silliness and seriousness, fantasy and reality, like Razor's threat of rape, their manipulation of Katrina takes us further into the territory of criminality and violation than we have been conditioned to expect. Their intended acts of sexual violation destabilize lines between the familiar worlds of fantasy they consistently refer to (video games, comics, "free cable porn") and one of troublingly real violence.

Katrina herself will make this overwhelmingly clear. In an initially consoling moment, the dampener wears off before she can perform the sexual favor. She is thus momentarily able to avoid being violated further, though she will soon lie dead, the Trio's first human victim. Katrina angrily voices what the audience may be feeling: "This is not some fantasy. It's not a game, you freaks! It's rape!" The word "rape" shocks Jonathan and Andrew, much as it shocked many viewers waiting for the scene to turn to humor. It produces disruption on both levels of the show, altering the characters' perception of events and also signaling a shift for the audience. Initially leading viewers to find the Trio funny and inept, in the characters' perpetration of real evil, the show violates expectations and seems to put its unstated contract with viewers into jeopardy. This one spoken word — "rape" — is a pivotal point for Season Six, piercing into the viewer's consciousness that this season may be funny at times, but it will be no joke.

Finally, the Trio's entry into real evil is underscored by their attempts to make Buffy believe that she has murdered Katrina. Once again altering Buffy's sense of reality, they engage Buffy in a fight in which she seems to have killed Katrina accidentally. Katrina's dead body becomes a thing from the moment Jonathan refers to her corpse as "it" (in the manner of Nazis referring to dead Jewish bodies as *figuren* in order to separate the material body from the idea of the human), and Buffy temporarily resembles one of Warren's robots, her mind controlled and her reality altered by the Trio. Later, in a troubling dream, Buffy sees herself alternately straddling Katrina and then Spike, handcuffing or penetrating them, or being penetrated herself, her positioning in the dream sequence mirroring her physical stance during the real events of earlier that night, and implying her belief that she is, like Spike, "dead inside." Buffy's dream literalizes the continuum between victims and perpetrators, the powerful and the powerless, the living and the dead that has been a frightening theme in Season Six. Measured according to their relationship to Katrina's body, a "dead thing" which has been manipulated, prostituted, defended, murdered, and dumped in a river by the time of the episode's conclusion, the capacity of any individual or individual body to occupy different spaces along that continuum is made all too powerfully clear.

Beyond their unexpected sexual violence, the Trio's ability to manipulate time and change reality made viewers uncomfortable by challenging the reality of the viewing experience, by making the suspension of disbelief impossible. Many Buffy fans like to think of demons and vampires as *possible*. However, as opposed to more or less traditional supernatural enemies, even though the Trio are normal human beings, they are also impossibly powerful. Their accomplishments in Season Six — disrupting time, discovering invisibility — are more dangerous than those of any of Buffy's other enemies, yet as more comic book villains than supernatural enemies, they seem frustratingly less believable to many viewers. The Trio again force a new reality on an unwilling subject, as to accept them into the context of the viewing experience is to accept such concepts as inconsistency and instability as part of the fabric of the show.

Dissolving definitions of good and evil, human and monster, and the unity of the soul are fully realized in the absent presence of The First in Season Seven, when the deconstruction of the unity of the body and the autonomy of the self that began in Season Six finds its negative expression in the incorporeal absent presence of the First. The body continues to be a site of contestation in Season Seven — note especially the ubiquity of bandages, casts, scars, and bruises. If holding onto the concept of the unity of the body is a guarantee of presence, then the absent and fluid nature of the First uses this instability to threaten the idea of order, and to increase our anxieties over the idea of the Other and of the post-human.

Prepared for by the destabilizing and chaotic effect of the Three, the First Evil is a force that is no-body and any-body, that exists as an unstable combination of the dead body that it occupies and the psyche of the person it appears to, and that very literally destabilizes the ground beneath our feet. However, in a reverse of what we might expect, while the Trio was unsettling in being too powerful to be believed, The First is a threat because it is too familiar and ultimately, in itself, powerless. Whether The First *created* evil or is created *by* evil is never completely clear. The First initially described itself as "beyond sin," "beyond understanding" and "the thing the darkness fears" ("Amends," 3.10). For Giles, "there's evil and then there's the thing that created evil" ("Bring on the Night," 7.10), but the other possibility is that the First, as Andrew says, is "made out of the Evil impulses of human beings" ("First Date," 7.14).

The villains of the final two seasons come together in the moment when the First appears as Warren to Andrew and convinces him to murder Jonathan in order to open up the Hellmouth. Operating through the physical bodies as well as the incorporeal presence of the Three is what allows the First to unleash its own physical, or embodied, force from the depths of the Hellmouth. The manner in which the Three and the First enact their ruptures into the narrative suggests the concepts of "radical evil" and "banal evil" developed in philosophical works by Hannah Arendt and, more recently, by Richard Bernstein. The First is radical because it cannot be explained by comprehensible motives, and the Three represent radical evil in that their actions disturb the ground of understanding of those affected by them. Both can be understood only outside of our metaphysical tradition, especially as it is represented by traditional television dramas, which depend on teleological narrative. Yet both evils are banal in that they represent the most ordinary or internal aspects of the human condition: they are essentially, and only, all of us. Although philosophers argue over whether these two formulations of evil are contradictory or compatible, in Seasons Six and Seven they are symbiotic, working together. Evil is banal and radical, boring (or funny) even as it forces absolute breaks in our understanding of ourselves and confronts viewers with the impossibility of philosophizing their own metaphysical existence.

In the End Is Chaos

Repeated figures of rupture — unexpected images of rape and violation, unsettlingly ambiguous and unstable images of good and evil, and disturbing breaks in the narrative and narrating process — are all part of what make Seasons Six and Seven an exploration into our need for order and our resistance to fragmentation. Buffy may tell the Potentials that they "have a reason" and that they are not "here by chance" ("Potential," 7.12), but that is exactly the kind of moral and cosmic certainty that Season Six and Seven continually question. Season Seven, especially, abounds in statements of uncertainty. In the episode "Selfless" (7.5), Spike says, "I don't trust what I see anymore." Buffy claims, "It is never simple. It is always different. It is always complicated," and Anya admits that "I'm not even sure there's a me to help," three questioning statements that express, respectively, a doubt in empirical knowledge, narrative, and the existence of an autonomous self. Throughout the season it is stressed that although we may desire balance, order, a sense of self, and a definition of good and evil, these things are ultimately denied us.

Andrew most clearly represents this desire for definition, order, and linear narrative, constructing charts in order to discern patterns and creating his own coherent narrative of events through a homemade documentary. A parody of that great symbol of television narrative, *Masterpiece Theater*, the episode "Storyteller" (7.16) with Andrew as the host, opens with a close-up of the spines of two leather bound books labeled "Nietzsche" and "Shakespeare," perhaps signifying the two great traditions of literature and philosophy. But while Shakespeare represents a paradigm of five-act narrative, for Nietzsche "unity, identity, permanence, substance, cause, being" are to be seen as only man-made "fictions" (*Twilight of the Idols*). Therefore, there is a sense in which Nietzsche and Shakespeare do not represent two great traditions, but opposing storytellers that cancel each other out and clear the playing field for new participants and a new type of story. Although, like Andrew, we want life to make sense as an organized coherent narrative, for us, like the gang in the final season of *Buffy*, there is no going back to a simpler more linear world. Buffy tells Andrew that "life isn't a story," and her character's arc in Seasons Six and Seven involves a gradual realization of the necessity of disorder and uncertainty.

The final seasons of *Buffy* force us to let go of our certainty, and to admit we don't and can't know. If Season Six is defined by the questions "Where did I go?" and "Is this Hell?" then the most important and often repeated answer to questions in Season Seven is "I don't know." This is Buffy's response to Dawn when she asks, "What does it mean that Spike is all soul-having?" ("Him," 7.6), to Spike's questions, "Why is it [the First Evil] doing this to me?" ("Sleeper, 7.8) and "What does this mean?" ("End of Days" 7.21), and to a potential's inquiry, "Are you, like, back?" ("End of Days," 7.21). This repeated response to questions of the importance of a soul, structure, plot, and meaning (and also the unstated answer to the final question of the series) pushes the season into a questioning, non-positivistic space of chaos. As Masterpasqua and Perna point out in *The Psychological Meaning of Chaos*, "a system in chaos takes the stance 'I don't know.' It is thus open to any number of evolutionary paths" (91). The study of chaos challenges "both the assumption that there is an objective verifiable universe and that there is a self-contained, individual self who can know the one truth" (Demastes, 10). The villains of Seasons Six and Seven destabilize and rupture our sense of a single reality, but rather than fight against that, we, and the characters on the show, must learn from them, learn to see and seek multiple paths and narrative. The new possibilities contained in the new, non-linear model are only possible after Seasons Six and Seven, after the Trio and The First.

To use chaos as a tool or metaphor of understanding is to develop new ways of processing complex information, and it is what allows Buffy to visualize her plan to defeat The First. In their final act together — performing a ritual that destroys the line of power passed on from one slayer's body to another, therefore giving every potential slayer the power of the chosen one — Buffy and Willow must defy the rule of a "bunch of men who died thousands of years ago" ("Chosen," 7.22). Our ideas of order, of power against chaos, all come from the rules of long-dead men: Aristotle, Moses, Jesus. Buffy and Willow's act can be seen as an act of anti-myth and as a dismissal of traditional metaphysical order, a releasing of chaos upon a cosmic order. If the many potential slayers in Season Seven were confusing for viewers, the shift to a world of thousands of slayers is incomprehensible. In this final act, Buffy attacks the socially constructed roots and apostolic succession of her own mythology and religion and rids her power of any sense of absolute essence. The body of the slayer, the space of conflict and magic (when Buffy's body died, another slayer was created), is now disseminated to a point of unintelligibility. The conclusion of Season Seven, and of the series, becomes, in this context, a metaphorical exploration of what it means to signify the end of a narrative, of the unity of the individual, of teleology, and of history — in short, it questions the ideas of origin, narrative, and continuity on which episodic television (and Western metaphysical traditions) have conventionally been based.

Works Cited

Brison, Susan J. *Aftermath: Violence and the Remaking of the Self.* Princeton: Princeton University Press, 2002.
Demastes, William W. *Theatre of Chaos.* Cambridge, UK: Cambridge University Press, 2005.
Farrell, Kirby. *Post-traumatic Culture: Injury and Interpretation in the Nineties.* Baltimore: Johns Hopkins University Press, 1998.
Freud, Sigmund. "The Uncanny." In *The Standard Edition of the Complete Psychological Works of Sigmund Freud.* London: Hogarth Press, 1955.
Herman, Judith. *Trauma and Recovery.* New York: Basic Books, 1997.
Jowett, Lorna. *Sex and the Slayer: A Gender Studies Primer for the Buffy Fan.* Middletown, CT: Wesleyan University Press, 2005.
Masterpasqua, Frank, and Phyllis A. Perna. *The Psychological Meaning of Chaos: Translating Theory into Practice.* New York: American Psychological Association, 1997.
Nietzsche, Friedrich. *Twilight of the Idols/The Anti-Christ* [1889; 1895]. New York: Penguin, 1990.
Rambo, Elizabeth. "'Lessons' for Season Seven of *Buffy the Vampire Slayer.*" *Slayage:The Online International Journal of Buffy Studies* 11–12 (2004). November 11, 2006. http://www.slayage.tv/essays/slayage11_12/Rambo.htm.

Simkin, Stevie. "'You Hold Your Gun Like a Sissy Girl': Firearms and Anxious Masculinity in *Buffy the Vampire Slayer*." *Slayage: The Online International Journal of Buffy Studies* 11–12 (2004). November 11, 2006. <http://www.slayage.tv/essays/slayage11_12/Simkin_Gun.htm>.

South, James. "On the Philosophical Consistency of Season Seven: or, 'It's not about right, not about wrong...'" *Slayage: The Online International Journal of Buffy Studies* 13–14 (2004). November 11, 2006. http://www.slayage.tv/essays/slayage13_14/South.htm.

Stafford, Nikki. *Bite Me! An Unofficial Guide to the World of Buffy the Vampire Slayer.* Toronto: ECW, 2002.

Reality Bites: Buffy in the UPN Years

LYNNE Y. EDWARDS AND CARLY HAINES

Introduction

Why is everyone so upset about Season Six and Season Seven? Sure, Buffy dies in "The Gift" (5.22), she comes back on UPN in "Bargaining, Part 1" (6.1) and "Part 2" (6.2), there is some unpleasantness with the Scoobies throughout most of Seasons 6 and 7, they work it out in "End of Days" (7.21), and then order is restored and they sing their metaphoric kumbayayas in "Chosen" (7.22). We've seen it all before — heck, Buffy even sings about it: same old trips, why should we care ("Once More with Feeling," 6.7)? After all, Buffy died and came back in "Prophecy Girl" (1.12), was extremely unpleasant toward the Scoobies, worked things out, and restored order in the second season on the WB ("When She Was Bad," 2.1). Technically speaking, Seasons 6 and 7 were downright déjà vu-y — yet, there was something different about Seasons 6 and 7.

When Buffy died in "The Gift" (5.22), we hoped — but we didn't know — that Buffy was definitely coming back and that she would still be our Buffy. And we were right to be concerned. The Buffy who came back to us in Season 6 was a far cry from the wise-cracking, ass-kicking slayer who boldly threw herself into an alternate dimension to save her sister and to save the world. In her place was a bewildered and disconnected soul whose teen-angsty high school battles seemed a generation away and whose primary concern now appeared to be getting through the day and paying her bills. In other words, our Slayer died and came back an adult — and an unhappy one, to boot. The Scoobies were also at a loss; by Season 6's premier, the Scoobies were all grown up and facing adult trials of their own. They had lost their "mother" Joyce ("The Body," 5.16), their "sister" Buffy ("The Gift," 5.22), and were saying goodbye to their "father" Giles who was heading back to England ("Bargaining, part 1," 6.1). Sunnydale's hell had become very real indeed.

To go from epic battles with The Master, with Adam, and with Glory to futilely and frantically trying to thwart the pathetic yet deadly misogynistic Trio seemed to be a colossal, and oddly ironic, fall to earth for Buffy. Three of the very civilians Buffy had risked her life to save in Seasons 2 and 3 became the very monsters she would spend Season 6 battling. Like Buffy's normal new life, the Geek Trio's mission[1] bordered on the mundane. And I couldn't get enough. After five seasons of training in Buffy's Scoobie dojo, I was ready for the biggest monster of all: real life. For five years on the WB, *Buffy*'s metaphoric monsters reflected the real world hell that most youths inhabited; for two years on UPN, *Buffy*'s monsters became the real world. This essay examines how Buffy's metaphoric monsters foreshadowed her very real world battles.

Death and Déjà Vu in Sunnydale

> "Buffy will meet the Master and she will die."
> — Giles ("Prophecy Girl," 1.12)

> "Death is your gift."
> — Spirit Guide ("Intervention," 5.18)

Several Buffyologists have explored the intricate relationship between death and the Slayer, equating it with sexual desire and with a feminist challenge to the patriarchal order of procession for heroes.[2] Jana Reiss has called *Buffy* one of the "more death-obsessed shows on television" and suggests that in *Buffy*, death functions as a "teacher" for viewers (25). From Jesse's siring and death in Season 1 ("The Harvest," 1.2) to Joyce's equally untimely death from a brain tumor in Season 5 ("The Body," 5.16), we were forced to face the horror of suddenly losing friends and loved ones without the comfort of knowing that they found peace in death:

> For such a deeply metaphysical show, *Buffy* says surprisingly little about the afterlife that it presumes to exist. However, the show has quite a bit to say about how the ultimate reality of death should inform the human experience here and now [Riess, 25].

Death may be something that Buffy is accustomed to dealing out, and even, to a certain extent, facing every day, but rebirth seemed to be the bigger struggle for her. Buffy rarely enjoyed the "hero's return" that Campbell describes; rather than boon, Buffy's return often brought pain and confusion. Buffy, and at least two other Slayers according to Spike, also seeks peace in death, subconsciously yearning to die and lay down her very singular burden. As Reiss notes, Buffy seems incapable of "feeling alive" and even the presence of her friends is not enough to bring her any joy in living.[3] Buffy's brief death in "Prophecy Girl" (1.12) was enough to thwart the prophecy in the Codex and to destroy the Master, but her victory over death did not bring her any peace. The Slayer, who could deal with anything, including death, was suddenly unable to deal with life. Buffy's death and resurrection also revealed an unexpected identity crisis, a bitter resentment of her friends' carefree lives in the face of her slayer destiny and a new identity crisis when her replacement, Kendra, arrived in Sunnydale and connected immediately with Giles ("What's My Line, part 2," 2.10).

Buffy's despair and loss are immediately evident upon her return to Sunnydale in "When She Was Bad" (2.1). Her father describes her as "brooding and sulking" during her summer visit with him, but it is Buffy's interactions with Cordelia and the Scoobies that provide our first indication that she is not our Buffy anymore. Willow and Xander are shocked when Buffy bitingly promises not to tell anyone that Cordelia is a "moron" after Cordelia loudly promises to keep Buffy's slayer identity a secret. Both Scoobies comment that the sting against Cordelia was a little "too good" coming from Buffy. Ironically, Cordelia also notes Buffy's cruel new nature and warns Buffy that she is in danger of losing her friends if she continues behaving this way: "Whatever is causing the Joan Collins 'tude, deal with it. Embrace the pain, spank your inner moppet, whatever, but get over it. 'Cause pretty soon you're not even gonna have the loser friends you've got now" ("When She Was Bad," 2.1). Buffy demands that the "civilians" (a.k.a. The Scoobies) butt out of Slayer business, even when her tunnel vision leads them into mortal danger—a danger so great that Xander even threatens to kill Buffy for putting Willow's life at risk.

Death and foreshadowing are frequent themes in *Buffy*, and Cordelia's words of reproach are repeated in Season 6 as Buffy once again struggles with re-entry and re-assimilation. The foreshadowing function of death in Buffy serves as a wonderful instructor in the real world since death is the one inevitability that we spend our real lives fighting and it is the one inevitability that *Buffy* regularly inverts through the use of vampires and through the moral ambiguity of concepts like heaven and hell. This inversion, however, presents a window into the part of the hero myth that we rarely consider in television: the return. Even a soulless demon like Cordelia ... er ... Spike ... can see that returns are problematic. The irony, of course, is that the return makes Buffy not only a hero but also more akin to the vampires she slays since they, too, are forced to return against their will and walk between the dark and the light: "Oh, poor little lost girl. She doesn't fit in anywhere. She's got no one to love" ("Smashed," 6.9).

In season 2, Buffy eventually works through her grief at facing her own mortality, only to come face to face with the primary consequence of her death: Kendra. Kendra's activation further drives home the consequences of Buffy's death and return. Even Giles is flummoxed by Kendra's presence in Buffy's town; Buffy; however, is freaked out: "What's the flum? It's a mistake, she isn't supposed to be here, she goes home! Look, no offense, I really don't mean this personally, but I'm not dead, and frankly having you around creeps me out just a little bit" ("What's my line, part 2," 2.10). This disruption in the Slayer line foreshadows Buffy's battles with Faith and the epiphany that they don't get along because two Slayers aren't supposed to exist at one time ("End of Days," 7.21). Buffy's death in "Prophecy Girl," therefore, doesn't merely signal the birth of this generation's next Slayer; co-existing with Kendra foreshadows the death of the "one slayer in each generation" myth. We were faced with the knowledge that Buffy, although she was the Slayer, was not the only Slayer in the world; the "word" isn't the "truth."[4]

Kendra's presence also offers Buffy the opportunity to seriously consider the prospect of having a normal life. In "What's My Line, part 1 (2.9), Buffy laments that her future is "sealed in fate": "Unless Hell freezes over and every vamp in Sunnydale puts in for early retirement, I'd say my future is pretty much a non-issue." However, Buffy begins to consider giving up the Slayer identity to Kendra and heading off to Disneyland. This willingness to cede her power to Kendra foreshadows the collective and collaborative battle waged by Sunnydale students against the mayor in "Graduation Day, part, 2" (3.22) and the activation of the Potentials in the series' finale. "So here's the part where you make a choice: What if you could have that power ... now? In every generation, one slayer is born ... because a bunch of men who died thousands of years ago made up that rule.... So I say we change the rule. I say my power ... should be our power [Buffy, "Chosen," 7.22]. The Scoobies had their own battles in Seasons 6 and 7 as they each came into their own power only to learn that they were unable to wield it. Xander's love for Anya, which had in essence, redeemed her demon deeds, unexpectedly became the impetus for her return to the vengeance fold when he left her at the altar ("Hell's Bells," 6.16). Willow's Wiccan power and love for Tara combined to create Dark Willow, a force as dark and apocalyptic as a hellgod, unleashed after Tara's senseless murder ("Villains," 6.20). Rack describes Willow as the "new power" in town whose rage will "blow the town apart" to get the man who killed Tara. Death in Sunnydale, apparently, not only foreshadows loss of *the* Slayer identity, but also that of her friends.

The Fox, the Frog, and the Failure...

Ironically, Buffy's death in "Prophecy Girl" also reflected the connection with death in *Buffy the Vampire Slayer* and network corporate realities. Buffy was initially a mid-season replacement on the WB for *Savannah*, a serial drama about three girlfriends and their troubled relationships set in the South. The Aaron Spelling prime-time soap opera started off strong on the WB, earning a 3.6 rating on average among 18-to-24-year-old women in 1996 before dropping down to an average 2.5 rating in its second and final year. In its final days, the WB fought hard to save Savannah, even sponsoring a contest offering 7 days and nights in a Southern mansion, complete with maids and servants.[5]

Poor ratings eventually killed *Savannah* and gave birth to *Buffy*, metaphorically connecting Buffy's arrival to the death not of another slayer but to the death of an unsuccessful program. Not that a program entitled *Buffy the Vampire Slayer* was a guaranteed hit, either:

> In the world of network television, being a midseason replacement on the WB was pretty much the bottom.... From the beginning, the title was an obstacle. The network tried to get Whedon to change it from *Buffy the Vampire Slayer* to *Slayer*, but Joss Whedon was adamant. "I believe that anyone who isn't open to a show with this title isn't invited to the party" [Havens, 33].

It was a time of change and revolution in the television industry[6] as advertising rates were rising while the television market was marked by an unprecedented fluctuation in the networks and growing competition from cable and other audience siphons. Into this market, two new mini-networks, The WB and UPN, launched within one week of each other in January 1995, battling for the same audience, the same advertisers and the same destiny: to be the fifth network.[7] To be competitive, the new networks offered cut rate advertising prices[8] as incentives for prospective advertisers and offered syndicated programming limited to only one night a week. In addition, the two minis offered creative revenue stream structures.

The two networks struggled to establish unique identities and a sufficient number of affiliates to successfully compete against each other. At its launch, UPN had signed 96 affiliates covering 79 percent of the country, while Warner Bros. had only 43 affiliates.[9] Airing only on Wednesday evenings, the primetime programs on the WB were a mixture of dramas, reality shows, and sitcoms that targeted black audiences. During the afternoons however, the focus age range was for a younger audience. While competitor networks like Nickelodeon based all of their programming on young children, the WB targeted children with their Saturday morning cartoons. On the other hand, the programs on UPN were primarily sitcoms and two signature programs—*Star Trek: Voyager* and the WWE program *Raw*—before branching out to *Buffy the Vampire Slayer* to draw a more youthful and female audience.

The younger demographic for Saturday mornings and afternoons was a big part of the WB's beginning. However, the WB made sure to continue a link with the younger teens and kids with the continuation of the weekday cartoons and family geared programming. This straddling method was later mirrored in the decision to continue airing *Angel* after *Buffy* moved to UPN. The two programs remained narratively connected, each drawing the same viewers, but with significantly different ratings. Both UPN and the WB followed Fox's cautious prime-time strategy in building their network schedules a few nights at a time. UPN paid $100 million for 44 episodes of *Buffy*, which was more than double what the WB had been paying for the series. Although UPN led in most prime-time comparisons, the WB had its greatest impact on the children's programming market. The WB doubled its advertising billings from $22 million to $43 million for children's programming across a single year's time. *Buffy*'s deal with UPN / Twentieth Century–Fox Television required the network to keep *Angel* on the air for at least two seasons if the WB cancelled it.

The move from the WB to UPN can almost be described as an act of sibling rivalry between two fledgling networks vying for the same audience, advertisers and network identity. Buffy the girl who fought Kendra and Faith for her identity as the Slayer suddenly became *Buffy* the program that fought for the UPN's changing identity from a bastion of whitemaleness. She became that symbol of change and the concomitant fears of her fans who feared the industry's impact on the storyline and its color.[10] The battle for *Buffy* makes sense because audiences see themselves as getting "free entertainment" while the programs they view produce huge profits and grant immense socio-cultural power to program producers.[11]

The UPN and WB launch strategies resemble the strategy employed by Fox when it first debuted — limited programming aimed at a very narrowly defined audience. Unfortunately, unlike Fox, UPN and WB failed in their bid to become the fifth network, due in large part to the markedly different market factors the two networks faced in comparison to much smaller media landscape faced by Fox in the mid–1980s.[12]

This strategy by the two networks was similar to Fox's strategy of targeting black audiences with ethnic programming to become the fourth network.[13] At the time, black viewers watched more network television than non-black audiences, due in part to their slower move to cable television than their white, and frequently more affluent counterparts.[14] It was successful, leading Fox to become the fourth network, joining NBC, ABC, and CBS. Ironically, Fox made the entry of the WB and UPN into the market even more difficult because of the number of affiliates the network maintained.

The UPN and WB also failed in their attempt to become the fifth network because the audience they targeted, teens, is far more difficult to pin down. In the real world, teens are faced with an ever-growing sense of alienation and risk as schoolyards become bullet-ridden battlefields, hallways become gauntlets of sexual harassment, and the Internet becomes a playground for predators. As parents, legislators, teachers, and police were wringing their hands at this generation's newest moral panic, they began to turn to their favorite boogeyman — the media. Like Joyce and Sheila Rosenberg in "Gingerbread" (3.11), adults in the real world frequently exist in a state of "collective denial"[15] that prevents them from exploring the murky and often contradictory causes for their teens' violence and victimization.

Asa Berger argues that "reality is socially constructed" (1). And there is no social group whose reality is as constructed or as contested as youths. Youths are also an entity whose cultural construction is intricately intertwined with their relationship with the media, a relationship that has been the subject of study and concern for parents and experts alike, a concern that is often legitimated and maintained by news coverage.[16] Advertisers try to capture them, programmers try to captivate them, and parents try to protect them. That elusive creature, the furtive youth, defies explanation, definition, and, more frighteningly for news and popular media producers, prediction. According to Henry Giroux, the construct "youth" "represents an inescapable intersection of the personal, social, political, and pedagogical" (3), and at this intersection are a conflicting chorus of experts from a variety of disciplines working to construct youths and their culture as problematic for us. Buffy's world, however, invited audiences to see youths differently in Seasons 1 though 5, but that message was lost in the frenzy of a new social construct, school shootings.

As problematic as the construction of youths is, it is intricately intertwined with our equally problematic construction as audiences. Audiences have been alternately constructed by the industry as passive masses of "isolated and unknown individuals," as "market" for advertisers, as "consumers" of media content and advertisers' products.[17] So youths are doubly problematized by the media industry. First, they are constructed as desirable targets for media content designed to entertain and persuade them to purchase consumer goods; not educated citizens but happy shoppers. Second, youths are constructed as victims of this same media content, titillated by televisual scenes of graphic sex and motivated by a torrent of violent images. And on April 20, 1999, this double bind was literally broadcast on television screens around the world. That morning, Eric Harris and Dylan Klebold killed 13 people and themselves at Columbine High School in Littleton, Colorado. That same evening, four former high school friends (Jack, Bob, Dickie, and Parker) returned from the dead to blow up Sunnydale High School in Sunnydale, California ("The Zeppo," 3.13). Although the Columbine shooting was a horrific news event and the Sunnydale bombing was a *Buffy* rerun, they shared a similar tale about monstrous teens whose actions defied logic and reason. What news and popular media didn't share, however, was the privilege to tell the tale. In the aftermath of the shooting, news outlets ran non-stop programming exploring every minute detail of the shooting, its planning, and its shooters. And then the new media turned on the popular media. Although *Buffy* postponed several episodes in response to Columbine ("Earshot," 3.18, "Graduation Day, Part 1," 3.21 and "Part 2," 3.22) and changed the content ratings from TV-PG to TV-14 for the "Graduation Day" episodes, the news media continued to scapegoat *Buffy* and other popular programs for Columbine.[18]

Despite all of this drama, "Graduation Day, part 1" and "Part 2," airing way after they were supposed to and basically, thereby, disrupting our narrative flow, the two episodes mirrored the soon-to-be recurring theme of shared power. Kellner notes there is usually a lag between "social experience and the world of television entertainment belatedly portraying social change after the turmoil has abated. Television thus often puts its benediction (or damnation) on changes after the fact."[19] One of the most brilliant elements about *Buffy* was the clear and obvious insight into teen angst and culture, so much so that the series metaphorically reflected more so than reported or represented teen crises; however, that same insight was used as a battering ram against the program when real-life teen crises led to monstrously fatal results.

Why this clash between news and entertainment programming? Although this battle is seemingly external as news and entertainment media compete for loyal audiences, it also reflects an internal battle as both news and entertainment programs air on the same networks. Networks, however, are caught between dueling drives as they attempt to give the public what it wants and what it needs without comprising their profit flow.[20] Therefore, to make a profit in the somewhat immediate future, networks will broadcast contradictory material in the news and entertainment programming, meaning, ironically, the same network that aired extensive news coverage of the Columbine shooting also aired entertainment programming that was blamed for the shooting.

Kellner and others argue that network television is an important social force in America and serves as "an instrument of social control, promoting capital commodities and consumerist values, social conformity, law and order, authority figures, and the family" (31). For this reason, parents' groups and the FCC pay special attention to programs presumed to target young audiences, particularly regarding representations of sex and violence. And these restrictions and concerns are centered on a living, real metaphor: youths. In news, the storyteller for the real world teens are eerily silent in stories about them or only select voices get through. They are talked about as if they are children who need to be protected from the mean media or as if they are deviants who use media to inspire their crimes and to boast about them after. Their silenced voices and virtual bodies are represented by expert sources in mediated construction sites that are privileged as political and factual (news) or stigmatized as popular and entertaining (*Buffy*).

Advertisers are also powerful enough to create an organization that would let them know, in essence, what programs to sponsor for their approval. The Family Friendly Programming Forum was founded in 1998 by major corporations, led by Procter & Gamble, to encourage the creation of series "that parents would enjoy viewing together with a child."[21] The Family Friendly Programming Forum is a group of over 40 major national advertisers, all members of the Association of National Advertisers and representing approximately 30 percent of all U.S. television advertising dollars, who want to increase family friendly programming choices on television. Programs deemed offensive are targeted and deemed family-unfriendly, as the youth construct stretches to include parents. And offense seems limited to language, sex, and violence broadcast in the home, so space is also part of this youth construct as being in need of protection. *Buffy* was blamed for violence, scapegoated and the same organization that charged *Buffy* with indecency also named it the third worst show in television. Like a real world Watcher's Council, the Parents Television Council identified Buffy as the third worst show in television for youths. But there was one small problem: youths are not the primary or majority audience for Buffy.[22] According to Hollywood executives, senators and many parents have a skewed notion of which programs children are watching. Such series as *Xena: Warrior Princess* and *Buffy the Vampire Slayer*, which were mentioned by some of the critics of Hollywood's R-rated marketing, are watched by far fewer under-age teenagers than many believe, about 18 percent for *Xena* and 26 percent for *Buffy*.[23]

More and more, television viewers are going their separate ways, lured by dozens or even hundreds of program choices. At the same time, the concept of television that is suitable for the whole family to watch together remains a pie-in-the-sky ideal of everyone from parents to politicians. The Parents' Council is misguided in believing that families view together, since cable, multiple television sets, computers and VCRs are all dividing and siphoning off viewers. Ultimately, the FCC rejected complaints filed by conservative groups, like the Parent Television Council, finding in two 5–0 votes that the shows didn't violate indecency rules.[24]

Conclusion

From Buffy's death(s) to rebirth(s), from big bads to the Geek Trio, from the WB to UPN, and from adolescence to adulthood, *Buffy* in the UPN years brought me full circle from Buffy's arrival in "Welcome to the Hellmouth" (1.1). Five years of *Buffy*'s metaphoric monsters, adolescent angst and danse macabre prepared fans for the show's final lessons in Seasons 6 and 7: reality bites. As fans collectively waited for Buffy to return to form (both literally and figuratively), we slowly and painfully realized what Angel had known for some time: re-entry is a bitch. As Season 6 unfolded, however, it became painfully clear to everyone that something was wrong with our slayer, that perhaps the torture of the hell dimension she was in had somehow changed her, like Angel ("Beauty and the Beasts," 3.4) or that she had come back wrong.

But maybe *we* were the ones who came back wrong; we were the ones who didn't see *Buffy the Vampire Slayer* for what it really was. We had plenty of warning from "When She Was Bad" that Buffy isn't pleasant when she returns from the dead. We knew from the Columbine High School shooting that the television industry would gladly muck with our beloved show, while happily selling us to their advertisers. And we knew from the loss of Jesse and Marcie (metaphorically) that we would be faced with more painful losses in later seasons, like Joyce and Tara. Thanks to its unique narrative, use of foreshadowing, and gut-wrenching pathos, *Buffy the Vampire Slayer* on the WB prepared us for the real pain that was to come on UPN. Yes, Virginia, vampires bite, but so does reality.

Notes

1. The Trio mission statement included: shrink rays, controlling the weather, miniaturizing Fort Knox, conjuring fake I.D.s, girls, girls and trained gorillas.
2. See "'Digging the Undead': Death and Desire in *Buffy*" by Elisabeth Krimmer and Shilpa Raval and "'Who Died and Made You Boss?': Patterns of Mortality in Buffy" in *Fighting the Forces: What's at Stake in Buffy the Vampire Slayer* for excellent explorations of the significance of death in *Buffy*.
3. Reiss, 31.
4. See Matthew Pateman's *The Aesthetics of Culture in Buffy the Vampire Slayer* for a fuller discussion of this knowledge and its control in *Buffy*.
5. Stanley, Mediaweek.com.
6. See Collette and Littman for a fuller discussion of changes and exchanges in network ownership. See also Steve Donohue, "'Weblet' Merger Sends Shockwaves," Betsey Sharkey, "Giving Shape to UPN: Two Marketing Execs Have Made Geometry a Winning Costar of the Maturing Net's Branding Effort," and James Hibberd, "Did Cable Topple UPN and The WB?; Netlets Chased Same Young Demos Targeted by MTV, Others; Merger May Boost Cable" for the details of the financial battle between UPN and WB.
7. Collette and Littman, p. 5.
8. Ibid., p.14.
9. Ibid., p.14
10. At the time of the big move, networks were under fire from the NAACP and other community leaders for the lack of diversity in their programming, specifically for using black audiences to launch a network and then switching to white audiences as advertiser interest grew. See Dusty Saunders' article in the *Rocky Mountain News* for further discussion of this topic.
11. Kellner, p. 39.
12. Collette and Litman, p. 10–11.
13. Interestingly enough, Fox didn't actually begin as a network. See Zook for a fuller discussion of Fox's status.
14. Zook, p. 3.
15. See Tracy Little's essay for further discussion of this active teens and oblivious adults in Sunnydale.
16. See Males for further discussion.
17. Ang, 209–211.

18. Seattle Times News Services, July 7, 1999.
19. Kellner, 43.
20. Kellner argues there are "frequent tensions and conflicts among [a] network's drive toward profit-maximization, its production of hegemonic ideology to engineer social consent, and its production of news and entertainment according to professional codes" (pp. 40).
21. Pennington, "'Family' Programming Continues to be a Hot Debate Topic."
22. Ibid.
23. Lyman, "Overhaul of R-Rated Movies Gets a C Rating: Confusing," *New York Times*, November 1, 2000.
24. Pennington.

Works Cited

Ang, Ien. "The Nature of the Audience." In Questioning the Media: A Critical Introduction. 2nd ed. Edited by John Downing, et al. Thousand Oaks, CA: Sage Publications, 1995.
Collette, Larry, and Barry R. Litman. "The Peculiar Economics of New Broadcast Network Entry: The Case of United Paramount and Warner Bros." *The Journal of Media Economics* 10, no. 4 (1997); 3–22.
Donohue, Steve. "'Weblet' Merger Sends Shockwaves." *Multichannel News*. 30 January 2006. Lexis-Nexis. Retrieved 21 February 2006. http://web.lexis-nexis.com/universe/document?_m=ae8484a27416effaaefl133a1b4394ab....
Havens, Candace. *Joss Whedon: The Genius Behind Buffy*. Dallas: Benbella Books. 2003.
Hibberd, James. "Did Cable Topple UPN and The WB?; Netlets Chased Same Young Demos Targeted by MTV, Others; Merger May Boost Cable." *Crain Communications*. 30 January 2006. Lexis-Nexis. Retrieved 21 February 2006. http://web.lexis-nexis.com/universe/document?_m=ae8484a27416effaaefl133a1b4394ab....
Jowett, Lorna. *Sex and the Slayer. A Gender Studies Primer for the Buffy Fan*. Middleton, CT: Wesleyan University Press, 2005.
Kellner, Douglas. *"Network Television and American Society: Introduction to a Critical Theory of Television."* Theory and Society 10, no. 1 (January 1981): 31–62.
Levine, Michael P., and Steven Jay Schneider. "Feeling for Buffy: The Girl Next Door." In *Buffy the Vampire Slayer and Philosophy: Fear and Trembling in Sunnydale*. James B. South, ed. Chicago: Open Court, 2003. 294–308.
Little, Tracy. "High School as Hell: Metaphor Made Literal in Buffy the Vampire Slayer." In *Buffy the Vampire Slayer and Philosophy: Fear and Trembling in Sunnydale*. James B. South, ed. Chicago: Open Court, 2003. 282–293
Lyman, Rick. "Overhaul of R-Rated Movies gets a C Rating." *New York Times*, 1 November 2000. Retrieved from Infotrac, 3 March 2004. http://web7.infotrac.galegroup.com/itw/infomark/931/160/78737224w7/purl=rcl_EAIM_0...
Males, Michael. "Bashing Youth: Media Myths about Teenagers." *Extra!* March–April 1994. Retrieved 3 March 2004. http://www.fair.org/extra/9403/bashing-youth.html.
Pateman, Matthew. *The Aesthetics of Culture in Buffy the Vampire Slayer*. Jefferson, NC: McFarland, 2006.
Pennington, Gail. "'Family' programming continues to be a hot debate topic." Post-Dispatch television critic, July 8, 1999. August 9, 2001.

Riess, Jana. *What Would Buffy Do? The Vampire Slayer as Spiritual Guide.* San Francisco: Jossey-Bass, 2004.

Saunders, Dusty. "Diversity on Network TV is Abysmal." *Denver Rocky Mountain News*, July 19, 1999. Retrieved from Infotrac 21 August 2007. http://web7.infotrac.galegroup.com/itw/infomark/931/160/78737224w7/purl=rcl_EAIM_0....

Seattle Times News Services. "Janet Jackson Gets Modest TV Exposure on Will & Grace; Buffy, Will & Grace beat indecency rap." *The Seattle Times*, 12 August 2004. Retrieved from Infotrac 21 August 2007. http://web7.infotrac.galegroup.com/itw/infomark/931/160/78737224w7/purl=rcl_EAIM_0....

Sharkey, Betsy. "Giving Shape to UPN: Two Marketing Execs Have Made Geometry a Winning Costar of the Maturing Net's Branding Effort." *MediaWeek*. 10 February 1997. Retrieved from Infotrac 21 August 2007. http://web7.infotrac.galegroup.com/itw/infomark/931/160/78737224w7/purl=rcl_EAIM_0....

Stanley, T.L. "When Ratings Sag, It's Contest Time." *Mediaweek*, 24 February 1997. Retrieved from Infotrac 21 August 2007. http://web7.infotrac.galegroup.com/itw/infomark/931/160/78737224w7/purl=rcl_EAIM_0....

Wilcox, Rhonda. "'Who Died and Made Her the Boss?' Patterns of Mortality in *Buffy*." In *Fighting the Forces: What's At Stake in Buffy the Vampire Slayer*. Rhonda V. Wilcox and David Lavery, eds. Lanham, MD: Rowman & Littlefield, 2002. 3–17

Zook, Kristal Brent. *Color By Fox: The Fox Network and the Revolution in Black Television.* New York: Oxford University Press, 1999.

SECTION 4. SEASONS
(AT SIXES AND SEVENS)

"Just a Family Legend":
The Hidden Logic of Buffy's
"Chosen Family"

AGNES B. CURRY AND JOSEF VELAZQUEZ

While he was still speaking to the crowds, his mother and his brothers were standing outside, wanting to speak to him. Someone told him, "Look, your mother and your brothers are standing outside, wanting to speak to you." But to the one who told him this, Jesus replied, "Who is my mother, and who are my brothers?" And pointing to his disciples, he said, "Here are my mother and my brothers! For whoever does the will of my Father in heaven is my brother and sister and mother."
— Matthew 12:46–50

I.

Introduction

Was that any way to treat his mother? And is it really possible to build a society (Christian or otherwise) while undermining those family relations on which societies have always been based?

But this paper is actually not going to be about Christ, but about the TV show *Buffy the Vampire Slayer*. For the show also contains what has come to be called a "chosen family," i.e., the circle of Buffy's followers-helpers-friends. And like the Gospel instructs, this chosen family comes to take precedence over the characters' natural families of biologically related parents and siblings.[1]

In fact, the show conducts an extended polemic designed to point out the failings of the traditional family and to extol the virtues of the chosen one. Biological families are, at best, fragmented and obtuse,[2] at worst, demeaning and controlling — or demonic.[3] In contrast, the Scooby Gang offers seemingly unconditional recognition and acceptance. That this is the message we're meant to absorb is suggested by the inclusion of the following remarks by Vivian Sobchack on a special feature accompanying the official Season Seven DVD:

> It [the series] seems to me much more about not only the longing for — the achievement — of community in amongst a disparate group of people, including some misfits or social deviants who become a group and a family. That's where its power and also where some of the larger ethical issues emerge, and where in fact it fulfils, it seems to me, a larger cultural need ["Buffy 101"].

The critics also have, by and large, fallen in love with the chosen family and with the idea that it is superior to the natural one. In fact, part of the motivation for this paper was one author's experience at a Buffy conference where the topic came up for discussion and was treated with the sort of reverence usually reserved for scriptural revelation or quotes by Gene Roddenberry.

But is the chosen family really as good as it looks? We must confess that we have our doubts.

A Brief Review of the Literature

The work of two scholars is especially relevant to our argument.[4] The most extended treatment is by Jes Battis in *Blood Relations: Chosen Families in Buffy and Angel*. Battis defines chosen families as "core family units that have nothing to do with heredity or biology" but are instead composed of a "surrogate sphere of friends who sometimes succeed, and sometimes fail, to recuperate ideas that the characters' biological families cannot properly transmit" (Battis, 12–13). And what is striking about Battis's response to such chosen families is how positive it is. For example, Battis talks, with obvious agreement, about how "both shows [*Buffy* and *Angel*] suggest that non-biological fathers can 'head' non-traditional families far better than their biological counterparts" (Battis, 111).[5]

Battis does note a series of complexities and hesitations in his approval. He explores how members of the chosen families on both shows not only disrupt, but also reproduce roles reminiscent of traditional families — Willow as a sort of middle child, Buffy and Cordelia as matriarchs, Giles and Angel as patriarchs, etc. Battis is sensitive to the possibility of multiple and contradictory readings. Likewise, he discusses how, as with all cultural productions, room for transgression in some directions is bought at the price of reinforcing other systems; he finds that while the family of *Buffy* is gloriously queer in its sexuality and acceptance of the monstrous, it remains tied to middle class consumerism and white privilege (Battis, Ch. 3). Nevertheless, and despite these complications, Battis clearly valorizes chosen families in general, and the Scooby Gang in particular.

In an earlier article, entitled "*Buffy the Vampire Slayer* and the Domestic Church: Revisioning Family and the Common Good," Reid Locklin hints at some of the specific satisfactions offered by the portrayal of the Scooby Gang as a family. He praises *Buffy* for its construction of "an alternative version of the North American family" that is notable for its refusal to oppose family life and "the common good" (par. 16) As such, Locklin argues, the show is in surprising concordance with strands of Catholic social teaching. Focusing on Season Five, Locklin emphasizes the significance of its eschatological framework. While there are obvious differences between the Scooby Gang and the sort of family valorized by Catholicism, the show's move to contextualize familial relations in terms of a supernatural mission entailing service to others parallels the theology of the family as "domestic church." And as such, Locklin argues, the new social order of the Scooby Gang "can be seen, not as an abrogation of traditional family ideals, but as a profound transformation and fulfillment of them" (Locklin, par. 6). Bypassing traditional bonds of birth kinship, self-interest or patriarchal law, Buffy, Xander, Willow, Giles, Dawn, Tara, Anya and Spike nonetheless exemplify the core values of genuine family: love, mutual responsibility, and "a saving relation to the world" (Locklin, par. 14).

Locklin, though, has his hesitations too. He notes that it's questionable whether the relationships within the chosen family are really all that mutual, since Buffy's mission has formed the family's raison d'être. Likewise, he wonders whether patriarchy has been rejected only to be replaced with another hierarchy.[6] Nonetheless, Locklin finds that *Buffy*'s family ideal is a major step in the right direction with its recognition of the transcendent, and its portrayal, at least on the symbolic level, of a family model that is emotionally compelling and positively counter-cultural.

Outline

As we stated earlier, we have our doubts about this chosen family idea. And we have organized those doubts into two levels.

In section II, we talk at the internal level. Here we analyze the show itself and ask what the internal structures of this chosen family really are.

In section III, we talk at the external level. Here we are worried not about the show itself but about society more generally. And we ask whether the chosen family really is a good ideal for society to be aiming at.

Acknowledgments

We would like to acknowledge Battis and Locklin of course. Much of what we have to say is an extension of their doubts and hesitations. We would also like to acknowledge Neil King and his work on the fascist dimensions of the Buffyverse, for we apply some of his ideas too.

II.

What Is the Glue?

Families are held together by a variety of what we might call "sociological glues." In the case of the natural family, these glues are the biological relations of sexuality and of parenthood, and also the kinship relations that define various family roles and responsibilities.[7]

But what are the sociological glues in the case of the chosen family on *Buffy*? Given that *Buffy* critiques the biological and kinship glues of the natural family, what sorts of bonding forces does it propose instead? We argue that there are three sorts: an eschatological glue, a proto-fascist glue, and a chosen people glue.

- The eschatological glue: the chosen family is held together by its mission of saving the world from apocalyptic evil.[8] This produces the type of bond that a group of disciples or soldiers would have—a group of disciples or soldiers bonding under the pressure of a mission of world-historical importance.
- The proto-fascist glue: the chosen family is held together by its opposition to a racially different and totally evil Other (paradigmatically the vampires, but the category can also accommodate demons). This produces an us-versus-them sort of bond (where the evil, ugly, and animalistic "them" constantly threatens to engulf the embattled, and therefore bonded, "us").[9]

- The chosen people glue: the chosen family is held together by its being set apart from ordinary (defenseless, sheep-like and unchosen) humanity. This produces the type of bond that a coterie of the elect would have. It also, given high school conditions, produces the type of bond that forms within marginalized groups.

It seems obvious enough that the show has eschatological, proto-fascist, and chosen people dimensions. What we want to insist, though, is that these dimensions do not just exist on the show, but are also the dimensions responsible for holding the chosen family together. Buffy and the Scooby Gang would not be such tight friends if they were not constantly warding off the apocalypse together, were not in constant conflict with the vampires, and were not set apart by their special knowledge from their schoolmates and so thrown constantly into each other's arms. The show itself, or more precisely the ideology of the chosen family that has grown up around the show, dissembles on this point. For this ideology can make it seem that what glues the chosen family together are friendship, loyalty, choice, love, and so on — a whole long list of unambiguously good things.[10] And the problem with this is that it ignores the more ambiguous glues that are actually at work beneath the surface.

The Children of Heaven

In the Gospels, Christ remarks, "For in the resurrection they neither marry nor are given in marriage, but are like angels in heaven" (Matthew 22:30). The point seems to be that the social arrangements of heaven (whatever they may be) take precedence over the social arrangements of earth (like marriage). And something similar seems true for *Buffy the Vampire Slayer*. It has been pointed out by Angie Burns that the show permits no member of the chosen family to achieve a long-term sexual relationship. Buffy's affairs with Angel, Riley, and Spike all end. The affairs of Xander with Cordelia, Willow, and Anya all end. Willow's affairs with Oz and Xander end, and her affair with Tara is ended by Tara's death. Giles's affair with Jenny is ended by Jenny's death.

While it's easy to attribute these sad states of affairs to the show's soap operatic dimensions, or to its focus on adolescence, we suggest a deeper reason. In a family held together by an eschatological glue, no other relationship can be allowed to take precedence over the eschatological mission. In a family held together by the proto-fascist and chosen people glue, no other relationship can be allowed to take precedence over the relationship to the (embattled and chosen) group. In a sense, it is not just that the relationships on the show fail, as relationships tend to do, but that they had to fail, given the underlying structures out of which the show is building its chosen family. These underlying structures demand that the individual's primary allegiance be to the mission and group rather than to a sexual partner.

Other natural relationships are lacking from the show as well. For example, except for Joyce, the parents of the chosen family members appear rarely, if at all — we see Willow's mother twice or so and Xander's parents once.[11] Even Joyce is generally confined to domestic space and not realized as a fully dimensional character. And then she is killed off. Her death makes room for new challenges for Buffy's independent maturation, but it also sidesteps the fact that most young women must contend with a living mother's often looming presence as they work to become themselves.[12] It also continues the pattern of dispensing with female role models noted by J.P. Williams.

A truly bleak portrayal of the contrast between eschatological mission and family relationships comes in Season Seven's "Lies My Parents Told Me" (7.17), where we are given a glimpse of another Slayer's focus on her mission at the expense of her motherhood.[13] Nikki Woods indoctrinates four-year-old Robin that they "got to work the mission. The mission is what matters." Robin loses his mother to that mission shortly thereafter when she is killed by Spike. And when, years later, he attempts to avenge his mother's murder by killing Spike, it is another Slayer who serves him notice. For Spike is on the side of the mission now. And that mission, Buffy informs Robin, *is* everything. And if he cannot see that, then she will just have to let Spike kill him.

The Show's Trajectory

The family dynamics change from the early seasons to the later ones. Initially, Buffy is much more vulnerable, much more in need of emotional help from the other members of the chosen family. In the later shows, she becomes much more the leader, much more sovereign. By Season Seven, she is explicitly presented as a sort of general, with the other members of the chosen family as her troops.

What is happening here seems to be a working out of the logic that was always implicit in the show, for if the show is going to work with protofascistic and eschatological glues, then it is going to have a tendency to authoritarian command structures. Actual fascistic and eschatological societies, after all, tend to be authoritarian ones, and so the use of eschatological and fascistic glues will, it seems, be bound to introduce this authoritarian tendency into the show's underlying logic.[14]

Carl Schmitt, a proto-fascist political theorist in Weimar Germany, argued that society is fundamentally based on the relationship between protection and obedience (*Concept,* 52, and *Leviathan,* 45, 72–77). The sovereign offers protection to his (or her) followers, and the followers respond by offering their unquestioning obedience to the sovereign. What is interesting about *Buffy the Vampire Slayer* is that, certainly by the time we reach Season Seven — and maybe even as early as Season Five — the chosen family is actually held together by this authoritarian social structure of protection and obedience.

A Pivotal Scene

To substantiate our claim, let us review the scene where the show most explicitly puts natural and chosen families in contrast. This scene comes from the episode in Season Five entitled "Family" (5.6) and has been cited as a positive example of chosen family values (Battis, Bradney, Locklin).

The background to the episode is that Tara, who is already involved with Willow, has had some difficulties feeling accepted, indeed has had some difficulties being accepted, by the group as a whole. "Family" recounts how Tara finally becomes a full-fledged member of the family.

In the episode, Tara's father and brother arrive to take Tara back home. Tara's father tells her that she is part demon and so needs to return to his custodial care because the demon part is scheduled to resurface soon, on her upcoming birthday. Tara, however, doesn't want to go. She loves Willow, of course. But, besides this, her father is an unkind and dictatorial man to whom she does not want to return.

In the climactic scene, the father shows up at the magic shop and demands that Tara go back with him. But Buffy interposes herself between Tara and her father, and refuses to let her father take Tara back. Buffy's exact words are, "You wanna take Tara out of here against her will? You gotta come through me." The rest of the Scooby Gang then line up in support of Tara too. And when Tara's father asks who they think they are to interfere with the affairs between Tara and her "blood kin," Buffy replies, "We're family."

A few moments later, Spike manages to reveal that the story about

Tara's being a demon is a lie her father was using to control her. And once the "family legend" is exposed, Tara's father and brother have no choice but to leave, and Tara is taken in by her new and chosen family.

A Frightening Subtext

On the surface, this episode seems a little propagandistic since it builds sympathy for the chosen family by picturing the opposing side, the natural family, in extreme and unattractive terms — as a father who convinces his daughter she's a demon. Not only that, but it also employs the classic trick of picturing the chosen family as the victim, for the chosen family is here pictured as experiencing a cruel and underhanded assault at the hands of the natural family.

But this is not the main (or the most troubling) point. The main or most troubling point is that it is Buffy — and not Willow — who is depicted as deciding whether Tara is part of the chosen family or not. Ordinarily, in today's context, Willow's choice of a partner or spouse would automatically make that partner or spouse a member of the family. The other family members might not like their new in-law, but their new in-law she would be. And what is striking about this scene is that Willow does not have this power. Only Buffy does. And Willow does not question Buffy's authority on this matter. She does not say that she has chosen Tara and that this makes Tara a member of the family, period. Rather, Willow waits, beseechingly but obediently, on Buffy's word. And once Buffy speaks then all the members of the chosen family follow.

In Season Seven, we have an episode ("Selfless," 7.5) where, in a similar situation, Buffy refuses to honor a choice by one of the family members: Xander's appeal for Anya's life. Admittedly, the situation is not exactly the same, as Anya is Xander's ex and not his present lover. Moreover, she really is a demon, having by this time returned to D'Hoffryn's fold[15] and also crossed the line into murder. Despite these differences, though, what is nonetheless the same is that here, too, it is Buffy who makes the decision as to Anya's fate. It is Buffy and Buffy alone who judges that Anya must die. And when Xander pleads to Buffy that he still loves Anya, and that "when our friends go all crazy and start killing people, we help them," Buffy rebuffs him, reminding him that she killed Angel when the occasion demanded it, and then sets out to kill Anya too. It is Willow who looks for, and finds, an alternative solution. And though Buffy is open to this alternative, and in a later episode even offers to protect Anya ("Him,"

7.6), she never indicates regret — the show's logic doesn't require her to indicate regret — about her initial decision to kill Anya.

Moreover, the show itself seems to confirm Buffy's initial sentence of death. For of all the characters, most of whom are in need of atonement, it is Anya whom the show singles out for a designedly[16] un-heroic death in the final episode.

Reversal of Patriarchy

The chosen family on the show is not just a chosen family as against a natural one. It is also a matriarchal family as against a patriarchal one. But it is often a matriarchal family in what Carl Schmitt would call an "essentially polemical" way (*Concept*, 30–32). This means that it is less concerned with what an actual matriarchy might look like, and more concerned with making an anti-patriarchal statement. For example, it seems pretty doubtful that an actual matriarchy would center on a female action hero. But this feature, however fantastic, is also polemically very satisfying (and a linchpin of the story).

One aspect of this "essential polemicism" is that the matriarchy on the show is too often just a reversed patriarchy. Whereas patriarchy said "man on top," this sort of matriarchy responds "woman on top" — and then forgets that the real issue might be to question the whole idea of top and bottom. To put it less metaphorically, there are instances where the show seems not so much to deconstruct the structures of patriarchal power as to simply redistribute them. Some of these instances seem to involve putting Buffy into the role of the patriarch.[17]

Buffy really does seem to wield a patriarchal sort of power. We have already seen one example of this in the power she has regarding Willow and Tara, for one prerogative of the paterfamilias, a prerogative Buffy here shares, is a control over the sexual choices of his (or her) family members. Another example is how her action-hero persona entitles her to command the other chosen family members, for this connection of brute force to authority is a standard bit of patriarchal logic.[18] But perhaps the best example of Buffy's patriarchal authority is her role as general in Season Seven. The point here is not just that a general's authority is of the patriarchal sort, but that the show actually imports this sort of authority into the internal structure of the chosen family.

Season Seven does, of course, explore some of the difficulties of exercising this military sort of authority. It even shows Buffy getting briefly deposed. But what it does not do is question the patriarchal truism that for some sorts of situations (the most important sorts of situations) hierarchical authority wielded by one person is essential. As Buffy states in "Empty Places" (7.19), "Democracies don't win battles. It's a hard truth but there has to be a single voice. You need someone to issue orders, and be reckless sometimes, and not take your feelings into account. You need someone to lead you." But perhaps Faith's experience is even more to the point, for when she is installed as leader in "Touched" (7.20) and tries to institute a more discussion-based structure, she quickly finds that this produces chaos. By mid-episode, she responds by silencing everyone and taking over command, saying, "I'm your leader. Which means, I go first, and I make the rules, and the rest of you follow after me. Is that clear?"

In addition, the series has a trajectory on these points. The early seasons can be read as an attempt to deconstruct at least the action-hero version of male power, for we see Buffy slamming vampires around and then, in a moment of delightful, deconstructive humor, worrying about her hair. But in the later seasons, this sort of humor stops and the show takes Buffy's action-hero persona very seriously. Instead of a deconstruction of this dimension of male power, we have a reversed re-affirmation of it: the action-hero persona is an unambiguously good thing as long as it is the woman who does the kicking.

Qualifications

We wish to stress that we are not arguing that the show is just a series of gender switches and nothing more. It is far too complicated and layered a text for that. All we are talking about is one gender switch that occurs sometimes, along with all sorts of other mechanisms, in one particular area of the show.

Also, we are decidedly *not* arguing that a feminist icon cannot be small, blonde and fashion-conscious. It is these dimensions of Buffy's persona that are in fact the most potentially deconstructive of both patriarchal and feminist orthodoxy. We *like* the fact that she is not only powerful but also cute.

Possible Objections

One possible objection has to do with Buffy's decision in the series finale, "Chosen" (7.22), to take control of and rewrite the Slayer ur-narrative so as to share the power of the scythe with all the young slayers in training. The objection is that this looks like a move away from an authoritarian and patriarchal power to a more democratic one.

Two things need to be said about this, however. First of all, the decision to share the power of the scythe is still Buffy's. This power is not won by a democratic revolution from below, but dispensed by the real power which still remains above. Secondly, as touching as are these climactic scenes of little girls getting empowered, the patriarchal orthodoxy linking power and violence remains intact.

Another possible objection has to do with Willow's powers as a witch, and with the important role these powers play—both generally on the show, and particularly in the final episodes. Since Buffy's plan to redistribute the power of the scythe depends essentially on Willow's regaining confidence and using her powers to their utmost, and given that witchcraft is usually coded as a feminine sort of power, it would seem that the show actually does not privilege masculine sorts of power only.

The show undercuts this reading, however, by framing Willow's growth in power in Season Six as a sort of addiction. One effect of the addiction narrative is that it renders palatable the idea that to be usable or stable, her feminine witch powers need to be contained or tethered by the more masculine Slayer power, exemplified by both Buffy and Kennedy. As Kennedy, positioned clearly as Willow's pursuer, says when she makes love to Willow in "Touched," "I'll be your kite string" (7.20). And this is actually a very traditional and patriarchal constellation: woman as the possessor of a dark and mysterious force, but an unruly force, that needs to be tamed by the clarity of man's authority and command.

Rhetorical Glue

If the reader wouldn't mind, we would like to make a few additional general remarks. We think that the show operates on a variety of levels (sociological, polemical and psychological). We also think that the show's coherence and power derive, in part, from the fact that all of these levels are producing a hidden or secret message that is more or less the same.

At the start, we saw how the show had sociological structures (eschatological, proto-fascist, and chosen-people) that made the chosen family surprisingly authoritarian in its under-the-surface orientation. Now we are seeing that the show has a rhetorical or polemical structure (the reversal of patriarchy) that is introducing a surprising dose of patriarchal logic into this seemingly matriarchal family. In the following section, we will see a similar (and similarly disturbing) sub-text being introduced at the psychological level too.

It might be a little tendentious to put it this way, but the show seems very consistent in that it is consistently liberal on the surface and consistently anti-liberal beneath the surface. And if the authors' experience is any guide, this is a mixture which is surprisingly appealing — and surprisingly appealing even (or especially?) to liberals like ourselves.

Longing for the Father

At the psychological level, what we have is a structure of unconscious yearning — an unconscious yearning for the father.

To begin with, the show is careful to sideline the fathers of the characters. Buffy's father is absent. Xander's father is alcoholic and a boor. Willow's father is not mentioned. (Neither is Spike's, Robin's or, with possibly one exception, Faith's.[19]) And yet these missing fathers are actually controlling much of the psychological action of the show.

Let's begin with Xander's case. What's obvious here is that Xander does not respect his father; this is manifest through the entire series. The flip side of this though, is that he must never have received any meaningful psychological support from such a father.[20] This lack of support seems to have left its traces on his personality, for his whole Xander goofiness is one long testimonial to his need for such support and to the uncertainties and oddities of behavior that result when it is not forthcoming. Moreover, this issue of support might also help explain why Xander's work as a carpenter becomes so important to him: success in this career goes some way to convincing him of his own manliness, a conviction which his father, sadly, seems to have done nothing to instill.

Buffy, too, misses her father in a very deep way. In his absence, she is the one who has constantly to be strong. In a normal family, it would be the father, and not the adolescent daughter, who would be responsible for fighting the vampires. But in Buffy's case this role falls on her, and the strain of it goes a long way to defining her character. There is, for example, the isolation and loneliness this burden imposes. There is what Holden, the psych-major vampire in Season Seven's "Conversations with Dead People" (7.7) describes as her inferiority complex about her superiority complex. There is also her choice of a series of older (often much, *much* older) boyfriends, as she seemingly searches for someone strong enough to help her shoulder the load. Of course the series' founding myth of the Slayer is meant as a gesture of empowerment to young women, but the attractiveness of this move should not lead us to overlook the ethical ramifications of shifting such grave responsibilities to a child.[21]

In Willow's case too something similar looks like it might be true. The show is less detailed here, and so this is speculative, but part of what Willow seems to miss is ever having been the apple of her father's eye. For all her intelligence and power and beauty, her personality is marked by an inability to believe that she is actually attractive.[22] A possible contributing factor for this (corroborated by the little we do know of Willow's family) is that her father may not have been emotionally close or affectionate enough to make her secure in her attractiveness.[23]

This is suggested by the fact that Willow has an almost neurotic need to please — and to please by the methods of following the rules and achieving scholastic success. Given the usual assumptions about rules-success being typically paternal demands, the excessive need to please in these areas could be read as an effort on Willow's part to flatter a paternal power whose approval was not as forthcoming as her psychology required. An exchange suggesting this — and the effects of its withholding — is in Season Six's "Flooded" (6.4). In conversation with Giles, Willow relates with some relish the horrors of the spell used to resurrect Buffy, structuring the tale as one of personal triumph: "And this pack of demons interrupted but I totally kept it together." When Giles responds, "You're a very stupid girl," she is shocked. When he continues by questioning her judgment, her first response is not to explain her decision to resurrect Buffy. Instead she says, "I thought you'd be impressed, or something." By the end of the exchange her disappointment has given way to anger, and now that she has power, the anger is accompanied by an explicit threat. The psychic importance of this conversation to Willow is suggested by her allusion to it when Giles returns to confront her in the season finale. Her claim that he is irrelevant notwithstanding, the link between her disappointment and anger is palpable in her later remark, "I used to think you had all the answers, that I had so much to learn from you" ("Chosen," 6.22).

It seems, then, that the members of the Scooby Gang are strongly marked by their longing for their fathers.[24] If it is permissible to interpret the show itself as a person with a psychology, one would have to say that the show exhibits a classic case of ambivalence on this point: a conscious rejection of the father coupled with an unconscious longing for him.

As is typical in such cases, the show handles this ambivalence by creating a disguised symbol of what it unconsciously longs for. This, for example, is how Freud says the dream works: the unconscious symbolizes its forbidden desire in such a hidden way that the conscious does not quite realize what it is seeing. In this case, the longing for the father produces a symbol of the patriarch — but a symbol disguised beneath the figure of a teenaged girl from Sunnydale, California. And yet, as with all such symbols, one can also see the hidden content peeking through the disguise, for this is a teenage girl with both a very commanding attitude and a very nasty left hook (with both the authority and the power appropriate to the patriarch).

The Case of Dawn

Besides Buffy's portrayal as a commanding general, another way that Buffy's role as patriarch shows up is in her protective relationship towards Dawn. We realize, of course, that Buffy's relationship to Dawn is complex and that her motivations for protecting Dawn are multilayered (Battis, 74–76), and we do not want to reduce all of this down to just one aspect. But we do want to say that as one part of this mix there is a certain paternal logic. Even the story of Dawn's origin places us into paternal logic since Dawn was formed magically out of Buffy's own body, and in this way the relation of Dawn to Buffy parallels the relation of Eve to Adam.[25]

Battis reads Buffy as a sort of "super mom" in her vigilance to protect Dawn, both in Season Five and later (Battis, 71). But she actually seems more like a "super dad." Buffy's chief role with regard to Dawn is to protect her. As part of this, she tries to impose on Dawn some rules and restrictions that are designed to keep her out of danger. Dawn's response to Buffy is ambivalent: she rebels against the rules and restrictions at the same time that she is grateful for the protection. The point is that this seems like a paternal relationship, particularly when there are surprisingly few instances of the corresponding maternal stereotypes. In Seasons Six and Seven, Buffy and Dawn do few stereotypically feminine things together. Nor do we see much of the sort of intimate and leisurely conversation which the maternal stereotypes call for. Often it is someone other than Buffy who performs the traditional maternal function of comforting Dawn when she is distressed; in Season Six, it is usually Tara, whereas in Season Seven it is usually Willow. At least on this symbolic level, then, it actually seems that Buffy is Dawn's father.

It is true that, for a little while, the show does try to rewrite the

Buffy-Dawn relationship into a more feminine key. In the Season Six finale, Buffy, finally reconciled to her return from heaven, tells Dawn, "I got it wrong. I don't want to protect you from the world. I want to show it to you. There's so much that I want to show you." The opener and first few episodes of Season Seven continue with this re-feminization of the Buffy-Dawn relationship. For example, the episode "Him" (7.7) has both an instance of intimate conversation and a dose of (enchanted) sisterly sexual treachery.

But this process of rewriting the relationship is not given a chance to develop very far, for by episode seven, preparations for battle have started, and Dawn's relationship to Buffy is quickly eclipsed by other concerns.

Moreover, in the later episode "Empty Places," we see Buffy once again taking a standard paternal "don't ask questions but just do as I say" attitude towards Dawn. She simply silences Dawn when Dawn asks about Xander. She then silences her again when Dawn tries to explain what happened at the Bronze, and when Faith tries to intervene on Dawn's behalf, Buffy responds violently and simply punches Faith. Here Buffy's relationship to Dawn certainly does not seem like one of those stereotypical maternal relationships based on talking things out, but seems to have returned to a paternal relationship based on command and silent obedience.

Buffy again plays the part of the patriarch when, in "End of Days," she instructs Xander to take Dawn away from Sunnydale before the final battle. This time Dawn takes matters into her own hands and returns, prompting one of the few unambiguously sisterly remarks of the season, as Buffy accepts the situation, saying, "If you get killed, I'm telling." This sort of remark is striking for its rarity.

Giles the Librarian

Giles is, of course, a paternal figure. On the one hand, this might seem like a confirmation of the position this paper is taking, for the fact that the Scooby Gang forms under his care can be read as a confession of their longing for the father. Perhaps one could even say that the fact that Giles's role is central while Joyce's role is less so is an indication that it is the father and not the mother who is really longed for here.

On the other hand, though, the role of Giles might seem to contradict our thesis. For if Giles is already a father figure, how can we be arguing that the show somehow needs to construct Buffy as a father figure too?

To answer this, it is important to note just what kind of father figure Giles is. He seems to be a refurbished father figure, i.e., one that has been remade along feminist lines. Especially at the start, Giles is kind, attentive, discreet, and not at all terrible. He is the sort of father that, if asked, the characters might say that they wanted.

But this also means that he is not a father figure who completely satisfies. No matter what they might say, it is not the nice and unterrible (the un–awe-inspiring) father that the characters are unconsciously longing for. What Buffy wants is someone stronger than she is, with a large measure of darkness — look at the boyfriends she chooses. Xander needs the approval not of someone kindly but of someone with the weight (the awe-inspiring weight) to pass judgments that are definitive. And Willow needs not just the circumspect affirmation she gets from Giles, but the emotional intensity of a father's love.

Thus the show does seem to require a father figure besides Giles, a father figure who has a greater dose of the patriarchal. It is Buffy (the father as general and action-hero) and not Giles (the father as wise counselor) who becomes the emotional center of the show.

Good Old Xander

Xander might also seem to be an objection to what we are saying here. In their own commentaries, the writers of the show insist that it is actually Xander who holds the chosen family together (Season Seven Disc 6). It is his quiet perceptiveness and his manifest concern which function as the real glue.

We do want to admit the truth of this assertion, but we do not think it is actually an objection to our thesis. Although Xander is frequently referred to as "the heart," the emotional component of the Scoobies (beginning with "Restless," 4.22), this is, after all, still the standard patriarchal structure, but just transposed: one authoritarian and commanding parent (usually the father, but here Buffy) and one emotionally perceptive and caring parent (usually the mother, but here Xander). In this standard structure, the family will actually be glued together twice: on the surface level by the strength of the authoritarian parent, and behind the scenes by the concern of the perceptive one — just as Buffy and Xander, each in his or her own role, glue the chosen family together.[26]

What we have in *BtVS*, in other words, is just one more example of that sort of reversal we talked about earlier: the basic structure of the patriarchal family, with its authoritarian dad and caring mom, has not changed;

all that has happened is that there has been a new choice about who goes into which of these standard roles.

III.

Here we move into a discussion of some larger social issues.

An Easy Pitch

In televisual culture *Buffy* is certainly not alone in its preference for a chosen family. Many other shows, from Whedon's other creations to *Seinfeld, Friends, Sex and the City, Queer as Folk,* and *Cheers* offer similar constellations. In an age of post-industrial mobility, the popularity of depictions of groups of friends who fill in for missing or inadequate family members is clearly tapping into a cultural longing. *BtVS* is explicitly structured so as to deal with the horrors of adolescent development, and thus it is set up to privilege the child's perspective. The show is both a reflection of the reality faced by children in households wracked with neglect, instability or abandonment, as well as a powerful replaying of that perennial children's fantasy: "I'm much more special than they see me, and I'll find another family who really appreciates me." For the child in each of us, inevitably disappointed by the families into which we landed, the seductions of such an alternative family model are palpable.

While there is indeed a cultural need for variety in our depictions of what counts as family, and for sympathetic portrayals of contemporary adolescence, one of the most difficult tasks of growing up is dealing with the family one got dealt — with the precisely unchosen aspects of our placement into the world. This involves recognizing the traces of others in the interstices of one's personality, and thus the ways one's self-definition turns out not to be a function of one's sovereign individuality. We take it as a given that narratives can aid in these sorts of tasks, and that popular culture can play a particularly powerful role in offering new possibilities for identification. For this reason it is important that audiences are offered variety in their pictures of human life, and that these portraits are not all pitched to the same social-psychological developmental level.

The Sartrean-style existentialism to which we know Whedon is attracted (described in some detail in Whedon's commentary track to *Firefly*'s "Objects in Space") may reinforce American assumptions of individualism on this score. Sartre, especially as he is popularly received in the American context, resonates with young people's dilemmas about choice and their tendencies to starkly dualistic thinking. Sartre's own complexities notwithstanding, the idea that we are constantly faced with existential choice fits into U.S. cultural presumptions that if a situation is not working, we can always just start over.

What Color Is God's Skin?

As noted above, part of the inspiration for this paper was one author's witnessing a group of fellow *Buffy* enthusiasts praise the show's re-visioning of the family. So she should disclose that the paper is a result of her attempts to discover and flesh out the sources for her strong sense of discomfort in this discussion. The discussion occurred in a session about race in the Whedonverse, and most of the participants seemed to identify as white. The authors wish to suggest that there is a connection between the valorization of the chosen family and rhetorical patterns of privileging or normalizing white people's experiences. For not all cultural groups experience or respond to the forces of social fragmentation in the same way. For example, Latinos, notoriously, often remain family-centered even at the cost of social mobility and mainstream success. From the dominant white culture, however, such allegiance to extended kinship groupings is seen as mere "clannishness" or "tribalism."

It is a commonplace that while racially marked people tend to include their racial designations in their basic descriptions of themselves, a white person will more often think of herself as just a person. What we wish to suggest is that it is easier to contemplate the idea that you can choose your family if you are invisible — not socially marked. Otherwise, the choice to leave the people with whom you share a fundamental and risky category of identity raises complex questions of loyalty to social struggle and even survival — cultural-symbolic and biological. While for some the choice to bond into another family involves painful breaks with particular others, a racialized person may face scrambling at extraordinarily deep levels involving one's relation to basic categories of existence (Lugones, "Hispaneando," "Playfulness"). In other words, one's attraction to the idea that we can choose our families may be an index of one's social privilege.

We certainly are not suggesting that racially marked people do not make such choices, or that they are painless for white people. Indeed, the term "chosen family" is often used to designate the alternative emotional units forged by those refugees of gender and sexuality of all races who have been rejected by their natural families. This association no doubt is the source of at least some of the term's current emotional resonance with liberal audiences. We share concerns about the injuries faced by those who do not fit into current gender constellations. But to overlook the dimensions of racial privilege operating in what people are able to envision as choices risks compounding those injuries even more.

The Cordelia Problem

Cordelia, of course, leaves Sunnydale by Season Four in search of stardom in Los Angeles. But her position in the Scooby Gang was marginal from the start. In spite of her relationship with Xander, Cordelia is never quite accepted by the other group members, who bring their own judgments to bear. Our point in bringing up Cordelia is to raise questions about what we can call the "structures of inclusion" operative in social groupings. Part of the rhetorical power of the idea of choosing your family is its contrast to the fact that families are often groups of people who would not have chosen each other if given the opportunity. But this lack of choice also connects to the reasons why families are the places where those struck by illness, accident, or other misfortunes have more of a chance of being cared for and genuinely accepted in their infirmities. Choices based on liking might be enough for a group of friends, but they seem neither decisive nor secure enough to support the sorts of care and security we search for in family relationships.

Another way to put this is that actual chosen families will have innate tendencies to become cliques. If the bond which holds the family together is choice based on liking, then we need to demarcate who is "in" and who is "out" in terms of personal affection — and that means cliques. Absent stronger structures of inclusion than affection, structures like biological relationship, shared long-term history, and moral obligations attendant upon specific roles (like "parent"), we wonder whether chosen families may have a tendency to overwork other structures, like the dominance of a single member or subgroup, in order to pick up the slack. To return for a moment to *BtVS*, the show obscures this problem by using the idea of eschatological mission to justify its cliquishness and Buffy's dominance. (In this way, too, the show panders to the adolescent within by offering a valorization of a comfortable, but unhealthy, adolescent bonding pattern.)

In this sense, it makes a big difference whether the chosen family is thought of as a sort of safety valve or as a dominant social ideal. As a safety valve, who could argue with the idea? We not naively suggesting that natural families work all the time. For those who are rejected by their own families, or who are isolated due to distance or misfortune, or who undertake to adopt children, the chosen family may be their best and only choice. But it is one thing to say that we need chosen family arrangements to pick up the slack when natural families fail, and quite another thing to say that the chosen family should be the dominant social ideal.

IV.

Conclusion

The philosopher J.L. Austin once said that philosophy has two bits: there's the bit where you say something and the bit where you take it back. And maybe it is now time for bit number two. We have so far been talking about *Buffy the Vampire Slayer* as if it were putting the chosen family forward as an ideal. But what if it were, instead, actually chronicling its collapse?

In the text, we interpreted Season Seven as the working out of the inner logic of the chosen family. It seemed to us that the patriarchal, the eschatological, the proto-fascist, the chosen people, and the yearning-for-the-father logics all here attained to their extreme form. We thought, in other words, that what we were seeing in Season Seven was the chosen family showing, at last, its hidden face.

But perhaps we were wrong in this. Perhaps Season Seven is actually supposed to show us the collapse of the chosen family. Of course, all the same people are still involved. But maybe what the show is trying to say is that these same people are not really a family anymore, but that their association has changed into some other sort of social structure: a military organization, or, perhaps, a business. And maybe the reason for this change is that the show has finally seen through the illusions of the earlier seasons and realized that the chosen family is actually not a stable alternate structure.

It would, in any case, be easy enough to make the case that what happens in Season Seven is that the family structure disappears and that a military one takes its place. Everything we said earlier about Buffy's role as a general, and which we then interpreted as showing a military logic within the family, could, it seems, be more naturally interpreted as showing that the family has simply been replaced by a military unit.[27] Developments in Whedon's subsequent comic book series seem to bolster this line of interpretation (Vineyard).

But in addition to this switch from family to military, there also seems to be a switch from family to business. In Season Seven, workplace metaphors abound: in "Selfless" (7.5) Anya accepts Buffy's decision to kill her as just part of their respective jobs, and in "Get it Done" (7.15), Robin refers to Buffy's slaying as her "other job," and so on. One could perhaps track the career of these usages through the final seasons.

The implication of such patterns might look like a very bleak vision. The early seasons showed us the inadequacy of the natural family and the need to replace it with the chosen family. But now in Season Seven we see this chosen family itself reduced to rubble and replaced by business and military forms of relation. Is the ultimate message, then, that the military-industrial complex will be our new mommy and daddy?

Notes

1. An interesting index of this precedence is how, in later seasons, the characters actually come to live with their chosen family rather than their natural ones. By Season Six, Willow and Tara have moved into the Summers residence and in Season Seven Spike and Anya become installed there as well. Xander may as well live there, too, for all the time he spends repairing the place.

2. Joyce, Buffy's mother, is the most central biologically related family member, and the most sympathetically portrayed. But her lack of connection and inability to recognize the oddity of her daughter's life is a strong theme of the early seasons (Williams). Cynthia Bowers discusses three early episodes foregrounding the failures in parenting by the adults in Buffy's life (including Giles) and notes that in response to adult incompetence and self-centeredness, the members of the younger generation adopt parental roles and skills with notable success.

3. In what we could describe as the doppelganger family to the Scooby Gang, relations between Darla, Angel, Drusilla and Spike are depicted as sorts of amplifications of the biological and erotic dimensions of human families-extending the metaphor of blood relationships to the literal and reveling in incestuous generational reversals (Kaveney, 8).

4. But see also Bradney.

5. The whole passage goes like this: "Both shows suggest that non-biological fathers can 'head' non-traditional families far better than their biological counterparts, primarily because they are able to share their parenting duties with the rest of the family, and that they understand that their coherence as 'father' depends just as much on the symbolic input, as well as the love and support, of their family members." See also Battis, 146–149.

6. Just as problematic, from the perspective of Catholic social teaching, is the show's almost exclusive focus on supernatural threat with little concern for economic disparities among people. Jeffrey L. Pasley echoes this critique in his non-theological examination of the politics of the Buffyverse. Although there are anticapitalist themes to be found, "the heroes have never developed any strong sense that the larger social order is unjust enough, or changeable enough, to overturn" (Pasley, 264). For a more positive assessment of the

show's critique of capitalism, see Brian Wall and Michael Zyrd. It should be noted that Season Six's "Flooded" has these nice lines from Willow, upon finding out that the bank has rejected Buffy's application for home refinancing: "But no, they're like, 'we're not going to give you money unless you prove you don't need it.' What kind of system is that?"

7. In describing some families as natural, we are certainly aware that kinship relations and responsibilities are wildly variable historically. Nonetheless, these various kinship relations are grounded upon heterosexual couplings and their initially small, bawling and pooping natural consequences.

8. This follows Locklin's point about how it's Buffy's mission that is the raison d'être for the chosen family.

9. It is here that Neil King's work is especially relevant.

10. The difference between our analysis and Reid's model of a domestic church seems to be as follows. In the model of the domestic church, what comes first is the bond between the family members. This is then expressed outwardly in some sort of social mission. And what changes in the sort of eschatological church we have on the show is basically the priority or direction of these two moments. For on the show it seems to be the mission that comes first and the bond between the family members that is a result of the mission.

11. To see how odd this is, compare it to the very un-eschatological chosen family on *Seinfeld* where we meet both of George's parents often, both of Jerry's parents often, Jerry's uncle Leo often, Jerry's great aunt once, Kramer's mother once, Elaine's father once, and Susan's parents several times (this list may not be exhaustive as it was compiled from memory).

12. Of course, someone might object that the episodes concerning Joyce's death are supposed to teach us that she was actually more crucial than anyone realized and that her absence is a blow not just to Buffy and Dawn, but to all the characters. On this point, see Kaveney (5). And we do agree, of course, that this is the message of these episodes. But we would also argue that this sort of belated realization of Joyce's importance is actually evidence that the show didn't really do justice to that importance earlier. And of course the show won't be able to do justice to her importance later since she will be simply gone.

13. That the single mom just happens to be black, well....

14. Here too we want to acknowledge Locklin and his idea that, because Buffy's mission is the raison d'être of the chosen family, the relations within that family are bound not to be mutual ones. On the whole idea of proto-fascistic command structures, King is of course relevant.

15. Notably, D'Hoffryn describes his cohort of vengeance demons as "a family of sorts."

16. Anya is hit from behind and goes down wordlessly. Of course the suggestion in the text is our suggestion about how Anya's death fits into the show's logic. And we should admit that Joss Whedon's explanations are different for he notes in the commentary accompanying this episode that he decided to have Anya die because somebody had to die, because it seemed unfair to kill Xander or any of the more core characters, and because he wanted to remind viewers that not all deaths are heroic.

17. Here we are sort of agreeing with Locklin's worry that Buffy rejects patriarchy only to replace it with another hierarchy. Our only difference from Locklin is the thought that Buffy actually replaces patriarchy with the same hierarchy just in a transposed (and disguised) form.

18. Whatever happened to civilian control of the military?

19. We don't actually remember a mention of Faith's father, but Lynne Edwards, whose expertise is greater than ours, says that she thinks she remembers one mention — a mention in which Faith says her father used to hurt her.

20. And this is a conservative claim. For given what we know of Xander's father, as evidenced in Season Six's "Hells Bells" it is likely that he did more than just fail to support his son's self-concept; it is likely that he said and did things to undermine it.

21. We're not claiming that the show itself does this. Much of the drama involves Buffy's

being overwhelmed by such world-historical responsibility. And in Season Seven we are given a nice critique of the coercion and sexual violence involved in the creation of the Slayer line. Indeed, in her speech outlining her plan to redistribute the power of the Scythe, Buffy emphasizes that the Potentials have a choice. Whether the speech opens a genuine space for individual choice or instead serves mainly as a vehicle for persuasion remains questionable, however.

22. Battis notes that her personality is marked by a certain fundamental hollowness and lability (31–34).

23. In tracing these links we're not suggesting that they form a complete or adequate analysis of Willow's character. For a fuller and more sophisticated discussion see South, 131–145.

24. We think that a similar point could easily be made for Faith, and probably for Tara and even Spike as well. There is not, however, space to develop all this here, and so we confined ourselves to the three core members of the chosen family.

25. Thanks to Agnes's husband for this observation.

26. This connects back to Battis's point that Buffy both produces and disrupts traditional family structures.

27. The military metaphors populating Season Seven continue to mount through to the final episode ("Chosen") with the potential Slayers distinguished from "civilians" and Dawn volunteering to "check out our field of engagement." The fact that Buffy remains in command even after her loss of status as the Chosen One is signalled in the series' final scene when Dawn and Willow continue to ask for her directives.

Works Cited

Battis, Jes. *Blood Relations: Chosen Families in Buffy and Angel*. Jefferson, NC: McFarland, 2005.
Bible. King James version.
Bowers, Cynthia. "Generation Lapse: The Problematic Parenting of Joyce Summers and Rupert Giles." *Slayage: The Online International Journal of Buffy Studies 2* (2001). http://slayageonline.com/essays/slayage2/bowers.htm.
Bradney, Anthony. "Choosing Law, Choosing Family: Images of Law, Love and Authority in *Buffy the Vampire Slayer*." *Web Journal of Current Legal Issues* (2003). http://webjcli.ncl.ac.uk/2003/issue2/bradney2.html.
Buffy the Vampire Slayer, Season Six. Fox DVD boxed set. Twentieth Century Fox, 2002.
Buffy the Vampire Slayer, Season Seven. Fox DVD boxed set. Twentieth Century Fox, 2004.
"Buffy 101: Studying the Slayer." *Buffy the Vampire Slayer*, Season Seven. Fox DVD. Disc 6, 2004.
Burns, Angie. "Passion, Pain, and 'Bad Kissing Decisions': Learning about Intimate Relationships from Buffy Season Six." Slayage: *The Online International Journal of Buffy Studies* 21 (2006). http://www.slayageonline.com/essays/slayage21/Burns.htm.
Kavaney, Roz. "'She Saved the World. A Lot': An Introduction to the Themes and Structures of *Buffy* and *Angel*." *Reading the Vampire Slayer*. Roz Kavaney, ed. London: Tauris Paperbacks, 2001. 1–36.
King, Neal. "Brownskirts: Fascism, Christianity, and the Eternal Demon." *Buffy the Vampire Slayer and Philosophy: Fear and Trembling in Sunnydale*. James B. South, ed. Chicago: Open Court, 2003. 197–211.

Locklin, Reid B. "*Buffy the Vampire Slayer* and the Domestic Church: Revisioning Family and the Common Good." *Slayage: The Online International Journal of Buffy Studies* 6 (2002). http://slayageonline.com/essays/slayage6/Locklin.htm.

Lugones, María. "Hispaneando y Lesbiando: On Sarah Hoagland's *Lesbian Ethics*." *Hypatia: A Journal of Feminist Philosophy* 5.3 (Fall 1990): 138–147.

_____. "Playfulness, World Traveling, and Loving Perception." *Hypatia: A Journal of Feminist Philosophy* 2.2 (1987). 3–19.

Pasley, Jeffrey L. "Old Familiar Vampires: The Politics of the Buffyverse." *Buffy the Vampire Slayer and Philosophy: Fear and Trembling in Sunnydale*. James B. South, ed. Chicago: Open Court, 2003. 254–267.

Schmitt, Carl. *Concept of the Political*. George Schwab, trans. Chicago: University of Chicago Press, 1996.

_____. *The Leviathan in the State Theory of Thomas Hobbes*. George Schwab and Erna Hilfstein, trans. Westport, CT: Greenwood Press, 1996.

South, James. "'My God, It's Like a Greek Tragedy': Willow Rosenberg and Human Irrationality." *Buffy the Vampire Slayer and Philosophy: Fear and Trembling in Sunnydale*. James B. South, ed. Chicago: Open Court, 2003. 131–145.

Vineyard, Jennifer. "ReBuffed: New Comic Book Series Resurrects Vampire Slayer." *MTV News* online, February 1, 2007. http://www.mtv.com/news/articles/1551286/20070131/index.jhtml.

Wall, Brian, and Michael Zyrd. "Vampire Dialectics: Knowledge, Institutions and Labor." *Reading the Vampire Slayer*. Roz Kavaney, ed. London: Tauris Paperbacks, 2001. 70–76.

Whedon, Joss. "Commentary for 'Objects in Space.'" *Firefly*. Fox DVD. Disk 4, 2003.

Williams, J.P. "Choosing Your Own Mother: Mother-Daughter Conflicts in *Buffy*." *Fighting the Forces: What's at Stake in Buffy the Vampire Slayer*. Rhonda V. Wilcox and David Lavery, eds. Lanham, MA: Rowman & Littlefield, 2002. 61–72.

Yeats's Entropic Gyre and Season Six

ELIZABETH L. RAMBO

> Turning and turning in the widening gyre
> The falcon cannot hear the falconer;
> Things fall apart; the center cannot hold.
> — W.B. Yeats, "The Second Coming" 1–3

One question was asked again and again in various forms during the sixth season of *Buffy the Vampire Slayer*, by fans and characters in the show itself: "What's wrong?" What's wrong with Buffy? "What's wrong here?" sang the band as Willow and Amy wreaked magical havoc in The Bronze ("Smashed," 6.9). What's wrong with Willow? What's wrong with Xander? What's wrong with Spike? What's wrong with Dawn? What's wrong with the show? Some, all right, maybe a lot of fans complained it was dark, depressing, fragmented, lacking in direction. Who's the season's villain, the big bad? Those three geeks? Please! What's going on? Buffy was back from the dead, the theme for the season, according to series creator-producer Joss Whedon and executive producer Marti Noxon, was supposed to be "Oh, grow up," so why did everyone seem to be behaving so badly, so immaturely? Clues were dropped all along, of course, but the key was episode 18, "Entropy," and Tara's almost off-hand allusion to Yeats's famous poem, "The Second Coming": "Things fall apart, they fall so hard.... You can't ever put them back the way they were" (6.18).

How do "things fall apart" in the poetic and visionary universe of Yeats, and how can this framework help us re-imagine Buffy's sixth season? The image of the "gyre"—the spiral or cone—became a central figure for Yeats's poetry and thought. A complete rendering of this symbol in Yeats's work consists of two interpenetrating cones or spirals within a sphere, representing the world of appearance, a world in which, as he says, "Consciousness is conflict." Wedded in antagonism, they symbolize any of the opposing elements that make up existence, such as sun and moon, day and night, life and death, man and God, man and woman ... on a more abstract level, they are permanence and change..., the natural and the supernatural worlds [Ellmann, 153].

Yeats also used this image to represent historic cycles; he believed each historic age had its own "character," which gradually erodes as its gyre expands; at the same time, the qualities of the next age are coming into focus as its gyre is narrowing (Yeats, qtd. in Jeffares). This is the vision we are given in "The Second Coming," along with the terrifying images of the resulting chaos and a "rough beast, its hour come round at last" that "slouches toward Bethlehem to be born" (21–22). The title of the poem alludes to the return of Christ, but the final image is of anti–Christ. Nevertheless, Helen Vendler comments that "Yeats, for all his fascinated horror, *approves* intellectually, if not emotionally.... The destruction of the known is always a terrifying experience and the clutching of the familiar is the greatest deterrent to new knowledge" (99). Thus, the widening gyre, and indeed, several images in "The Second Coming," symbolize loss of innocence, irresistible change, and although most are associated with fear, destruction and chaos — in short, entropy — the end result, as with *Buffy* Season Six, may be less disastrous than expected.

Thus, although the episodes of Season Six may seem to have lacked direction, in fact, the apparent disorderliness and repetition of themes from episode to episode reflects the widening gyre of the Scooby Gang's collective consciousness, their ethos, if you will, while at the same time Buffy, the Slayer, the hero of this fictional world, begins the season in chaos and despair, at the widest cycle of her gyre, and slowly spirals back to the center of her own reason for being. The changes of Buffy and her friends — and her enemies — as they face or attempt to evade their individual challenges of growing up may be seen as variations on Yeats's two interpenetrating, antithetical gyres. For all of them in each expanding or narrowing cycle, "the clutching of the familiar is the greatest deterrent to new knowledge" they need for true maturity or rebirth (Vendler, 99).

Most *Buffy* seasons begin with Buffy needing to reclaim her identity or her sense of calling as the Slayer: consider Season Two's "When She Was Bad"— Buffy, after dying briefly in "Prophecy Girl" (1.12), is a "bitca" until she "[works] out her issues" (2.1) — or "Anne" (3.1) — Buffy, having abdicated Slayer duty altogether, abandoned Sunnydale, and changed her name, triumphantly confronts the forces of evil again with, "I'm Buffy.

The Vampire Slayer. And you are...?" (3.1). At the start of Season Six, however, Buffy has been dead and buried for about three months; anyone who thought she could bounce back in one episode, or even three, must have thought this was *Charmed*. If we consider the storyline of Season Six with Yeats's antithetical gyres as our model, Buffy claws her way out of her grave at the widest cycle of her gyre; newly resurrected, she strays through the hellish streets of demon-infested Sunnydale which symbolize her inner confusion. She sees her robotic image torn limb from limb, a scene one writer has called "*the* visual metaphor for [Season Six's] deconstruction and destruction and violation of self" (Tague); Bronwen Calvert comments on the reverse mirror imagery of Buffy and the Buffybot: "The dismemberment of the Buffybot is almost contemporaneous with Buffy's resurrection, during which the reconstruction of Buffy's decaying physical body marks her return to 'real' life, and the Buffybot's 'death' is viewed through Buffy's blurred vision, so that it becomes part of the 'hell' in which Buffy now believes herself to be" (par. 18). Everything appears to her through a haze, and the first turn of her gyre brings her back to the last place where things made sense to her, the top of the crazy tower built by Glory's minions for Dawn's sacrifice, the site where Buffy gave her own life instead. She asks Dawn, "Is this hell?" then, when told it's not, murmurs: "It was so ... clear ... on this spot. I remember ... how ... shiny ... and clear everything was. But ... now ..." ("Bargaining," 6.2). Whether Buffy is about to throw herself off again or is simply attempting to gain some inner clarity when Dawn finds her there remains unresolved; in any case, from this point of her highest physical, mental, and emotional chaos, the season's remaining episodes take Buffy in a narrowing spiral back down to where she at last regains her sense of self and mission.

The spiral structure is highlighted in miniature in episode 5, "Life Serial," in which Buffy cycles through three different, unsuitable occupations—student, construction worker, and sales clerk at the Magic Box—while the season's ostensible villains, the Trio, or Nerds of Doom test her skills. The last test is an actual time-loop, with Buffy forced to repeat the same sequence of events again and again until she finds a way to succeed. She ends this episode by attempting to drown her sorrows with Spike at a demon poker game. The whole episode is played for humor but foreshadows the season's cyclical structure and should warn us not to be surprised when it sometimes seems repetitive: for Yeats, a key element of the gyre imagery is recurrence (Ellmann, 154). Another version of the gyre in Yeats's work is a spiral staircase in a tower, in which each turn brings one around again to similar scenes (read: metaphors, images, issues), but with a new perspective that is further up or down the winding stair. The falcon of "The Second Coming," rising as it turns in its "widening gyre," illustrates the same type of vertical spiral.

In the turning gyre of Season Six, Episode 7, "Once More, with Feeling," is considered by many thoughtful viewers to encapsulate the entire season's story arc, reiterating the story so far and hinting at developments to come through staging, oracular lyrics, and other means. It does take Buffy through another cycle, as her spell-induced song, "Something to Sing About," reveals to her friends that they brought her back, not from hell, as they've believed, but from heaven, and as she gives in to her desire "just ... to feel" by kissing Spike, giving him what he's wanted madly for nearly a year (6.7). As an example of significant staging and choreography in this episode, Spike is the first to break away from the final chorus of "Where Do We Go from Here?" ("Once More, with Feeling," 6.7), and he will be the first character (other than Giles) to leave Sunnydale altogether, in "Seeing Red" (6.19), and his gyre will spiral on outward from this point, starting with the next episode, "Tabula Rasa" (6.8).

In fact, "Tabula Rasa" is the decisive break-point for the other characters' outward-spiraling gyres, after Willow's carelessly cast memory-wipe spell causes amnesia for everyone, including herself. After the comic interlude that briefly reveals each character's strengths, hopes, fears, and flaws,[1] the spell is broken, and two key departures occur: Giles flies back to England and Tara moves out of the Summers house, breaking up with her lover, Willow. If any character can be identified as "the falconer," Giles seems the obvious choice, but a case can also be made for Tara. Tara was something of a cipher in Seasons Four and Five, but in Season Six, she becomes the voice of wisdom and strength, the one character who seems to have already completed the "Oh, grow up!" spiral and could be trusted to take care of Dawn, make pancakes, use magic responsibly, make the hard decisions—no matter how painful to herself and her loved ones—and show compassion to the lost.

For the other characters, Season Six begins with all the slayerettes, except Dawn, and including Spike, working together efficiently to slay vampires, under the magical guidance of Willow. As soon as Buffy returns, the others begin spiraling away from each other and from her. Consider Willow, for example: Although Giles speaks for viewers, as well, in saying that "Having Buffy back in the world makes me feel ... indescribably wonderful" ("Flooded," 6.4), it seems likely that Willow's determination to resurrect the Slayer may spring primarily from her inability to deal with change and her own sorrow, as Paul McDonald notes:

Over the course of the series, it has become apparent that Willow does not handle loss well. Magic provides her with the perception of an outlet, and she uses it after Oz leaves in season four [to] near disastrous effects.... Willow probably never dealt with her pain on any conscious level. The possibility of bringing Buffy back perhaps held her in a kind of emotional stasis. It is not until the ritual is over and the Urn of Osiris is destroyed that Willow realizes her friend is truly "gone" and she looks horror-stricken.

Willow's abuse of magical power will eventually drive away the person she's come to value most, her lover Tara (the character who seems to have found her center much sooner than anyone else), and will finally lead her, shockingly, to extremes of evil that few would have predicted who remember the hesitant girl who had to put on her "resolve face" to convince people she was serious ("Becoming," 2.22) and was "very seldom naughty" ("Restless," 4.22). However, if one reviews the series, clues to Willow's developing attraction for dark magic and power go at least back to Season Two (Battis, South).

Tara is Willow's center, and her death blows Willow's entropic gyre wide open, but the primary center that was removed for the *Buffy* gang in Season Six was Giles, Buffy's Watcher, mentor, father-figure. In fact, using Yeats's poem as our guide, it may be more effective to read Buffy as "the falcon" and Giles as "the falconer." In the pivotal musical episode, "Once More, with Feeling," Giles finally decides that his presence was preventing Buffy from making her own decisions, growing into her own responsibilities, "Your path's unbeaten and it's all uphill / And you can meet it, but you never will / And I'm the reason that you're standing still" ("Once More, with Feeling," 6.7).

Giles has also been Willow's teacher in magic, and she's surprised that he's not completely pleased with the way she brought Buffy back; instead he chides her for her foolhardy irresponsibility. "The magicks you channeled are more ferocious and primal than anything you can hope to understand, and you are lucky to be alive, you rank, arrogant amateur!" (Giles, "Flooded," 6.4). Giles' departure to England removes his authoritative voice from Sunnydale. Oddly, no one ever calls him on the phone, although it seems an obvious choice. Why not? Perhaps out of misguided pride — a determination to prove that they can do this on their own, be grown-ups? Nevertheless, when Giles does finally return to Sunnydale, he tells Buffy, "Sometimes the most adult thing you can do is ask for help when you need it" ("Grave," 6.22).

The episodes "Hell's Bells" (6.16) and "Entropy" (6.18) see the engaged couple Xander and Anya spun away from each other by Xander's fears of his own inability to break his family's cycles of abuse and alcoholism (his glance at his bickering, drunken parents seems to drive the final nail in his decision not to go through with the wedding in "Hells Bells"), his lingering unresolved feelings about Buffy, and by Anya's cycling back to her familiar role of vengeance demon, aided by her vengeance demon mentor, D'Hoffryn, the closest thing Anya has to a father-figure, and by Spike, who's just about to reach his own outermost gyre in "Seeing Red." Although Anya and Spike both indicate that their encounter in the Magic Box is not about revenge (Anya says, "[I]t was just a thing. I felt bad, he was just there" ["Entropy," 6.18]), vengeance is the effect. At the end of this episode, all the characters are as far away from each other emotionally and physically as possible, except Willow and Tara, who finally reunite as Tara, after her "things fall apart" comment, insists on skipping the process of putting them back together: "Can you just be kissing me now?" ("Entropy," 6.18). It would seem that the level-headed, centered Tara has at this point spun out on her own small antithetical gyre of passion, as much as we sympathize, and of course, we know what follows: "the center cannot hold"—through not fault of her own, "mere anarchy," in the form of Warren's wild gunshot, will end Tara's life.[2]

And what about Warren? Do the three villainous geeks — the Trio, the Legion of Dim, the nerds of doom, the evil troika — have their own widening gyre? Or are Jonathan, Warren, and "the other one[3] just cardboard excuses for trouble while Buffy and her friends battle their own inner demons? In fact, the trio have their own parallel antithetical gyres. When we are first introduced to them after their first successful demon-assisted crime, they are presented as boys playing at being "super-villains."

They seem to have decided to "take over Sunnydale" on a whim, more or less out of boredom, with a mission statement centered around acquiring money and women ("Flooded," 6.4). Each succeeding crime swings them a turn closer to the murder they considered in "Flooded." Andrew and Jonathan vote against killing Buffy, but Warren, while appearing to accept the democratic decision, acts alone — his own entropic gyre of evil is already much wider than Andrew's and Jonathan's. Andrew becomes Warren's shadow, fascinated by the "coolness" of literally "[getting] away with murder" ("Dead Things," 6.13), but ultimately ineffective: in "Seeing Red," he has a jet-pack just like Warren's, delivers what should be a devastating parting speech ("Well played, Slayer.... This round to you. But the game is far from over"), then zooms up into the roof overhead, knocking himself unconscious (6.19); it's a deliciously ludicrous moment. Andrew never understands why there are consequences to his actions, continuing to insist, "But we didn't do anything" ("Two to Go," 6.21). At the same time, Jonathan, though never quite strong enough to break away from the other two, becomes increasingly aware that their crimes have real repercussions, that they are harming real people, including some people that he knows and likes: Buffy, Willow and Xander. If "Superstar" (4.17) is any indication, in his ideal world, Jonathan would be part of (or leader of) the Scoobies, not a super-villain. In "Dead Things," Jonathan is truly horrified by the concepts of rape and murder, and from that point on is only cooperating until he can end the partnership while still saving his own skin — his cowardice is his tragic flaw. Nevertheless, Jonathan gives Buffy the key to Warren's super-strength, the "orbs of Nezzla-khan" while pretending to attack her in "Seeing Red" (6.19), and when he and Andrew are in jail, attacked by the vengeance-bound Willow, Jonathan realizes they're reaping what they've sown. "Why is she doing this? Tell her, we didn't do anything," Andrew exclaims, to which Jonathan replies, "Yes, we did. We signed on, we teamed up, we wanted to see where our plans would take us. Well, take a look." ["Two to Go," 6.21].

In Season Six, the villains' gyres just keep expanding — and perhaps this is only fitting, as they represent evil and chaos. One writer notes that Warren's out-of-control pursuit of revenge "accidentally manage[s] to transform Willow into the very person he was trying to be. She truly has [bought] a commission into the Forces of Darkness. The fact that she's willing to end the world to end the pain of that empowerment just proves how much Warren underestimated the bill" (kdS). Jonathan has a brief moment of righteousness as he holds Andrew to accountability at swordspoint ("We're not leaving Sunnydale. When this is over, you and I are going back to jail to do our time" ["Two to Go, 6.21]), but it all spins away when he loses Xander's social reinforcement and Buffy's guardian strength; Jonathan and Andrew exchange glances and run for Mexico.[4] The "challenge to the audience" in the portrayal of the evil Trio, according to "kdS," is that, since Warren, Jonathan and Andrew are represented as "fans," they are

> remarkable as possibly the most hostile portrayal of an element of its audience a TV series has ever attempted. In addition to the usual stereotypes of "cult TV" and SF fandom (social ineptness, sexual inexperience and unemployability) ME portrays the Troika as genuinely malevolent, dangerous, and in Warren's case, [sociopathic]. Yet apart from one (very mild) expression of concern by Paul Cornell in *SFX* magazine, very little offense seems to have been taken ["A small appendix"].

"kdS" goes on to ask:

> If we're so repelled by Warren, what does it say that we're fascinated by sexier characters who do things that are just as bad? In seeing the dreadful failure of

Warren's fantasies of power, we're forced to question our own chortling identification with the acceptable face of darkness and any power fantasies that we may have. Warren shows us the truly terrifying face peeking through the kitsch Halloween mask, the trail of blood hidden by the tails of Spike's trenchcoat ["Re: Mary Sue"].

None of the three geeky villains reach the epiphany or rebirth that should be the result of Yeats's completed gyres; they just spiral outward until they're gone, one way or another, at least as Season Six concludes. We will, of course, see all three again in Season Seven, but that is another essay.

As Season Six winds through ever darkening coils, Dawn whirls through her own isolated chaotic spiral or gyre to a new beginning, which she shares with Buffy.[5] Joss Whedon may have been thinking of Dawn's Season Six spiral when he commented recently, "Everybody knows Dawn complains. I kept having her be sad because her reality was so crushingly horrible. She kept losing parental figures over and over and over" ("Slay Ride"). In Season Five, Dawn experienced the deaths of her mother and her elder sister, and while it must be noted that most of Dawn's memories of those relationships were constructed as part of her creation to disguise her original identity as "the Key" ("No Place Like Home," 5.5), they are nonetheless affective. Thus, while it may be accurate to call Dawn "Buffy's virtual sister" (Mendlesohn, qtd. in Jowett, 52), this label cannot be applied meaningfully beyond Season Five. In Season Six, Dawn also loses Tara, the most parental of the Scoobies.

Whatever virtuality Dawn may have had, its relevance fades as Season Six begins. As Dawn reminds Spike, "I'm fine alone. It's not like anyone's coming after me. I'm not the key. Or if I am, I don't open anything any more. It's over. Remember?" ("Bargaining" part 1, 6.1). Dawn is not fine alone, as she tries to convince Spike (and herself), but not because she needs protection. Lorna Jowett says Dawn's "bad behavior" (most of which occurs in Season Six) is "coded clearly as teenage rebellion or a cry for help rather than as morally 'evil'" (55), but it's more complicated than that: Dawn, although no longer a key, needs to find a purpose for her existence and to feel assured that her relationships are real. She is fifteen, the same age as Buffy when she became a slayer, yet the gang still think of her as "young" and "delicate," ("Blood Ties," 5.13) as illustrated in this scene with Tara from "Flooded" in which Dawn declares herself mature enough, at fifteen, to do research. "You know, if you don't let me look at the pictures, I'm gonna learn everything I know about demons on the street." she points out.

When Tara responds "Knock yourself out," Dawn attempts to prove her point—"Thank you. See? No biggie. I can totally handle it. [opens the book] That's a weird place for a horn. [closes the book] That's not a horn ... "Flooded" 6.3. Yes, Dawn is somewhat naïve, but in this episode she returns to research and she, rather than the more experienced Willow and Xander, succeeds in finding the bank-robbing M'Fashnik demon ("Flooded" 6.3). Recall that Dawn begins Season Six by saving the resurrected Buffy from the same tower of doom where Buffy saved her at the end of Season Five. Although Dawn is nearly ravished by musical demon Sweet in "Once More, with Feeling" (leading Buffy to sigh metatextually, "Dawn's in trouble? It must be Tuesday"[6]), when Spike stops Buffy from dancing herself into flames, it is Dawn who recalls Buffy's own words to her again: "The hardest thing in this world ... is to live in it." Dawn's turning point in Season Six coincides, significantly, with Buffy's birthday (always a bad day[7]), when a vengeance demon grants Dawn's wish that she "could just make [people] stop [g]oing away" ("Older and Far Away" 6.14). She's making restitution to Anya and other storekeepers for her shoplifting by episode 18 "Entropy" (note that this is the episode in which almost every other character falls completely apart, as the title suggests). Buffy finally acknowledges that protection is not what Dawn needs as a new day dawns over Sunnydale: "I want to see you grow up. The woman you're gonna become.... I got it so wrong. I don't want to protect you from the world—I want to show it to you." ("Grave," 6.22). Although this speech may not be one of the most brilliantly written, its message is clear: Dawn is no longer an endangered puppet whom magical genetics compel Buffy to guard. She has her own path.

Meanwhile, Buffy's personal gyre has been spiraling closer to the center point of recovering herself and, thus, moving on to the next level of understanding, the next age, in Yeatsian terms. Regarding the interpenetrating gyres as "transvaluation of values" (Harrison), Yeats wrote, "A primary dispensation looking beyond itself towards a transcendent power is dogmatic, levelling, unifying, feminine, humane, peace its means and end; an antithetical dispensation obeys imminent power, is expressive, hierarchical, multiple, masculine, harsh, surgical" (*Vision*, 263). Not every adjective applies, but surely we can recognize elements of Buffy in the primary dispensation, and Spike in the antithetical dispensation, though each has some elements of the other, and Yeats would not find this surprising— mirrors and other types of reflecting images also figure prominently in *A Vision*.

It has been a painful, wild journey, for both, mostly revolving around a passion Buffy expressed when she first gave in to it at the end of "Once

More, with Feeling" with "This isn't real, / But I just want to feel" (6.7), while Spike's ambivalence may be judged by his lines, "First I'll kill her then I'll save her / ... / No I'll save her then I'll kill her" (6.7). Yet the undead vampire does save Buffy, in the end.

Yeats's comment in *A Vision* regarding the antithetical gyres seems to sum up the Spike-Buffy relationship perfectly: "Here the thought of Heraclitus dominates all: 'Dying each other's life, living each other's death'" (68). Spike greeted the newly resurrected Buffy tenderly, but from episode 3 ("Life Serial") onward gyrated between fairly aggressive, even violent seductions—"You belong in the shadows ... with me" ("Dead Things," 6.13)—and more charming or humble approaches, such as the brief exchange before Anya and Xander's disrupted wedding when he tells her, "It's nice to watch you be happy. For them, even. I don't see it a lot. You, uh ... you glow." "But it hurts?" he then asks. "Yeah," she replies, to which he simply responds, "Thanks" ["Hell's Bells," 6.16].

Until the "Entropy" episode introduced the final "falling apart" of the season, Buffy and Spike more than any other relationship epitomized Yeats's lines.

> The blood-dimmed tide is loosed, and everywhere
> The ceremony of innocence is drowned;
> The best lack all conviction, while the worst
> Are full of passionate intensity ["Second Coming" 5–8].

Nothing ceremonious or innocent about their house-shattering, erotic battle in "Smashed" (6.9) or their rough-house and implied bondage play in "Dead Things" (6.13),[8] and from the typed shouting matches on fanboards, one would be hard-pressed to decide whether Spike or Buffy should be identified as "best" or "worst"—probably both in one episode or another, depending on your point of view. But at the end of "As You Were," Buffy finally gains sufficient conviction to end it: "I can't love you. I'm just ... being weak, and selfish..." "Really not complaining here," Spike interjects, and she ends with, "... it's killing me" (6.15). She's able to stick with this decision, much to Spike's chagrin and frustration, until Spike spins completely out of control, resulting in the attempted rape of "Seeing Red" and his departure from Sunnydale promising, "It's all gonna change" (6.19).

"Seeing Red" was an enormously controversial episode, but within the pattern of the entropic gyres, its events might have been expected. According to Harrison, "Violence, which for Yeats was symptomatic of the end of era and the birth of another, becomes widespread as the inverted cone reaches its point of greatest expansion." Thus Spike becomes the "rough beast, its hour come round at last, / Slouch[ing] towards Bethlehem to be born" (Yeats, "Second" 21–22), or rather, towards Africa, considered the cradle of humanity, where he will have his soul returned to him ("Grave," 6.22). What that means, if we take Yeats as our guide, should not be envisioned in conventional apocalyptic terms, expecting the monstrous beast of biblical Revelation. Rather, Vendler notes that for Yeats, influenced by William Blake, the beast "symbolizes, literally, a new birth, a passing to another level, leaving behind all that has been developed and refined in the old state" (101). Thus, the ensouled Spike of Season Seven, moving through madness to compassionate heroism, while still retaining his edge, is very much the type of development that might emerge from a Yeatsian personal apocalypse.

With each turn of her narrowing gyre, Buffy spirals inward towards her identity as the Chosen One. In some episodes, she seems to swing out towards the chaotic—"Smashed," "Gone"—but almost every one also brings her back around and down towards a new grip on life, some reaffirmation of her calling as the Slayer, although she may lose track of it in the next episode: the end of "Wrecked" finds her huddled in her bedroom, clutching a cross and surrounded by wreathes of garlic, determined never to let Spike near her again (6.10); that resolve vanishes along with all her other inhibitions in "Gone," but as Buffy returns to visibility, she also sees for the first time that "I didn't ... I don't ... wanna die.... That's something, right?" ("Gone," 6.11). Significantly, this episode is halfway through the season, but she'll have to cycle through despair again, in the ennui of the "DoubleMeat Palace" (6.12), the agonizing revelation in "Dead Things" (6.13) that she has not "come back wrong" but is merely human after all, and the nearly fatal hallucinations of "Normal Again" (6.17), in which Buffy tells Dawn things are "coming apart" (6.17), but finally pulls herself together by accepting her (internalized) late mother's wisdom. "Buffy, fight it. You're too good to give in ... I know you're afraid. I know the world feels like a hard place sometimes, but you've got people who love you. Your dad and I, we have all the faith in the world in you. You've got ... a world of strength in your heart.... Believe in yourself (Joyce, "Normal Again," 6.17). Buffy rises up and saves her friends from the demon she has set upon them, much as she did at the end of "When She Was Bad" (2.1). This cycle has taken much longer, and there are still a few turns left, but Buffy has finally "spank[ed] her inner moppet" ("When She Was Bad," 2.1). As Riley told her in "As You Were": "Wheel never stops turning, Buffy. You're up, you're down ... it doesn't change what you are. And you are a hell of a woman" (6.15). The wheel, though most obviously a reference to the Wheel of Fortune, may also be an allusion to a complementary image also used by Yeats, "the Great Wheel, representing everything, [which] represented as well the ... phases of any single life" (Unterecker, 27).

The widening gyre of chaos and even active rejection of the accepted or existing values that results in achievement of what Blake might have understood as "a state beyond experience," Vendler notes (101), was described by Yeats in "A Prayer for My Daughter": "All hatred driven hence, / The soul recovers radical innocence" (65–66). This process describes the final outward spiral and resolution of Willow, who, driven by grief and vengeance, once again reveals overwhelming depths of anger and cruelty beneath her usual, sweet "homework gal" persona ("Doppelgangland," 3.16). Lines like, "I'm not coming back" ("Villains," 6.20) and "Willow doesn't live here any more" ("Grave," 6.22) imply that Willow has become another falcon that "cannot hear the falconer." Willow can be called back only by one who has always been something of an innocent himself, Xander, here playing the Holy Fool, who faces her at the edge of the cliff with nothing supernatural, only his heart full of love. In the same way, Spike, having failed to force his antithetical passion on Buffy, must spiral outward emotionally, spiritually, and geographically to have his soul returned with a Yeatsian "lightning flash" (quoted in Unterecker, 166) to become "what [he] was" and give Buffy "what she deserves" ("Grave," 6.22), while Buffy's inward gyre brings her back to a grave and she fights her way out of it again — this time voluntarily: "I'm not just gonna sit here while Willow incinerates what I'm chosen to protect" ("Grave," 6.22), a line we might have expected to hear in episode one in any other season,[9] Buffy is finally able to say now, at the end of Season Six. In many ways, the entire sixth season seemed like what I like to call "the anti–*Buffy*," but in Yeats's mysterious world of opposing spirals, that is the only way to fully come back from the grave, the only way to win one's soul, the only way to get past vengeance to forgiveness.

Finally, the really interesting thing is that the "Second Coming" references, and thus perhaps this gyre structure, are continue in Season Seven of *Buffy*, where Willow, though recovering, "isn't finished" ("Same Time, Same Place," 7.3) and for Spike, getting his soul back is only the first turn in a long spiral back to "what [he] was" and more; while Season Four of *Angel* includes at least one episode title that alludes to Yeats's poem, "Slouching towards Bethlehem" and a definite apocalyptic theme throughout. For *Buffy* Season Seven, with a theme Mutant Enemy writers have described as "back to the beginning," and given Yeats's general theory of the gyre as symbolic image of both history and individual lives, the final season of the show also reflects certain elements of Season Six, including certain primary and antithetical gyres.

Notes

1. One could write an entire essay on this episode alone-together with "Once More, with Feeling," it's the "Restless" of Season Six. And in fact, several articles have been written, including Rhonda Wilcox, "Singing and Dancing and Burning and Dying: Once More with Textual Feeling," and Richard S. Albright, "'[B]reakaway pop hit or ... book number?': 'Once More, with Feeling' and Genre."
2. Early in the show's history, Buffy creator Joss Whedon explained in a Fresh Air interview that important, even beloved characters would die on Buffy and Angel "because I want people to understand that everything is not perfectly safe.... If somebody objects ... I know I've done the right thing.... It does inflame emotions sometimes, but that is in fact what I'm trying to do." Tara's death caused more controversy than any previous regular character's death, however, because Willow and Tara had been almost the only long-term lesbian couple on network television. The Mutant Enemy producers and writers were accused of perpetrating the "dead-evil lesbian cliché," in which one member of fictional a lesbian couple is killed or dies and the other member reacts by going insane or committing some crime, usually murder. The history of the "death of Tara" controversy is recorded extensively elsewhere.
3. It becomes a recurring joke that no one can remember Andrew's name.
4. As previously represented on Buffy, South America seems to be a popular refuge for the demonic and other forces of chaos.
5. Bates et al. discuss Dawn's isolation in Season Six in some detail.
6. Recall that BtVS actually aired on Tuesdays. Now, thanks to DVDs, any day can be Buffy day.
7. Some bad Buffy birthdays of seasons past: "Surprise"/"Innocence"-Buffy sleeps with Angel, he loses his soul; "Helpless"-the Watchers Council tests the slayer with near-fatal results; "A New Man"-Giles is turned into a demon, and Maggie Walsh tries to eliminate Buffy; "Blood Ties"-Dawn finds out she's "the Key"... you get the idea.
8. Though some will argue that ritual is involved in bondage, it seems unlikely that Yeats had anything involving handcuffs in mind when he conceived of "the ceremony of innocence."
9. Except for the part about Willow!

Works Cited

Albright, Richard. "'[B]reakaway pop hit or ... book number?': 'Once More, with Feeling' and Genre." *Slayage: The Online International Journal of Buffy Studies* 17 (June 2005). http://www.slayageonline.com/essays/slayage17/Albright.htm.
"Anne." 3.1. Written and directed by Joss Whedon. *Buffy the Vampire Slayer.* WB. 29 September 1998.
"As You Were." 6.15. Written and directed by Douglas Petrie. *Buffy the Vampire Slayer.* UPN. 26 February 2002.
"Bargaining" (part 2). 6.2. Written by Marti Noxon and David Fury. Directed by David Grossman. *Buffy the Vampire Slayer.* UPN. 10 October 2001.

Battis, Jes. "'She's Not All Grown Yet': Willow Rosenberg as Hybrid, Hero and Middle Child of the Scooby Family." *Blood Relations: Chosen Families in Buffy the Vampire Slayer and Angel* Jefferson, NC: McFarland, 2005. 25–43.
"Becoming" (part 2). 2.22. Written and directed by Joss Whedon. *Buffy the Vampire Slayer*. WB. 19 May 1998.
Calvert, Bronwen. "Going Through the Motions: Reading Simulacra in *Buffy the Vampire Slayer*." *Slayage: The Online International Journal of Buffy Studies* 15 (December 2004). slayageonline.com/essays/slayage15/Calvert.htm.
"Dead Things." 6.13. Written by Steven S. DeKnight. Directed by James A. Contner. *Buffy the Vampire Slayer*. UPN. 5 February 2002.
"Doppelgangland." 3.16. Written and directed by Joss Whedon. *Buffy the Vampire Slayer*. WB. 23 February 1999.
"DoubleMeat Palace." 6.12. Written by Jane Espenson. Directed by Nick Marck. *Buffy the Vampire Slayer*. UPN. 29 January 2002.
Ellmann, Richard. *The Identity of Yeats*. New York: Oxford University Press, 1964.
"Entropy." 6.18. Written by Drew Z. Greenberg. Directed by James A. Contner. *Buffy the Vampire Slayer*. UPN. 5 February 2002.
"Flooded." 6.4. Written by Douglas Petrie and Jane Espenson. Directed by Douglas Petrie. *Buffy the Vampire Slayer*. UPN. 16 October 2001.
Gilstrap, Andrew. "Death and the Single Girl: Buffy Grows Up." 10 June 2002. 12 December 2002. http://www.popmatters.com/tv/reviews/b/buffy-the-vampire-slayer3.shtml.
"Gone." 6.11. Written and directed by David Fury. *Buffy the Vampire Slayer*. UPN. 8 January 2002.
"Grave." 6.22. Written by David Fury. Directed by James A. Contner. *Buffy the Vampire Slayer*. UPN. 21 May 2002.
Harrison, John R. "'What rough beast?': Yeats, Nietzsche and Historical Rhetoric in 'The Second Coming.'" *Papers on Language and Literature* 31.4 (Fall 1995): 362 ff. 11 October 2002. http: //lion.chadwyck.com.
"Hell's Bells." 6.16. Written by Rebecca Rand Kirschner. Directed by David Solomon. *Buffy the Vampire Slayer*. UPN. 5 March 2002.
Jeffares, A. Norman. *A Commentary on the Collected Poems of W.B. Yeats*. Palo Alto, CA: Stanford University Press, 1968.
Jowett, Lorna. *Sex and the Slayer: A Gender Studies Primer for the Buffy Fan*. Middletown, CT: Wesleyan University Press, 2005.
kdS [Philip Eagle]. "A small appendix on the Troika and SF." Online posting. 31 October 2002. ATPoBtVS&AtS Discussion Board. http://www.voy.com/14567/72296.html.
___. "Re: Mary Sue goes septic: Warren, the audience and Villainy (Part II)." Online posting. 31 October 2002. ATPoBtVS&AtS Discussion Board. http://www.voy.com/14567/72292.html.
"Life Serial." 6.5. Written by David Fury and Jane Espenson. Directed by Nick Marck. *Buffy the Vampire Slayer*. UPN. 23 October 2001.
McDonald, Paul F. "To Heaven and Back: The Return of Buffy the Vampire Slayer." *Existential Scoobies Fictionary Corner*. 4 November 2001. 13 June 2002. http://www.hereticstudios.com/fictionary/e011104A-DED.asp.
"Normal Again." 6.17. Written by Diego Gutierrez. Directed by Rick Rosenthal. *Buffy the Vampire Slayer*. UPN. 12 March 2002.
Noxon, Marti. Interview. "Growing Up." Matt Springer. *Official UK Buffy Magazine*. May 2002.

"Older and Far Away." 6.14. Written by Drew Z. Greenburg. Directed by Michael Gershman. *Buffy the Vampire Slayer*. UPN. 12 February 2002.
"Once More, with Feeling." 6.7. Written and directed by Joss Whedon. *Buffy the Vampire Slayer*. UPN. 6 November 2001.
"Prophecy Girl." 1.12. Written and directed by Joss Whedon. *Buffy the Vampire Slayer*. WB. 2 June 1997.
"Restless." 4.22. Written and directed by Joss Whedon. *Buffy the Vampire Slayer*. WB. 23 May 2000.
"Same Time, Same Place." 7.3. Written by Jane Espenson. Directed by James A. Contner. *Buffy the Vampire Slayer*. UPN. 8 October 2002.
"Seeing Red." 6.19. Written by Steven S. DeKnight. Directed by Michael Gershman. *Buffy the Vampire Slayer*. UPN. 7 May 2002.
"Slay Ride: Joss Whedon Assembles a Squad of All-Star Slayers to Stake His Claim on Buffy's 'Season 8" Comic Series." *Wizard*. 2 March 2007. 10 March 2007. http://www.wizarduniverse.com/magazine/wizard/003709924.cfm.
"Smashed." 6.9. Written by Drew Z. Greenberg. Directed by Turi Meyer. *Buffy the Vampire Slayer*. UPN. 20 November 2001.
South, James B. "'My God, It's Like a Greek Tragedy': Willow Rosenberg and Human Irrationality." *Buffy the Vampire Slayer and Philosophy: Fear and Trembling in Sunnydale*. James B. South, ed. Chicago: Open Court, 2003. 131–145.
"Superstar." 4.17. Written by Jane Espenson. Directed by David Grossman. *Buffy the Vampire Slayer*. WB. 5 April 2000.
"Tabula Rasa." 6.8. Written by Rebecca Rand Kirschner. Directed by David Grossman. *Buffy the Vampire Slayer*. UPN. 13 November 2001.
Tague, Nancy. "Re: Bargaining II revisionism." Online Posting. 3 December 2002. SunnydaleU. 12 December 2002. http://groups.yahoo.com/group/SunnydaleU/message/10432.
Unterecker, John. *A Reader's Guide to William Butler Yeats*. New York: Octagon Books, 1971.
Vendler, Helen Hennessy. *Yeats's Vision and the Later Plays*. Cambridge, MA: Harvard University Press, 1963.
"Villains." 6.20. Written by Marti Noxon. Directed by David Solomon. *Buffy the Vampire Slayer*. UPN. 14 May 2002.
Whedon, Joss. Interview with David Bianculli. *Fresh Air*. National Public Radio. 8 November 2002; 9 May 2000. *http://freshair.npr.org/guest_fa.jhtml*.
Wilcox, Rhonda. "Singing and Dancing and Burning and Dying: Once More with Textual Feeling." *Why Buffy Matters: The Art of Buffy the Vampire Slayer*. New York: I.B. Tauris, 2006. 191–205.
"When She Was Bad." 2.1. Written and directed by Joss Whedon. *Buffy the Vampire Slayer*. WB. 15 September 1997.
"Wrecked." 6.10. Written by Marti Noxon. Directed by David Solomon. *Buffy the Vampire Slayer*. UPN. 27 November 2001.
Yeats, W.B. "A Prayer for My Daughter." *Norton Anthology of English Literature*. 7th ed. Vol. 2. Edited by M.H. Abrams, et al. New York: Norton, 2000. 2107–2109.
____. "The Second Coming." *Norton Anthology of English Literature*. 7th ed. Vol. 2. Edited by M.H. Abrams, et al. New York: Norton, 2000. 2106–2107.
____. *A Vision*. Rev. ed. New York: Collier, 1966.

Special thanks to the members of the "SunnydaleU" e-mail discussion list and the "All Things Philosophical on *Buffy the Vampire Slayer* and *Angel: the Series* Discussion Board," http://www.voy.com/14567/. Although I have only cited three of you directly, this essay would not have been possible without you.

Season Six and the Supreme Ordeal

PAUL HAWKINS

"[A] people without myths is already dead."
— Georges Dumezil, *The Destiny of the Warrior*

"Here, in this moment, is the chance to win all or die. No matter what you come for, it's Death that now stares back at you. Whatever the outcome of the battle, you are about to taste death and it will change you."
— Joseph Campbell, *The Hero with a Thousand Faces*

At the beginning of Season Six, *Buffy the Vampire Slayer* had undergone many changes. It had made a high-profile switch to UPN and, more importantly, Buffy's death meant it no longer had either a character named Buffy or indeed a character who was a vampire slayer. When Buffy's friends magically restored her to life in "Bargaining" (6.2) the difference was palpable. It was revealed that Buffy had been torn out of a heavenly place into the comparative Hell of Earth and it took the full 22 episodes of Season Six for her to find the desire to be alive again.

Meanwhile, the fantastical narratives of the early seasons gave way to a slew of real-world issues — such as Willow's addiction, Spike's attempted rape of Buffy and Xander's failed wedding to Anya — and Buffy herself seemed confused, directionless and lacking in her own sense of purpose. In the course of a few months she had had gone from having no real world responsibilities to being surrogate single parent to her younger sister. She was unable to find gainful employment, struggled to make ends meet and was grieving not only the loss of her mother but also the aftermath of her own death. The perky Buffy of Season One long gone, she was now depressed, lacking in emotion, having sex with her former nemesis Spike simply to feel something. Where Buffy once seemed capable of anything, now even a leaky pipe in the basement ("Flooded," 6.4) presented an ordeal too difficult to tackle.

At first glance this seemed to be a drastic and radical shift in direction from the show and certainly a number of fans and critics felt that the show had lost some of its spark and vitality. "Buffy's sixth series ... tried for minimalist realism at its core and, having for the most part succeeded, then faffed about playing games with the audience's tolerance for depressing storylines" (Topping, 38). However, depressing as the season arguably was, the bleakness of the themes was not a random or unexpected change of direction but a logical step in examining the journey of Buffy as a heroine and the complexities and paradoxes of the myth underpinning the series. It was perfectly understandable that Season Six would see Buffy suffer for she was suffering from the consequences of the supreme ordeal — the darkest, most challenging point in the monomyth of Hero's Journey. Examining Buffy's relationship to the monomyth and specifically how Season Six relates to the consequences of the Hero's Supreme Ordeal,[1] doing so can provide an explanation as to why the bleakness of Season Six was not only a natural step for the series but one that was essential to the arc and structure of the overall show.

The Significance of Myth

> "At the heart of every story is a confrontation with death.... They (the hero) may survive it, proving that death is not so tough. They may die (perhaps only symbolically) and be reborn, proving that death can be transcended. They may die a Hero's death, transcending death by offering up their lives willingly for a cause, an ideal of a group" [Vogler, 38].
>
> "*Buffy* is made by a bunch of writers who think very, very hard about what they are doing in terms of psychology and methodology.... When somebody says there is a philosophy behind *Buffy*, that is the truth. When they say there is symbolism and meaning in what we're doing, that's true too" [Joss Whedon].

The word "myth" applies to any story that serves an allegory appropriate to the audience's culture and world. In his book *The Hero with a Thousand Faces*, Joseph Campbell argues that the need for myth is innate in humankind: "Throughout the inhabited world, in all times and under every circumstance, the myths of man have flourished and they have been the living inspiration of whatever else may have appeared out of the activities of the human body and mind" (Campbell, 3). Furthermore, Campbell proposed the idea of a "monomyth" — one over-arching story of human experience of which all other myths are a variant or re-telling, resulting in all myths in all cultures containing similarities in their patterns, structures and symbolism and any differences across culture, time and place being "much less great than is popularly and politically supposed" (Campbell, xiii). Certainly research bears this out. Propp studied 100 Russian fairy stories and found 35 common narrative functions. Fiske applied Propp's ideas to an episode of *The Bionic Woman* (1976) and concluded Propp's structure "underlies the television narrative with remarkable consistency" (Fiske, 138).

Whereas Propp limited his work to stories from one culture, Campbell was influential in linking stories, folklore and dreams from all cultures into one universal monomyth. Although Campbell's prime interest within his work was to discover the monomyth's relevance in psychoanalysis and specifically the interpretation of dreams, it was soon noted that his work applied to (and indeed influenced) modern films and television. George Lucas openly utilized Campbell's ideas in the *Star Wars* (1976) trilogy and in 1992 Christopher Vogler wrote about how Campbell's work applied to films: "All stories consist of a few common structural elements found universally in myths, fairly tales, dreams and movies. They are known collectively as the hero's journey"[2] (1).

Buffy and the Monomyth

> "We're doing these sort of mythic-hero journeys in our minds" [Joss Whedon, quoted in Wilcox and Lavery, 86].
> "It is not difficult to find the monomyth pattern for the hero Buffy.... Buffy refuses her call to slay and then accepts it, she faces trial after trial, crosses over to death and then returns. In fact, there are smaller and larger versions of the monomyth pattern throughout Buffy" [Wilcox, "Pain," 38].

Buffy also has a monomyth over-arcing the entire course of the seven seasons.[3] Indeed the overall story of Buffy's seven seasons ties in closely with Vogler's model of the Hero's Journey[4]:

Buffy begins in the ORDINARY WORLD as a shallow LA teenager. She receives her CALL TO ADVENTURE when she is approached by a watcher and told she has been chosen to be the slayer. When the watcher is killed and her slaying gets her kicked out of high school and relocated to SUNNYDALE, she REFUSES THE CALL and decides to go back to an ordinary life.[5] In Sunnydale she meets her MENTOR, the Watcher Giles, and when her newfound friends are in danger, she CROSSES THE THRESHOLD and commits herself to vampire slaying. Over seven seasons, she faces a number of TESTS, ALLIES AND ENEMIES, some of whom (such as vampires Angel and Spike) fluctuate between being ally and enemy. Over the course of the end of Season Four and the whole of Season Five, Buffy APPROACHES HER INNER-MOST CAVE as she loses her mother and confronts her own mortality and desire for death, encounters the First Slayer, and learns more about the slayer myth.

At the end of Season Five she faces her SUPREME ORDEAL when she gives her life by leaping from a tower to save her sister, Dawn, and indeed the whole world. After obtaining the REWARD of peace in death, she returns three months later to face the consequences of her ordeal and embark on the ROAD BACK. During the course of Season Seven, she finally masters her RESURRECTION back into the role of vampire slayer and savior of the world when she confronts the First Evil and RETURNS WITH THE ELIXIR— the ability to unlock the potential in all the would-be slayers across the world, imbuing them with her powers and finally freeing herself from the sole responsibility that had burdened her. Within this over-arching monomyth structure, Season Six detailed the consequences of the Road Back from the Supreme Ordeal.

Buffy's Supreme Ordeal

> "The simple secret of the ordeal is this: Heroes must die so that they can be reborn. The dramatic moments that audiences enjoy more than any other is death and rebirth. In some ways in every story, heroes face death or something like it.... Most of the time, they magically survive this death and are literally or symbolically reborn to reap the consequences of having cheated death. They have passed the main test of being a hero" [Vogler, 159–160].

Buffy's death is her supreme ordeal. The time between the supreme ordeal and the resurrection must be the darkest time for the characters. Their hope is shattered, evil prevails and they question the value of their journey. Season Six marked the "returning to the starting point or continuing on the journey to a totally new locale or ultimate destination. We are still down in the basement and it will take some push to get back into the light" (Vogler, 193). Season Six was, both metaphorically and literally, this push back into the light. Indeed Buffy's last action of the series was to pull herself out of the ground into daylight:

> Many fans have complained about the grimness of Season Six, with its stories of addiction, attempted rape, broken weddings.... Social Services employees and

fast food jobs, but ... the series is simply reflecting the difficult return element of the monomyth ... the reaction to the hero's death should weigh heavily.... It should not be too easy for Buffy to return from that plunge from the tower; death should not be cheaply cheated.... year of mourning seems appropriate [Wilcox, "Pain," 39].

By the end of Season Six, Buffy had begun to rediscover a reason for being but, as one might expect, it was not easy. The Road Back can be difficult and the sheer scale of the experiences faced by the Hero means she returns to the world changed and often no longer feels comfortable within her original environment.

Death and the Slayer

In order to consider the difficulties Buffy faces on the Road Back, it is first necessary to consider how she does not perceive death as a negative experience. In contrast, Buffy found death to be a peaceful, happy place and a respite from the complexities and uncertainties of the everyday world. Of her experience she sings, "There was no pain, no fear, no doubt 'til they pulled me out of Heaven" ("Once More, With Feeling," 6.6) For a vampire slayer, death is a constant and inescapable presence. Buffy is the latest in a long line of vampire slayers, of whom very few (if any) survive into their late twenties. From the moment she is called, Buffy knows on some level that death at a young age is almost inevitable — like all slayers before her she will be killed and a new slayer will be called to assume the role of fighting evil:

> The basic myth that underlies the narrative logic of ... *Buffy* can be described as Manichaean. The term refers to a model of the universe ... for whom the cosmos is a site of an endless dualistic battle between good and evil ... humans are merely pawns in a larger game so, in order to break the bonds of fate, a hero is introduced. Unlike most Hollywood heroes, Buffy [is] only partially free from the constraints of fate ... Buffy is "chosen" ... actions and choices are constrained by extrinsic factors [Krzywinska, 179–180].

In the course of the first five seasons Buffy, along with the audience, is constantly reminded of her own mortality. Indeed, as early as "Prophecy Girl" (1.12) she is briefly killed at the hands of the master. She is also briefly killed in two "alternate reality" episodes: "Nightmares" (1.10) during which — in a nightmare-turned-real — she becomes a vampire and Season Three's "The Wish" (3.9), when she is killed in an alternate reality. On several other occasions Buffy is only saved from death by an error by an opponent or a timely intervention of a friend (most notably in Season

Five's "Fool for Love" (5.7) where Buffy slips up fighting an ordinary vampire and only the arrival of her boyfriend Riley Finn saves her from an unexpected and, by her standards, ignoble death. Throughout the show, viewers are constantly reminded of how mortal Buffy actually is: "The only reason you've lasted as long as you have is you've got ties to the world ... your Mum, your brat kid sister, the Scoobies. They all tie you here but you're just putting off the inevitable" (Spike, "Fool For Love," 5.7). The fact that Buffy will ultimately die and be replaced lends an unusual transience to her status as a hero. She is a "chosen" girl with skill, speed and strength who is called to fight evil in her teens and must continue to do this until her death. However, should she fail and die she will immediately be replaced by somebody else who can now do the job in her place. This presents Buffy's role as hero as simultaneously indispensable and utterly disposable.

Furthermore, the role of slayer is not one Buffy is ever keen to accept. The slayer is chosen rather than vice-versa. She is the only person who can save the world and refusal would not only be ethically difficult to contemplate, as guilt over the consequences of failure to act would be a difficult burden to bear, but also self-defeating (as it would result in the word ending) so she must bear sole responsibility for saving the world. However, Buffy's identity is tied up with her powers, and when, on her 18th birthday, she fears she has lost her powers, she feels a great loss. Although Buffy struggles to cope with being a vampire slayer, she finds the burden of no longer being a vampire slayer to be an equally difficult one to bear.

Buffy's imprisonment within an identity she neither wants nor can live without reaches into the heart of the show's mythology — Buffy cannot possibly win. She fights the forces of evil, she saves the world but the evil always returns. Even Buffy's mother points out that the Hellmouth is not "running out of vampires" ("Gingerbread," 3.11). Helford notes, "The entire reason for a Slayer's coming is that evil can never be completely vanquished" (25). Yet Buffy still must continue to fight to save evil from winning entirely, thus rendering Buffy's actions essential but ultimately futile.

This complicates the show's myth as it turns "Buffy *the* Vampire Slayer," the girl who can fight vampires into "Buffy, *a* vampire slayer," one of several girls through history who has been able to fight vampires and who does so for a limited period of time. While it is not unusual for heroes to risk vast sacrifice in order to save the world, Buffy's sacrifice is inevitable and, though vital in the short-term, an irrelevance in the long-term as, after her death, the world will be threatened again only for somebody else to avert the crisis.

The difficulties of being a vampire slayer are also highlighted by the fate of the two other slayers featured in the show — Kendra and Faith. "Kendra is trained; Kendra is ... killed. Buffy is educated; Buffy survives" (Playden, 127). Whilst Kendra's reliance on following rules to the letter leads to her demise, Faith is undermined by a refusal to follow the rules at all. Emotionally detached and convinced her powers render her above the law, Faith turns to crime and winds up in prison. Between them Kendra and Faith highlight just how limited Buffy's options are. Given that a slayer experiences an inescapable ethical dilemma, an inability to gain relationships, a normal life or peer acceptance, and the consequences of slaying appear to be death, emotional detachment or blind subservience to authority, it is not altogether surprising that death is presented as a viable, and even positive decision.

James B. South marks Buffy's death as the ultimate act of self-erasure and destruction of the slayer myth. By choosing to end her life she rejects the idea that the slayer is controlled by external forces and takes what is perhaps the only decision she is truly free to make. "She is refusing to play the 'slayer game' and accede to the constraining social relations that go along with being the slayer. It is then, and only then in her death, that she becomes Buffy, not Buffy the Vampire Slayer" (South, 12)

The Aftermath of the Supreme Ordeal

"Death is your gift" [The First Slayer's words to Buffy in "Intervention, 5.18].

The Supreme Ordeal is typically followed by a reward. In fact, as we have seen, Buffy's death was reward in itself. Buffy's death finally gave her the chance to rest and absolve herself from the responsibilities of being a slayer — it provided her with an easy (and heroic) way out of her quest. However, Buffy's quest is not yet over. Her brief death in Season One had seen her pass on her succession to Kendra, whose own death saw Faith called as the Slayer and, as a result of this unusual situation, no slayer was called to replace Buffy when she died a second time. With Faith imprisoned and not in a position to save the world, Buffy is called back from death to once again fight the forces of evil. What saved Buffy, as is often the case for heroes surviving death, were the allies who she surrounded herself with. Vogler talks of "an elastic band that connects a hero with loved ones. A hero may venture out into madness and death but is usually pulled back by those bonds" (171). Indeed, Willow does manage to pull Buffy back from death, but not to a place that Buffy wants to be.

The twenty-two episodes of pain and readjustment that make up Season Six are a consequence of Buffy being deprived of her reward and being plunged back into her quest. Unsurprisingly Buffy finds this an almost-unbearably hard readjustment. Vogler talks of post-ordeal distortions where "heroes may be tainted by the very death or evil that they came to fight. Heroes can enter the mental world of their opponents and get stuck there" (189). Indeed for much of the season, Buffy—as is often the case with heroes upon surviving the ordeal—finds herself pursued by the forces she faced. The temptation of death and escape from her quest still appealed to her and it was an escape Buffy was keen to take. Indeed as late as "Normal Again" (6.17) Buffy is still ready to accept any possible escape from having to fight evil, even finding the suggestion that she is in fact an inmate of a mental hospital hallucinating about being a slayer preferable to having to face up to the responsibilities of her heroism.

The battle between Buffy's supernatural powers and humanity are at the heart of her struggles in Season Six. At the end of Season Five, she made the positive decision to sacrifice herself and finally, so she thought, achieve her destiny, reconciling the human and supernatural aspects of her character. When she returns, these two elements are more unbalanced than ever: "Buffy is ... unable to acknowledge the latent content of the enigmatic signifier 'vampire slayer'.... Buffy feels the onerous weight of being the vampire slayer because she does not *want* to be the slayer ... Buffy sees her being a slayer as a burden and regularly contrasts her life as a slayer with being normal" (South, 6). The conflict between Buffy's supernatural powers and her desire to be human is certainly not unique to Season Six. From as early as the first season, the show has contrasted Buffy's desire to live the life of a normal girl with her duties as a slayer. However, in Season Six this conflict took on an intensity far beyond that previously seen in the series: "To begin with, the series rested on the contrast between Buffy's night-time life as world saviour and her daytime life as teenage girl, worrying about boys and clothes and school. But now what's at stake ... are the larger questions of what makes us human, how to be good and why we should bother; and whether we should stay alive at all" (Hanks, 17). Despite Buffy's desire to not to be a slayer, it is in fact humanity which she lacks most in Season Six. Buffy lacks the desire to live and finds herself increasingly disconnected from humanity—preferring to seek the company of the vampire Spike than to spend time around her ordinary friends. This sense of disconnection from humanity is enhanced when it becomes apparent that Spike, who has a chip in his brain preventing him from harming humans, is able to attack Buffy, thus raising the question over whether she is literally still human. Buffy is torn between the world of the living and the world of the dead; she is Campbell's "master of two worlds" (229), yet she cannot belong in either.

An Outsider

In many ways it could be said that Buffy has never truly belonged in Sunnydale and her attempts to fit in have always involved endeavoring to keep her identity a secret. Of course secrecy plays a part in many superhero mythologies. For example Superman, Batman and Spider-Man (along with most conventional superheroes) all use a secret identity as a valuable tool in fighting evil. In addition to the key defensive function of ensuring enemies do not discover the hero's identity and use this knowledge to threaten them and their loved ones, the secrecy allows the hero a normal job and life away from their heroism. Crucially, in spite of not knowing the true identity of the heroes, in all three cases each hero's respective townsfolk all acknowledge that a superhero exists and defend the hero from the dangers to which he or she might otherwise be exposed.

In *Buffy the Vampire Slayer*, secrecy fulfils a vastly different function. The secret Buffy keeps from the people of Sunnydale is not her identity, something which is known by most of her foes, thus cancelling out the traditional advantages of secrecy, but the existence of the dangers she fights to protect them from. If nobody knows who the vampire slayer is, it is only because they are not aware that there are vampires that need to be slain. In this sense, the function of the slayer's existence is not only to protect people from evil but also to protect them from the knowledge that evil must be fought, thus denying herself the gratitude, respect and support that might give her the ability to maintain a dual existence as slayer and as human being. Furthermore, the nature of Buffy's secrecy does not extend to her maintaining a separate identity, thus meaning that it is much harder for Buffy to separate her normal life from her hero life in the same way as, say, Clark Kent.

In fact Buffy's slaying (and perhaps more acutely the secrecy surrounding her slaying) actually prevents her from living a normal life. It impinges on her ability to hold down a steady job: "Life Serial" (6.5) sees her attempt three different types of work, only for her slaying responsibilities to earn her the sack from each one. It threatens her ability to act as a surrogate parent to Dawn: "Gone" (6.11) sees a social worker concerned for Dawn's welfare, arguably largely because Buffy's slaying duties prevent her from being there. And her work as a slayer arguably acted as the catalyst for the failure of all three normal human relationships — Owen, Scott, and, most significantly, Riley — that she either enters into or contemplates entering into during the history of the show.

Furthermore, should Buffy's work as a slayer be revealed, it would most likely see her rejected by the people of Sunnydale. In the episode "Gingerbread" (3.11), the people of Sunnydale have a temporary, distorted vision of the level of evil in Sunnydale and promptly try to burn Buffy at the stake (along with witches Willow and Amy). Even Buffy's own mother proclaims, "For too long we've been plagued by unnatural evils. This isn't our town anymore. It belongs to the monsters and the witches and the slayers."

Buffy has a great power, drawn from dark forces, and she must use it to fight for people who cannot accept her while they remain oblivious to the sacrifice she makes. Yet as Buffy fights the darkness, she also fights herself as, should the reality of the evils of the world be revealed to the people of Sunnydale, they would see her too as part of the same darkness. In "Dead Things" (6.13), Spike asks Buffy, "What would they think of you ... if they knew who you really were...? That's not your world. You belong in the shadows with me."

The Enemy Within

Certainly, for much of the series, Buffy was part of the darkness and she spent much more time battling her inner conflicts than she did battling evil. Season Six was the first season in which her character did not feature in either the first or last image of the season and, more crucially, the first season that did not end with Buffy saving the world.[6] Instead Buffy is still fighting her own battles; she is still not ready to fight for the world as well.

Indeed, at first glance, there was no great evil that challenged Buffy through the course of the series. From Season One to Season Five, there was a progression in the levels of the big bad with each perhaps more deadly and complex than the last, from an admittedly extremely powerful vampire in Season One through a jilted lover, a politician, a creation of the U.S. government and finally a god in Season Five. These enemies were all clear, external dangers posing a severe threat to Buffy's existence. Buffy's Season Six enemies were the Troika: three incompetent high school nerds with vague desires to take over the world and very little idea of how to achieve it, whose main threat came through their own incompetence. Ultimately, Buffy's enemy thoughout the season was not supernatural strength but human weakness and these three weak humans represented this perfectly.

The nerd Troika's lack of credible threat was no coincidence but a move to switch the emphasis to Buffy's struggle with herself and to display how humanity was presently more of a danger to her than the supernatural. Indeed, when the Troika attempt to take Buffy's life ("Seeing Red," 6.19) they do so with a revolver, a human weapon. Buffy is almost killed and only Willow's supernatural powers can save her. Ultimately, however, this magic is a false savior. Whereas Buffy's strength has a supernatural origin, her sense of purpose and motivation has always come from her inner humanity and that of those who surround her. The earlier quote from Spike in "Fool for Love" (5.7) is revealing in more ways than one: "The only reason you've lasted as long as you have is you've got ties to the world ... your Mum, your brat kid sister, the Scoobies. They all tie you here but you're just putting off the inevitable." Buffy is tied to the world by humanity and it is the friends who pulled her back from death who will also ultimately give her the desire to remain in the world.

However, Buffy does not realize the value of her humanity until the supernatural powers, which had previously been used as a source for good, swing out of control putting the world in danger. Toward the series end, Willow is addicted to magic and eager for revenge against the Troika, who had killed her lover. As with Buffy's struggles, Willow's addiction and desire for vengeance also represent facets of human weaknesses. She attempts to destroy the world in order to end pain and suffering. Buffy's battle with her friend represented Buffy battling with herself and her own humanity.

The Return

> Although the episodes of Season Six may seem to have lacked direction, in fact, the apparent disorderliness and repetition of themes from episode to episode reflected the widening gyre of the Scooby gang's collective consciousness, their ethos, if you will; while at the same time Buffy, the Slayer, the hero of this fictional world, begins the season in chaos and despair ... and slowly spirals back to the center of her own reason of being [Rambo, 3].

Like Buffy, who by the end of the season finally overcomes her desire to remain dead, Willow is saved only by humanity. For once, Buffy's supernatural powers cannot save the world and it is the human Xander's love for Willow that stops the world from plunging into oblivion. Despite the destructive nature of the human weakness that surrounds him, Xander is able to prove that humanity can also be a force for good, both on a global scale and within Buffy herself. The threat of the end of the world is enough to shock Buffy back into realizing her desire to live. Rhonda Wilcox contrasts the first image of Buffy in the season, where she climbs out of a hole in the ground into the darkness and the last image of Buffy in the season, where she climbs out of a hole in the ground into the light ("Pain," 39).

Buffy finally understands the lesson she was taught by Angel, her vampire ex-boyfriend who was also a mentor figure to Buffy: "We never will (win). That's not why we fight. We do it because there's things worth fighting for" ("Gingerbread," 3.9). Angel takes this further on his own spin-off show as he realizes "when nothing you do matters, all that matters is what you do" ("Epiphany," *Angel* 2.3). By the end of Season Six, Buffy too has begun to understand that continuing to fight against all hope carries within itself a hope of its own, for it must imply that while the world is full of evil and darkness, good and hope must exist. In this sense, Buffy realizes that, as a slayer, she may be part of the darkness but she is also part of the light and, instead of trying to hide younger sister Dawn from the horrors of the world, resolves to try and show her the beauty within it.

Ultimately, Buffy does not (and indeed cannot) find a solution for her outsider status or for the ethical and psychological dilemmas she suffers through being a slayer. Neither is she able to create a situation where she wins outright and rids the world of evil, for this cannot be possible.

However, the fact that Buffy finds the will to fight regardless reveals the strength of her character, and indeed the strength of the mythology of the show. *Buffy the Vampire Slayer* makes use of a Manichaean philosophy, of duality between the forces of good and evil, to turn what could be a simplistic B-movie plot style into a mythical story about a character whose "heroism is defined not as a radical quest to eliminate evil but rather an existential determination to fight it" (Wall and Zyrd, 59). In this sense, the structure of *BtVS* creates a rich and powerful allegory encompassing the value of morality in a complex, uncertain world and the importance of individual decisions to keep fighting, even when the odds imply victory to be impossible. Though operating in a fantasy genre, *BtVS* is able to use mythical structures to relate its stories to the real world.[7]

By the end of Season Six, Buffy had travelled along the road back to the ordinary world and appears to have reconciled the darkness and light within her and stands ready to be resurrected as a human. While there is no solution to her outsider status, Buffy at least appears to have accepted returning to the world and her cause on her own terms. She has survived death and accepted her survival. She has rededicated herself to the quest and is ready for the Resurrection stage of the monomyth. She is ready to live again.

Appendix One — The Stage of the Hero's Journey

Not all stages are always present or in this order

1. **Ordinary World** — The hero has *limited awareness* of a problem or void in her life.
2. **Call to Adventure** — Something *increases* the hero's problem (or *awareness* of the problem) and an opportunity arises to solve it.
3. **Refusal of the Call** — Aware of the risks, the hero will refuse or be *reluctant to change*.
4. **Meeting with the Mentor** — The hero receives guidance which persuades her to *overcome her reluctance*. The problem may intensify.
5. **Crossing the First Threshold** — The hero *commits to change* and agrees to take on the challenge. She enters the special world of the story.
6. **Tests, Allies, Enemies** — The hero *experiments with first change* and attempts to solve the problem. She makes allies and enemies (who may be unclear in their allegiances). She faces a variety of tests.
7. **Approach to Inmost Cave** — The hero *prepares for big change* as she starts to approach her first major test.
8. **Ordeal** — The character *attempts big change* and faces her shadow (*see below*). This may result in a death, either of herself, an ally, an enemy or simply her old self.
9. **Reward (Seizing the Sword)** — The hero faces *consequences* of the ordeal, both *improvements and setbacks* and gain a reward for her efforts. This will often be financial, sexual or simply a newfound wisdom.
10. **The Road Back** — The hero journeys back toward the ordinary world often pursued by, or in pursuit of, her shadow. Having not fully resolved into problem, the hero finds it comes back to haunt her. She must *rededicate herself to change* necessary to overcome it.
11. **Resurrection** — The hero *finally attempts big change* and either overcomes her problem or dies. Her old self or selves are shed and a "new self" emerges
12. **Returning with the Elixir** — The hero *finally masters the problem*, and often returns to the ordinary world with a token of her journey;

perhaps an artifact, a new love or wisdom that changes her life and the lives of those around her.

Notes

1. The stage of the monomyth where the hero faces his toughest challenge and attempts *big change*, often resulting in a death — be it a literal death of the hero or an ally or simply the metaphorical death of the person he used to be. For a full list of stages of the hero's journey, please see Appendix One.
2. Although Joseph Campbell's work is extremely significant in the formulation of the theories within this chapter, I shall use the terminology of Christopher Vogler simply because his phraseology is clearer and simpler to understand, as well as being more specifically tailored towards the visual medium.
3. The completion of the monomyth in Buffy was helped by the fact it ran for the number of seasons Joss Whedon had always claimed he had initially planned it to run.
4. Again, for a complete list of stages please see Appendix One.
5. It is not until this point that the television series begins, although the earlier narrative can be gauged from the backstory about Buffy revealed in the show and the events of the 1992 film starring Kristy Swanson. Although many details about Buffy's life differ between the film and TV show, the principal backstory appears to be largely similar.
6. The character who speaks the first line in the teaser of 6.1 and who appears last in episode 6.22 is Spike. Xander, of course, saves the world.
7. LC Patton has discussed how *BtVS* can be therapeutic in treatment of depression as it reflects the unappreciated strength people feel they need just to get through an ordinary day.

Works Cited

Campbell, Joseph. *The Hero with a Thousand Faces*. Glasgow: Fontana, 1993.
Dumezil, Georges. *The Destiny of the Warrior*. Chicago: University of Chicago Press, 1966.
Fiske, John. *Television Culture*. London: Routledge, 1987.
Hanks, R. "Deconstructing Buffy." *The Independent Review*, January 7, 2002, 16–17.
Helford, Elyce Rae. "'My Emotions Give Me Power': The Containment of Girls' Anger in *Buffy*." In *Fighting the Forces: What's at Stake in Buffy the Vampire Slayer?* Lanham, MD: Rowman & Littlefield, 2002. Rhonda Wilcox and David Lavery, eds. 18–34.
Krzywinksa, T. "Hubble-Bubble, Herbs and Grimiores: Magic, Manichaenism and Witchcraft." In *Fighting the Forces: What's at Stake in Buffy the Vampire Slayer?* Lanham, MD: Rowman & Littlefield, 2002. Rhonda Wilcox and David Lavery, eds. 178–194.
Patton, Lori C. "'What Else Are We Gonna Do?': Finding 'the Courage to Be' with *Angel* and *Buffy*." Paper presented at the Slayage Conference on *Buffy the Vampire Slayer*, Nashville, May 2004.
Playden, Zoe-Jane. "What You Are, What's to Come: Feminism, Citizenship and the Divine." Reading the Vampire Slayer: *An Unofficial Critical Companion to Buffy and Angel*. Roz Kaveney, ed. London, New York: Taruris Parke, 2001. 120–147.

Rambo, Elizabeth L. "Yeats' Entropic Gyre and Season Six of *Buffy the Vampire Slayer.*" Unpublished conference paper, 2002.
South, J. B. "'They show up, they scare us, I beat 'em up and they go away': The Dialectic of Self-Knowledge in *Buffy the Vampire Slayer.*" Paper presented at Blood, Text and Fears: Reading Around *Buffy the Vampire Slayer.* University of East Anglia. Norwich, UK. 19–20 October 2002.
Topping, K. "So Let Me Rest in Peace!" *TV Zone* 158. 2002.
Vogler, C. *The Writer's Journey: Mythic Structure for Storytellers and Screenwriters.* 2nd rev. ed. London: Pan Books, 1998.
Wall, Brian, and Michael Zyrd. "Vampire Dialectics: Knowledge, Institutions and Labour." *Reading the Vampire Slayer: An Unofficial Critical Companion to Buffy and Angel.* Roz Kaveney, ed. London, New York: Tauris Parke, 2001. 53–77.
Whedon, Joss. AOL Chat. November 10, 2002. 30 July 2007. http://www.geocities.com/soporjoe77/josschat.html.
Wilcox, Rhonda. "'Pain as Bright as Steel': Mythic Striving and Light as Pain." *Why Buffy Matters: The Art of Buffy the Vampire Slayer*, 30–45. London: I.B. Tauris, 2005.
_____, and David Lavery, eds. *Fighting the Forces: What's at Stake in* Buffy the Vampire Slayer? Lanham, MD: Rowman & Littlefield, 2002.

Kiss Kiss, Stake Stake: Storytelling and the Philosophical Pleasures of Season Seven

JAMES B. SOUTH

"Storyteller," an episode from *Buffy the Vampire Slayer*'s seventh season written by Jane Espenson, provides the viewer with a story about storytelling in which the show explicitly confronts its own practice of telling stories, and in telling the story of this episode, it suggests, I hope to show, that stories can point to what stands behind the story; call it, for the moment anyway, an experience. The episode opens with the narrative voice of one of the odder characters in the series, Andrew. We are provided with parody of *Masterpiece Theatre*. We see a mishmash of leather books, antique furniture, and pop cultural ephemera (*Star Wars* action figures). And then Andrew speaks.

> Oh, hello, there, gentle viewers. You caught me catching up on an old favorite. It's wonderful to get lost in a story, isn't it? Adventure and heroics and discovery — don't they just take you away? Come with me now, if you will, gentle viewers. Join me on a new voyage of the mind. A little tale I like to call: *Buffy, Slayer of the Vampyrs,* ["Storyteller," 7.16].[1]

In having Andrew provide us with a characterization of the series' thematics — adventure and heroics and discovery — this particular episode provides us with a curious perspective from which to view the entire series, but, perhaps even more so, a perspective from which to view the last two seasons of the series.[2] It is this perspective that I want to trace out in what follows. In using the slightly ludicrous, childlike, hero-worshipping, and, indeed, parroting Andrew, the episode draws our attention to the dangers of certain ways of relating to it.[3] These dangers are also ones that philosophy warns us against, and in setting these dangers out, I want to alert the reader to an intriguing connection between the way this episode asks us to think about the series and certain impulses that have typically motivated philosophers.

The title of my essay refers, obviously enough, to the famous collection of Pauline Kael essays, *Kiss Kiss Bang Bang*, which are words she once saw on an Italian movie poster. In remarking on these words, she tells us that they "are perhaps the briefest statement imaginable of the basic appeal of movies." In agreement with Kael, I suspect the basic appeal of *Buffy* is all the kissing and staking that goes on, as well as adventure, heroics and discovery. It is sometimes forgotten, though, that Kael goes on to caution, "This appeal is what attracts us, and ultimately what makes us despair when we begin to understand how seldom movies are more than this." The challenge of this caution is what I want to address in what follows. Is there more to *BtVS* than the kissing and staking, or, more specifically, is there anything philosophical in all the kissing and staking?

I am grateful to find myself with this opportunity to reflect on a connection between philosophy and *BtVS*. The timing may seem odd, since I previously edited a collection of essays on the topic and published a couple of other articles on the show. It would seem that I have already addressed the caution. Thus, I can understand the reader's criticism that I have this sequence of events a bit backwards; surely, some general reflection on this challenge should have occurred prior to the writing of papers on particular topics. But this paper is not a general reflection on the philosophical value of *BtVS*, or what claim the series might have on the discipline of philosophy. Others have done some nice work on this topic — I think particularly of Andrew Aberdein's fine reflection in an unpublished paper on philosophy and *BtVS*, and I do not want to rework his remarks (Aberdein). Instead, in what follows, I simply want to try to open up a bit more space for the interaction of two apparently radically disparate areas of activity that I confess to finding pleasurable.

Robert Warshow has written tellingly about the need to find a connection between his enjoyment of a Bogart movie and his enjoyment of a novel by Henry James, although he admits that he has no idea what that connection might be. He does not want to say that they are simply both pieces of art since that is too simple an answer. Any search for a connection, he argues, must be through self-reflection or self-knowledge since, in his words, "A man watches a movie and the critic must acknowledge that he is a man" (Warshow, xli). Following Warshow, then, I am the same person who watches *BtVS* and the person who reads Plato, Aquinas, Suárez, and so many other philosophers. I want to try to tease out basic connections between these two activities. I do not want to beg the question and claim that watching *BtVS* is identical to doing philosophy. At the same time, though, I do not want to cordon off my watching of *BtVS* from my activity of reading, writing, and teaching philosophy.

The most important objection the reader of this essay is likely to have, I suppose, is to the suggestion that there is any connection between *BtVS* and philosophy as anything more than a topic philosophy can address, as it typically and magisterially addresses any topic. But my essay is not about the philosophy of *BtVS*, whatever that might be, and I am not going to be discussing *BtVS* in the way that a philosopher might talk about mind or knowledge. Also, I am not addressing *BtVS* from some subdiscipline of philosophy, for example, aesthetics. Nor am I going to use *BtVS* to illustrate or augment a topic within philosophy, for example, the metaphysical status of fictional characters. In sum, I am not going to argue that we can learn philosophically from *BtVS* in the way that we can learn from some body of theory or set of facts. There is no direct route from watching *BtVS* to developing a substantive ethical theory.

After so many negations, here is a positive assertion: there is something valuable philosophically about *BtVS*, but for my purposes here, that value has more to do with the impulse to philosophy and its practice than with some version of philosophy or philosophical theory. Following Warshow, then, I want to show that there is a sense in which watching *BtVS* can provoke and nourish a philosophical attitude.

I still remember a class I took in the first semester of my Ph.D. program. The professor spoke of the danger of presentism — the privileging of present ways of doing philosophy over alternative ways. An awareness of this danger was supposed to be one of the virtues of studying the history of philosophy. Of course, doing history of philosophy within a philosophy department heavily invested in present ways of doing philosophy can be a dicey affair. Certainly, one of the lessons I learned from studying the history of philosophy as the history of *philosophy*, and not a catalog of errors, is that any present conception of philosophy is likely to look both cramped and contingent. At the same time, though, I recognize that there is an ideological use of the term presentism available that would allow us to ignore that which is current practice. My use of presentism in this paper, then, should be seen not as a way to exclude contemporary insights, but as a reminder that we can learn today from the past, or, indeed, from alternative currents of today's practiced philosophy.

Let me juxtapose that warning to a neophyte student about presentism with a remark by a contemporary philosopher. In his "Epilogue" to the collection of essays by Warshow, Stanley Cavell laments the unfortunate sense of the phrase "ordinary language philosophy." He states: "What it [ordinary language philosophy] contrasts with, rather, is a *fixated* philosophical language which precisely would preempt the extraordinary from disturbing customary experience" (Cavell, "Epilogue," 293).

In this description, Cavell has given us a nice account of a danger attendant on presentism — the cultivation of an attitude that preempts the disturbing of customary experience. So, as a historian of philosophy, let me just raise the possibility that one origin for the impulse to do history of philosophy is precisely some experience of the extraordinary coupled with a suspicion that one task of contemporary philosophy is to preempt such experiences. Of course, I can only speak for myself, but it is worth considering just what the sources are that motivate those of us who do history of philosophy, assuming it is not some mere attachment to dogmatism of some sort or a merely antiquarian pursuit. There must be both an attraction to a fixated language, since we do learn our history within philosophy departments, and at the same time some sort of non-conformist thinking, since we turn our backs at least partially from that fixated language. But the impulse cannot be merely aversive; rather there must be something about that philosophy occurring *then* that we historians find extraordinary. And those of us who wend our way through that most neglected (by philosophers) of periods, the Renaissance, must be drawn to something there that cannot be captured by the fixated language of philosophy today.

Earlier, I quoted Andrew's invitation to the viewer at the beginning of "Storyteller." After the invitation, he proceeds to describe an encounter between Buffy and some vampires from the previous night: "Ouch! My goodness! Things look bad for the Slayer, don't they? She didn't see that second vampire, concealed by cover of darkness, ready — (there's a knock at the door; Andrew ignores it) ready to attack and make her his own vampirical spawn." The knock on the door disturbs Andrew, causing him momentary confusion before trying to talk over it, but also warns the viewer that there is another perspective from which to view what Andrew recounts. Indeed, point of view changes with a cut to Andrew, sitting on a closed toilet seat, camera in front of him. The viewer now realizes Andrew is not in charge of the story we will be watching. Anya opens the door and asks Andrew what he has been doing in the bathroom for thirty minutes. "Entertaining and educating," is his response. To which Anya says: "Why can't you just masturbate like the rest of us?"

Andrew's answer and Anya's response get to the central issue of this essay: can telling a story entertain and educate? The fact that the episode so clearly brings this issue up for our consideration in turn suggests that there is not an obvious affirmative answer. If there is to be an affirmative answer, though, we have been put on warning to resist a certain kind of story, the sort with which Andrew began and which is effectively equivalent to masturbation. The remainder of the episode, then, might provide us with an alternative story, one in which Andrew is educated into a different perspective. Thus, one philosophical task of this episode is to provide Andrew, and by extension, any viewer, a counter-story to some standard story in much the same way that some venues of doing philosophy provide a counter to presentism. It is this concern about a fixated philosophical language that encourages me to think about *BtVS* as providing us with some philosophical work to do. I want to worry about this work in two ways. The first issue I want to worry about is the issue of experience. Warshow is concerned to explore the ways that experience is blocked by "customary experience." The point is that customary experience is not real experience after all, and what we must do is fight against the ways that the customary forms of thought militate against what Warshow calls "the immediate experience."

Consider the following passage from John Stuart Mill's *On Liberty*:

> In our times, from the highest class of society down to the lowest every one lives as under the eye of a hostile and dreaded censorship. Not only in what concerns others, but in what concerns only themselves, the individual, or the family, do not ask themselves — what do I prefer? or, what would suit my character and disposition? or, what would allow the best and highest in me to have fair play, and enable it to grow and thrive? They ask themselves, what is suitable to my position? what is usually done by persons of my station and pecuniary circumstances? or (worse still) what is usually done by persons of a station and circumstances superior to mine? I do not mean that they choose what is customary, in preference to what suits their own inclination. It does not occur to them to have any inclination, except for what is customary. Thus the mind itself is bowed to the yoke: even in what people do for pleasure, conformity is the first thing thought of; they like in crowds; they exercise choice only among things commonly done: peculiarity of taste, eccentricity of conduct, are shunned equally with crimes: until by dint of not following their own nature, they have no nature to follow: their human capacities are withered and starved: they become incapable of any strong wishes or native pleasures, and are generally without either opinions or feelings of home growth, or properly their own. Now is this, or is it not, the desirable condition of human nature? [Mill, 61–62].

In choosing the customary, in conforming to what is commonly done, we block ourselves from experience as Warshow talks of it. In Mill's terms, we lose peculiarity of taste and eccentricity of conduct. In short, we lose a sense of ourselves as manifested in our capacities and talents. Anya's accusation against Andrew's *Masterpiece Theatre* version of *Buffy, Slayer of the Vampyres* (both entertaining and educational!) is that it is masturbatory — a nice gloss on Mill's claim that conformity renders us "incapable of any strong wishes or native pleasures."

The problem with "immediate experience," though, is that words typically fail to capture it. Warshow talks of the writer having to invent his own audience for describing experience and adds that there is simply no vocabulary available in which to discuss such experience (p. xlii). This strikes me as an extreme version of the complaint alleged against presentism, but it seems true of my experience of many things relating to *BtVS*. And that leads me to the second issue: how can I show that *BtVS* is worth the effort? Again, a quote from Cavell (we historians stand behind our quotations in both obvious senses of "stand behind" — what we quote, who we quote, says more than we think we can say directly — an analogous concern to Warshow's lack of a vocabulary): "Nothing can show this value to you unless it is discovered in your own experience, in the persistent exercise of your own taste" (*Conditions,* 10–11). And now we're at the thorny question of taste and its objects. In the words of Chris Lehmann, "Taste [is] a function of subjectivity; cultural hierarchy is a gauge of that subjectivity's erosion" (63). In Mill's terms, then, there is no peculiarity of taste without resistance to conformity, and taste as typically exercised subsumes the individual's taste under some group's taste. Often, indeed, as Mill points out, that taste is the taste of "persons of a station and circumstances superior" to the one who exercises a judgment of taste. Taking my cues then, from Mill, "Storyteller," and Warshow, I will resist one way of conforming. While I can recognize that *BtVS* is not Plato, there is no reason why I should not bring my philosophically trained taste to bear on it as I do Plato. Of course, if my taste is legitimately mine, and not one belonging to some other group, it is not therefore baseless. At the same time, though, I cannot assume anyone else will share that taste unless I show them its basis. My approach to *BtVS* might be idiosyncratic, but no less philosophical, unless we consider only the fixated philosophy current among us.

Barry Stroud put his finger on one good reason to be wary of conforming to today's philosophical atmosphere when he wrote: "But I think the professionalized, scientistic conception that many people now have of how to proceed in philosophy is unfortunate.... I would say that it is compatible at a certain point with the absence of philosophy. It has led to what I think is a certain complacency, even a certain blindness, in the face of what remains philosophically important," (Stroud, 38–39). Now, I juxtapose Stroud's comment with a passage from Montaigne's *Of physiognomy*:

> Almost all the opinions we have are taken on authority and on credit. There is no harm in this: we could not make a worse choice than our own in so feeble an age. The version of the sayings of Socrates that his friends have left us we approve only out of respect for the universal approval these sayings enjoy, not by our own knowledge. They are beyond our experience. If anything of the kind were brought forth at this time, there are few men who would prize it.
> We perceive no charms that are not sharpened, puffed out, and inflated by artifice. Those which glide along naturally and simply easily escape a sight so gross as ours. They have a delicate and hidden beauty; we need a clear and well-purged sight to discover their secret light. Is not naturalness, according to us, akin to stupidity and a matter for reproach? [792].

The "blindness" that Stroud speaks of echoes Montaigne's claim that some charms, which are not inflated by artifice, "escape our sight." Stroud's "complacency" parallels Montaigne's "universal approval," and both are in the same conceptual territory as Mill's "conformity." Both Stroud and Montaigne are clearly inhabiting a world in which judgments ought not be subsumed under some other group's judgment. Thus, there is an interesting congruence in their respective complaints about the practice of philosophy current in their times, one that is captured nicely by Mill's concern about the "hostile and dreaded censorship" of conformity. Both Stroud and Montaigne offer an anchoring point from which to bring peculiarity back to philosophy. For Stroud, "There must be something we are involved in that is not philosophy. In reflecting on such things philosophically we have to have the strength to recognize and hold on to such things, and not to distort or deny them, in the face of philosophical reflection" (43–44). For Montaigne, it is those charms that "glide along naturally and simply." Both authors, then, contrast what is natural to the damage that philosophical artifice can do to our experience. They both point to a reality that is apparently available to experience and that is pre-philosophical. But here's the thing: Montaigne is nothing if not an artful writer, a thinker who uses multiple rhetorical tricks to drive home the lesson that the best we can do is remain within our powers and follow nature. Stroud, in turn, is a well-respected contemporary philosopher. There's something suspiciously paradoxical here. The construction of Warshow's hoped-for vocabulary is a philosophical, or at least theoretical task, but if philosophy itself blocks the possibility of that vocabulary, what are we to do?

"Storyteller" has a comparable set of concerns to those found in Warshow, Cavell, Mill, Montaigne, and Stroud: the ways that artifice blocks experience, thereby promoting blindness and an avoidance of the natural, or, perhaps better, the pre-theoretical. "Storyteller" begins by entertaining and educating in the *Masterpiece Theatre* manner. Andrew's narration of Buffy's actions are accurately characterized by Montaigne's terms: sharpened, puffed out, and inflated by artifice. Anya's subsequent deflating of Andrew's artifice as masturbatory is unsettling. Haven't viewers been watching the show for six and a half seasons precisely for "adventure and heroics and discovery?" Surely, the kissing and the staking have been essential to the pleasures viewers have taken from the series, but the higher pleasures of educational television have been present as well. Viewers have applauded the moral complexity of the show, and have seen various characters as role models.

Anya's deflation of pretension sets the stage for the theme of the episode: a self-reflective, highly critical account of the way the stories we tell, call them fixated ideas, are worth less than something simple and natural. It also seems to have a big idea present in it as we see Andrew's quest for redemption. Accordingly, for all its apparent criticism of stories, the episode also tells a story. As the episode progresses, we continue to see Andrew inflating his own story and the story of the other characters. Thus, we see Andrew the supervillain, the Andrew who once defeated Dark Willow. So, too, we see Spike being filmed by Andrew. Spike's response, which seems consistent with a standard story about his character, "I thought I told you to piss off with this bloody camera, yet here you are again with that thing in my face. Would you sod off (flicks the cigarette at Andrew) before I rip your throat out and eat —" is cut off when Andrew explains that the lighting was wrong. We see that Spike is as invested in an artificial image as Andrew.

We, the loyal viewers, recognize these fabrications as we see them, thus thinking that we are in on the joke. On that level, the story is simply funny. We go on, though, to find out that in the "real" world of the show, students at Sunnydale High are acting bizarrely, but bizarrely in a recognizable way. It turns out that they are behaving in ways that students behaved in earlier seasons of the show. In those earlier episodes, Buffy and her friends were victorious. Now, we are being asked to call into question those earlier stories. Did they end as neatly as we thought they did? The joke we thought we were in on is suddenly a little less funny, and we are made a bit uncomfortable in our ready acceptance of those prior stories.

The narrative of "Storyteller" includes an additional confrontation with storytelling in dealing with the relationship between Xander and Anya. In their taped conversation with Andrew on the one year anniversary of Xander's decision to leave Anya at the altar, Xander keeps dodging the question of whether he still loves Anya. In frustration, Anya states, "And here's where we hop on the merry-go-round of rotating knives. I blame you, and you blame me, and we both end up all cut to shreds. Please just tell — Do you still love me?" Xander replies that he does, but that he does not "know if that means anything for us anymore." Anya confirms that she still loves Xander, but concludes: "I don't know if that means anything either." Even with an attestation of their unique love for one another, there is no story to be told of their relationship. Andrew, who both accepts and tells stories rewatches the conversation on tape, crying all the while. Yet later in the episode, when we see Xander and Anya in bed after "one more time sex," we understand that there will be no happy ending for them. Within the overall theme of the episode, what we get in this sub-plot is a reminder that happy endings are the stuff of stories. More tellingly, perhaps, they are patterns of conformity. If one loves someone and that love is returned, surely the "happily ever after follows." Yet Xander and Anya represent a more natural, less artificial, experience of love. Anya's final line in this scene is especially striking: "I think maybe we're really over. Which is — it's good, right? I mean, now we can move on." Despite her experience of "one more time" sex with Xander, she insists on subsuming the experience under a story — their is experience is good because it means they can move on. Yet, as we know, that's not what happens. Within a few episodes, Anya is killed, which makes the poignancy of her inability to appreciate the experience for what it was all the more painful in rewatching.

The main story of this episode about storytelling, though, remains. It is the story of Andrew's "redemption." In an attempt to close the "seal of Danzalthar," the conduit for the evil causing the mayhem at the high school, Buffy and her friends discover that Andrew himself was responsible for opening the seal. Under the influence of another story told by the First Evil, he had killed his friend Jonathan at the seal and Jonathan's blood was the mechanism by which the seal was opened. The promise of the story told to Andrew was that once Jonathan was sacrificed, Andrew, Jonathan, and their friend Warren would "live as gods." Buffy takes Andrew back to the seal where she tells him, "Yeah, Willow did a little research. Turns out, the blood of the person that awoke it — you — different kind of deal. It reverses the whole thing." Andrew replies "So, this is my redemption at last? I buy back my bruised soul with the blood of my heart. But-but not enough to kill."

Here we have Andrew telling himself a story about the notion of redemption. Buffy calls him on it: "You always do this. You make everything into a story so no one's responsible for anything because they're just following a script."

The warning is clear: telling a story about our life can be a matter of following a script and, thus, a way of avoiding responsibility, denying experience. Indeed, Andrew goes on to try to displace responsibility for his actions. He claims that he was told Jonathan would be OK and that Jonathan's death would be temporary. And in listening to that story, he "lost his friend." Notice that he continues to avoid responsibility: he was deceived, and by that deception, he lost his friend. Buffy rightly points out in response that Andrew murdered his friend, and he admits it. He then points out that he also believes Buffy's stories that she has been telling those she was training to fight with her. Buffy's response is pointed: "This isn't some story where good triumphs because good triumphs. Good people are going to die! Girls. Maybe me. Probably you. Probably right now." Buffy tells stories and she knows that those stories are false, that they conceal the reality of the situation. In this exchange, it becomes clear that Buffy's storytelling is a counterpart to the storytelling of the First Evil. How are we to decide between the stories? How is Buffy's storytelling any less culpable that that of the First Evil? Presumably, there is a question of intent. The First wanted Andrew to murder Jonathan while Buffy does not want to murder those under her command. It is refreshing, though, to know that Buffy does not believe her stories, but unsettling to see that she uses stories knowingly even though "life is not a story."

Andrew's "redemption" is now at hand, but it does not take the form he expects. "When your blood pours out, it might save the world. What do you think about that? Does it buy it all back? Are you redeemed?" Buffy asks him. "No," he replies, "because I killed him. Because I listened to Warren, and I pretended I thought it was him, but I knew — I knew it wasn't. And I killed Jonathan. And now you're gonna kill me. And I'm scared, and I'm going to die. And this — this is what Jonathan felt." Again, we see Andrew cry, but this time it is not under the influence of a story. It turns out, in a neat bit of storytelling, that the seal needed to be closed by tears, not blood. It was the genuineness of the tears Andrew shed that closed the seal. Even more, though, there is here an implicit commentary on a pervasive *BtVS* theme. Repeatedly throughout the series, as is befitting a show that features vampires, we have heard story after story about blood. Indeed, a season finale hinged around the recognition that "it's always gotta be blood" ("The Gift," 5.22). Yet here, no blood is shed, only tears. Note, also, that Andrew does not tell a story. He does not try to describe what Jonathan felt, he simply experiences it. His "this" points to that which is unspeakable because our vocabulary cannot do it justice. Our fixated concepts would betray the experience. While the strict dichotomy between thought and feeling implied in Andrew's "redemption" is a bit too neat, nonetheless, the episode makes it clear that there is no story to be told about redemption.

The episode concludes the same as it began, with Andrew sitting in front of his video camera telling a story—but a very different one Andrew states: "Here's the thing. I killed my best friend. There's a big fight coming, and I don't know what's going to happen. I don't even think I'm going to live through it. That's, uh, probably the way it should be. I guess I'm—" And then he turns off the camera. One aspect of this final sequence worth remarking is that Andrew has not yet given up on stories. He thinks that dying is probably the scripted result of redemption. Again, the viewer who knows how Season Seven concludes will recognize the foreshadowing here and realize that Andrew does survive the big fight, thus putting a lie to even this residual commitment to categorizing experience according to stories much. Notice that this is the same failure that befell Anya. The series puts a lie to her story that she could finally "move on," just as it puts a lie to Andrew's story that he should probably die due to his past actions. He has begun to learn Montaigne's lessons—do what is within your power, do not be charmed by false stories, and, that most famous of Socrates charms, know thyself. Andrew turns off the camera leaving us to fill in the blank after the "I guess I'm...." The mid-sentence ending of the episode challenges us to fill in the blank, but how can we trust ourselves to do so? The promise the episode holds out here, I take it, is that through stories we can learn the inadequacy of stories, just as Montaigne tells us his task: "I do not portray being; I portray passing. Not the passing from one age to another, or, as people say, from seven years to seven years, but from day to day, from minute to minute" (Montaigne, "Of repentance," 610–11). If we were to fill in the blank, we would be playing the part of the gods, a stance explicitly mocked in the episode.

In conclusion, then, let me return to a distinctively philosophical pleasure I take in *BtVS*. First, all the kissing and staking is fun, and the stories the series tells are entertaining. But, fortuitously, *BtVS* is more than entertaining kissing and staking. In this essay, I have explicated this "more" in terms of the series' refusal to conform to certain expectations related to storytelling. In its refusal, for example, to conform to a standard theory of true love or redemption, the episode "Storyteller" points to a particular aspiration of philosophy. And the abrupt ending of this episode foreshadows the conclusion of Season Seven: Dawn's asking Buffy "What are we gonna do now?" and Buffy's response of an enigmatic smile. I do not want to claim that the theme I have traced in Montaigne, Mill, Warshow, Cavell, and Stroud are the only aspirations available to a philosopher. But it is a persistent theme in the Western philosophical tradition, and it is present in "Storyteller."

In a famous interview before the beginning of Season Six, Joss Whedon notoriously claimed that his mandate as a storyteller was, "Don't give people what they want, give them what they need" (Whedon). That statement has been a focal point of fan debate ever since. While one can argue with particular writing decisions, this essay has shown that there is a good philosophical impulse behind this mandate as such. Giving people what they want can support conformity. Thus, *BtVS* appeals to me for much the same reason that doing history of philosophy does. *BtVS* prompts me to question my categorization of experiences and it helps to provide me with a new vocabulary for dealing with experience. It does both these tasks not by making a claim but by pointing to its inability to make claims that warrant our conformity. *BtVS* may be, in Andrew's words "educating and entertaining," but in "Storyteller," it is not so in the sense that we can learn from it—instead we can learn through it. That is an unusual goal to ascribe to a TV show, but, honestly, as Warshow, Cavell, and Stroud point out, it is also an unusual goal for philosophy today.

Notes

1. All subsequent quoted dialogue is from this same episode unless otherwise noted.
2. In what follows, I will resist making general claims about Seasons Six and Seven, though the very presence of this volume is an argument that something changes in these two seasons. The essays by Adams, Edwards, Rambo, and Wilcox are particularly concerned to trace those differences in more detail than I could hope to achieve. I will return to the question of the unity of these two seasons in the final paragraphs of this essay.
3. The essay by Ira Shull and Anne Shull in this volume provides a very good overview of the uses of Andrew's character. Among the many uses, my focus is on a variation of their discussion of Andrew as Candide. Their quoting of Voltaire from his article on ignorance nicely supplements the rather different sources I draw upon in this essay.

Works Cited

Aberdein, Andrew. "'Insane Troll Logic': Popular Culture as Philosophical Heuristic." Paper presented at the Slayage Conference on *Buffy the Vampire Slayer*, Nashville, May 2004.
Cavell, Stanley. *Conditions Handsome and Unhandsome: The Constitution of Emersonian Perfectionism. Paul Carus Lectures.* Chicago: Open Court, 2000.

_____. "Epilogue: After Half a Century." In Robert Warshow, *The Immediate Experience: Movies, Comics, Theatre, and Other Aspects of Popular Culture*. 1962. Cambridge, MA: Harvard University Press, 2002. 289–300.
"Chosen." Written and directed by Joss Whedon. *Buffy the Vampire Slayer*. UPN. 20 May 2003.
Kael, Pauline. "A Note on the Title." *Kiss Kiss Bang Bang*. New York: Atlantic-Little Brown, 1968.
Lehmann, Chris. *Revolt of the Masscult*. Chicago: Prickly Paradigm Press, 2003.
Mill, John Stuart. *On Liberty and Other Writings*. Edited by Stefan Collini. Cambridge: Cambridge University Press, 1989.
Montaigne, Michel de. *The Complete Essays of Montaigne*. Translated by Donald M. Frame. Palo Alto, CA: Stanford University Press, 1958.
"Storyteller." Written by Jane Espenson. Directed by Marita Grabiak. *Buffy the Vampire Slayer*. UPN. 25 February 2003.
Stroud, Barry. "What Is Philosophy?" In C. P. Ragland and Sarah Heidt, eds., *What Is Philosophy*. New Haven, CT: Yale University Press, 2001. 25–46.
Warshow, Robert. "Preface." In *The Immediate Experience: Movies, Comics, Theatre, and Other Aspects of Popular Culture* [0]. Cambridge, MA: Harvard University Press, 2002. xxxvii–xliii.
Whedon, Joss. Interview with Tasha Robinson. *The Onion*. 5 September 2001. http://www.avclub.com/content/node/24238.

Appendix: Episode Guides for Buffy the Vampire Slayer and Angel

Buffy the Vampire Slayer

Season One

Episode	Airdate	Title	Writer
1/1	3/10/97	Welcome to the Hellmouth	Joss Whedon
1/2	3/10/97	The Harvest	Joss Whedon
1/3	3/17/97	Witch	Dana Reston
1/4	3/25/97	Teacher's Pet	David Greenwalt
1/5	3/31/97	Never Kill a Boy on the First Date	Rob Des Hotel/Dean Batali
1/6	4/7/97	The Pack	Joe Reinkemeyer/ Matt Kiene
1/7	4/14/97	Angel	David Greenwalt
1/8	4/28/97	I Robot... You Jane	Ashley Gable/ Thomas A. Swyden
1/9	5/5/97	The Puppet Show	Rob Des Hotel/Dean Batali
1/10	5/12/97	Nightmares	David Greenwalt/ Joss Whedon
1/11	5/19/97	Out of Mind, Out of Sight	Thomas A. Swyden/ Ashley Gable/Joss Whedon
1/12	6/2/97	Prophecy Girl	Joss Whedon

Season Two

Episode	Airdate	Title	Writer
2/1	9/15/97	When She Was Bad	Joss Whedon
2/2	9/22/97	Some Assembly Required	Ty King
2/3	9/29/97	School Hard	David Greenwalt/ Joss Whedon

Episode	Airdate	Title	Writer
2/4	10/6/97	Inca Mummy Girl	Matt Kiene/Joe Reinkemeyer
2/5	10/13/97	Reptile Boy	David Greenwalt
2/6	10/27/97	Halloween	Carl Ellsworth
2/7	11/3/97	Lie to Me	Joss Whedon
2/8	11/10/97	The Dark Age	Dean Batali/Rob Des Hotel
2/9	11/17/97	What's My Line?, Part One	Howard Gordon/ Marti Noxon
2/10	11/24/97	What's My Line?, Part Two	Marti Noxon
2/11	12/8/97	Ted	David Greenwalt/ Joss Whedon
2/12	1/12/98	Bad Eggs	Marti Noxon
2/13	1/19/98	Surprise	Marti Noxon
2/14	1/20/98	Innocence	Joss Whedon
2/15	1/27/98	Phases	Rob Des Hotel/Dean Batali
2/16	2/10/98	Bewitched, Bothered, and Bewildered	Marti Noxon
2/17	2/24/98	Passion	Ty King
2/18	3/3/98	Killed by Death	Rob Des Hotel/Dean Batali
2/19	4/28/98	I Only Have Eyes for You	Marti Noxon
2/20	5/5/98	Go Fish	David Fury/Elin Hampton
2/21	5/12/98	Becoming, Part One	Joss Whedon
2/22	5/19/98	Becoming, Part Two	Joss Whedon

Season Three

Episode	Airdate	Title	Writer
3/1	9/29/98	Anne	Joss Whedon
3/2	10/6/98	Dead Man's Party	Marti Noxon
3/3	10/13/98	Faith, Hope and Trick	David Greenwalt
3/4	10/20/98	Beauty and the Beasts	Marti Noxon
3/5	11/3/98	Homecoming	David Greenwalt
3/6	11/10/98	Band Candy	Jane Espenson
3/7	11/17/98	Revelations	Douglas Petrie
3/8	11/24/98	Lovers Walk	Dan Vebber
3/9	12/8/98	The Wish	Marti Noxon
3/10	12/15/98	Amends	Joss Whedon
3/11	1/12/99	Gingerbread	Thania St. John/ Jane Espenson
3/12	1/19/99	Helpless	David Fury
3/13	1/26/99	The Zeppo	Dan Vebber
3/14	2/9/99	Bad Girls	Douglas Petrie
3/15	2/16/99	Consequences	Marti Noxon
3/16	2/23/99	Doppelgängland	Joss Whedon
3/17	3/16/99	Enemies	Douglas Petrie
3/18	9/21/99	Earshot	Jane Espenson
3/19	5/4/99	Choices	David Fury
3/20	5/11/99	The Prom	Marti Noxon
3/21	5/18/99	Graduation Day, Part One	Joss Whedon
3/22	7/13/99	Graduation Day, Part Two	Joss Whedon

Episode Guides for Buffy the Vampire Slayer *and* Angel   213

Season Four

Episode	Airdate	Title	Writer
4/1	10/5/99	The Freshman	Joss Whedon
4/2	10/12/99	Living Conditions	Marti Noxon
4/3	10/19/99	The Harsh Light of Day	Jane Espenson
4/4	10/26/99	Fear, Itself	David Fury
4/5	11/2/99	Beer Bad	Tracey Forbes
4/6	11/9/99	Wild at Heart	Marti Noxon
4/7	11/16/99	The Initiative	Douglas Petrie
4/8	11/23/99	Pangs	Jane Espenson
4/9	11/30/99	Something Blue	Tracey Forbes
4/10	12/14/99	Hush	Joss Whedon
4/11	1/18/00	Doomed	Marti Noxon/ David Fury/Jane Espenson
4/12	1/25/00	A New Man	Jane Espenson
4/13	2/8/00	The I in Team	David Fury
4/14	2/15/00	Goodbye Iowa	Marti Noxon
4/15	2/22/00	This Year's Girl	Douglas Petrie
4/16	2/29/00	Who Are You?	Joss Whedon
4/17	4/4/00	Superstar	Jane Espenson
4/18	4/25/00	Where the Wild Things Are	Tracey Forbes
4/19	5/2/00	New Moon Rising	Marti Noxon
4/20	5/9/00	The Yoko Factor	Douglas Petrie
4/21	5/16/00	Primeval	David Fury
4/22	5/23/00	Restless	Joss Whedon

Season Five

Episode	Airdate	Title	Writer
5/1	9/26/00	Buffy vs. Dracula	Marti Noxon
5/2	10/3/00	Real Me	David Fury
5/3	10/10/00	The Replacement	Jane Espenson
5/4	10/17/00	Out of My Mind	Rebecca Rand Kirshner
5/5	10/24/00	No Place Like Home	Douglas Petrie
5/6	11/7/00	Family	Joss Whedon
5/7	11/14/00	Fool For Love	Douglas Petrie
5/8	11/21/00	Shadow	David Fury
5/9	11/28/00	Listening to Fear	Rebecca Rand Kirshner
5/10	12/19/00	Into The Woods	Marti Noxon
5/11	1/9/01	Triangle	Jane Espenson
5/12	1/23/01	Checkpoint	Douglas Petrie/Jane Espenson
5/13	2/6/01	Blood Ties	Steven S. DeKnight
5/14	2/13/01	Crush	David Fury
5/15	2/20/01	I Was Made to Love You	Jane Espenson
5/16	2/27/01	The Body	Joss Whedon
5/17	4/17/01	Forever	Marti Noxon
5/18	4/24/01	Intervention	Jane Espenson
5/19	5/1/01	Tough Love	Rebecca Rand Kirshner
5/20	5/8/01	Spiral	Steven S. DeKnight

Episode	Airdate	Title	Writer
5/21	5/15/01	*The Weight of the World*	Douglas Petrie
5/22	5/22/01	*The Gift*	Joss Whedon

Season Six

Episode	Airdate	Title	Writer
6/1	10/2/01	*Bargaining, Part One*	Marti Noxon
6/2	10/2/01	*Bargaining, Part Two*	David Fury
6/3	10/9/01	*After Life*	Jane Espenson
6/4	10/16/01	*Flooded*	Jane Espenson/Douglas Petrie
6/5	10/23/01	*Life Serial*	David Fury/Jane Espenson
6/6	10/30/01	*All the Way*	Steven S. DeKnight
6/7	11/6/01	*Once More, with Feeling*	Joss Whedon
6/8	11/13/01	*Tabula Rasa*	Rebecca Rand Kirshner
6/9	11/20/01	*Smashed*	Drew Z. Greenberg
6/10	11/27/01	*Wrecked*	Marti Noxon
6/11	1/8/02	*Gone*	David Fury
6/12	1/29/02	*Doublemeat Palace*	Jane Espenson
6/13	2/5/02	*Dead Things*	Steven S. DeKnight
6/14	2/12/02	*Older and Far Away*	Drew Z. Greenberg
6/15	2/26/02	*As You Were*	Douglas Petrie
6/16	3/5/02	*Hell's Bells*	Rebecca Rand Kirshner
6/17	3/12/02	*Normal Again*	Diego Gutierrez
6/18	4/30/02	*Entropy*	Drew Z. Greenberg
6/19	5/7/02	*Seeing Red*	Steven S. DeKnight
6/20	5/14/02	*Villians*	Marti Noxon
6/21	5/21/02	*Two to Go*	Douglas Petrie
6/22	5/21/02	*Grave*	David Fury

Season Seven

Episode	Airdate	Title	Writer
7/1	9/24/02	*Lessons*	Joss Whedon
7/2	10/1/02	*Beneath You*	Douglas Petrie
7/3	10/8/02	*Same Time, Same Place*	Jane Espenson
7/4	10/15/02	*Help*	Rebecca Rand Kirshner
7/5	10/22/02	*Selfless*	Drew Goddard
7/6	11/05/02	*Him*	Drew Z. Greenberg
7/7	11/12/02	*Conversations with Dead People*	Jane Espenson/ Drew Goddard
7/8	11/19/02	*Sleeper*	David Fury/Jane Espenson
7/9	11/26/02	*Never Leave Me*	Drew Goddard
7/10	12/17/02	*Bring on the Night*	Marti Noxon/Douglas Petrie
7/11	1/7/03	*Showtime*	David Fury
7/12	1/21/03	*Potential*	Rebecca Rand Kirshner
7/13	2/4/03	*The Killer in Me*	Drew Z. Greenberg
7/14	2/11/03	*First Date*	Jane Espenson
7/15	2/18/03	*Get It Done*	Douglas Petrie

Episode	Airdate	Title	Writer
7/16	2/25/03	Storyteller	Jane Espenson
7/17	3/25/03	Lies My Parents Told Me	David Fury/Drew Goddard
7/18	4/15/03	Dirty Girls	Drew Goddard
7/19	4/29/03	Empty Places	Drew Z. Greenberg
7/20	5/6/03	Touched	Rebecca Rand Kirshner
7/21	5/13/03	End of Days	Douglas Petrie/ Jane Espenson
7/22	5/20/03	Chosen	Joss Whedon

Angel

Season One

Episode	Airdate	Title	Writer
1/1	10/5/99	City of...	Joss Whedon/ David Greenwalt
1/2	10/12/99	Lonely Hearts	David Fury
1/3	10/19/99	In the Dark	Douglas Petrie
1/4	10/26/99	I Fall to Pieces	David Greenwalt
1/5	11/2/99	Rm w/a Vu	Jane Espenson
1/6	11/9/99	Sense and Sensitivity	Tim Minear
1/7	11/16/99	The Bachelor Party	Tracey Stern
1/8	11/23/99	I Will Remember You	David Greenwalt/ Jeannine Renshaw
1/9	11/30/99	Hero	Howard Gordon/Tim Minear
1/10	12/14/99	Parting Gifts	David Fury/ Jeannine Renshaw
1/11	1/18/00	Somnambulist	Tim Minear
1/12	1/25/00	Expecting	Howard Gordon
1/13	2/8/00	She	David Greenwalt/ Marti Noxon
1/14	2/15/00	I've Got You Under My Skin	Jeannine Renshaw
1/15	2/22/00	The Prodigal	Tim Minear
1/16	2/29/00	The Ring	Howard Gordon
1/17	4/4/00	Eternity	Tracey Stern
1/18	4/25/00	Five by Five	Jim Kouf
1/19	5/2/00	Sanctuary	Tim Minear/Joss Whedon
1/20	5/9/00	War Zone	Garry Campbell
1/21	5/16/00	Blind Date	Jeannine Renshaw
1/22	5/23/00	To Shanshu in L.A.	David Greenwalt

Season Two

Episode	Airdate	Title	Writer
2/1	9/26/00	Judgment	David Greenwalt
2/2	10/3/00	Are You Now or Have You Ever Been	Tim Minear

Episode	Airdate	Title	Writer
2/3	10/10/00	*First Impressions*	Shawn Ryan
2/4	10/17/00	*Untouched*	Mere Smith
2/5	10/24/00	*Dear Boy*	David Greenwalt
2/6	11/7/00	*Guise Will Be Guise*	Jane Espenson
2/7	11/14/00	*Darla*	Tim Minear
2/8	11/21/00	*The Shroud of Rahmon*	Jim Kouf
2/9	11/28/00	*The Trial*	Douglas Petrie/Tim Minear
2/10	12/19/00	*Reunion*	Tim Minear/Shawn Ryan
2/11	1/16/01	*Redefinition*	Mere Smith
2/12	1/23/01	*Blood Money*	Shawn Ryan/Mere Smith
2/13	2/06/01	*Happy Anniversary*	David Greenwalt
2/14	2/13/01	*The Thin Dead Line*	Shawn Ryan/Jim Kouf
2/15	2/20/01	*Reprise*	Tim Minear
2/16	2/27/01	*Epiphany*	Tim Minear
2/17	4/17/01	*Disharmony*	David Fury
2/18	4/24/01	*Dead End*	David Greenwalt
2/19	5/1/01	*Belonging*	Shawn Ryan
2/20	5/8/01	*Over the Rainbow*	Mere Smith
2/21	5/15/01	*Through the Looking Glass*	Tim Minear
2/22	5/22/98	*There's No Place Like Plrtz Glrb*	David Greenwalt

Season Three

Episode	Airdate	Title	Writer
3/1	9/24/01	*Heartthrob*	David Greenwalt
3/2	10/1/01	*That Vision Thing*	Jeffrey Bell
3/3	10/8/01	*That Old Gang of Mine*	Tim Minear
3/4	10/15/01	*Carpe Noctem*	Scott Murphy
3/5	10/22/01	*Fredless*	Tim Minear/Jeffrey Bell
3/6	10/29/01	*Billy*	Jane Espenson
3/7	11/5/01	*Offspring*	David Greenwalt
3/8	11/12/01	*Quickening*	Jeffrey Bell
3/9	11/19/01	*Lullaby*	Tim Minear
3/10	12/10/01	*Dad*	David H. Goodman
3/11	1/14/02	*Birthday*	Mere Smith
3/12	1/21/02	*Provider*	Scott Murphy
3/13	2/4/02	*Waiting in the Wings*	Joss Whedon
3/14	2/18/02	*Couplet*	Tim Minear/Jeffrey Bell
3/15	2/25/02	*Loyalty*	Mere Smith
3/16	3/4/02	*Sleep Tight*	David Greenwalt
3/17	4/15/02	*Forgiving*	Jeffrey Bell
3/18	4/22/02	*Double or Nothing*	David H. Goodman
3/19	4/29/02	*The Price*	David Fury
3/20	5/6/02	*A New World*	Jeffrey Bell
3/21	5/13/02	*Benediction*	Tim Minear
3/22	5/20/02	*Tomorrow*	David Greenwalt

Episode Guides for Buffy the Vampire Slayer *and* Angel

Season Four

Episode	Airdate	Title	Writer
4/1	10/6/02	Deep Down	Steven S. DeKnight
4/2	10/13/02	Ground State	Mere Smith
4/3	10/20/02	The House Always Wins	David Fury
4/4	10/27/02	Slouching Toward Bethlehem	Jeffrey Bell
4/5	11/3/02	Supersymmetry	Elizabeth Craft/Sarah Fain
4/6	11/10/02	Spin the Bottle	Joss Whedon
4/7	11/17/02	Apocalypse, Nowish	Steven S. DeKnight
4/8	1/15/03	Habeas Corpses	Jeffrey Bell
4/9	1/22/03	Long Day's Journey	Mere Smith
4/10	1/29/03	Awakening	David Fury/Steven S. DeKnight
4/11	2/5/03	Soulless	Elizabeth Craft/Sarah Fain
4/12	2/12/03	Calvary	Jeffrey Bell/Steven S. DeKnight/Mere Smith
4/13	3/5/03	Salvage	David Fury
4/14	3/12/03	Release	Steven S. DeKnight/Elizabeth Craft/Sarah Fain
4/15	3/19/03	Orpheus	Mere Smith
4/16	3/26/03	Players	Jeffrey Bell/Elizabeth Craft/Sarah Fain
4/17	4/2/03	Inside Out	Steven S. DeKnight
4/18	4/9/03	Shiny Happy People	Elizabeth Craft/Sarah Fain
4/19	4/16/03	The Magic Bullet	Jeffrey Bell
4/20	4/23/03	Sacrifice	Ben Edlund
4/21	4/30/03	Peace Out	David Fury
4/22	5/7/03	Home	Tim Minear

Season Five

Episode	Airdate	Title	Writer
5/1	10/1/03	Conviction	Joss Whedon
5/2	10/8/03	Just Rewards	David Fury/Ben Edlund
5/3	10/15/03	Unleashed	Elizabeth Craft/Sarah Fain
5/4	10/22/03	Hell-Bound	Steven S. DeKnight
5/5	10/29/03	Life of the Party	Ben Edlund
5/6	11/5/03	The Cautionary Tale of Numero Cinco	Jeffrey Bell
5/7	11/12/03	Lineage	Drew Goddard
5/8	11/19/03	Destiny	David Fury/Steven S. DeKnight
5/9	1/14/04	Harm's Way	Elizabeth Craft/Sarah Fain
5/10	1/21/04	Soul Purpose	Brent Fletcher
5/11	1/28/04	Damage	Steven S. DeKnight/Drew Goddard
5/12	2/4/04	You're Welcome	David Fury
5/13	2/11/04	Why We Fight	Drew Goddard/Steven S. DeKnight

Episode	Airdate	Title	Writer
5/14	2/18/04	*Smile Time*	Ben Edlund
5/15	2/25/04	*A Hole in the World*	Joss Whedon
5/16	3/3/04	*Shells*	Steven S. DeKnight
5/17	4/14/04	*Underneath*	Elizabeth Craft/Sarah Fain
5/18	4/21/04	*Origin*	Drew Goddard
5/19	4/28/04	*Time Bomb*	Ben Edlund
5/20	5/5/04	*The Girl in Question*	Steven S. DeKnight/ Drew Goddard
5/21	5/12/04	*Power Play*	David Fury
5/22	5/19/04	*Not Fade Away*	Jeffrey Bell/Joss Whedon

About the Contributors

Michael Adams teaches in the English Department at Indiana University at Bloomington. He has written *Slayer Slang: A Buffy the Vampire Slayer Lexicon* (2003), which received the first Mr. Pointy Award for the Best Book in *Buffy* Studies; *How English Works: A Linguistic Introduction* (with Anne Curzan, 2006); and *Slang: The People's Poetry* (2008), as well as many articles on the history of English language. For several years, he was editor of *Dictionaries: Journal of the Dictionary Society of North America*; he is currently editor of *American Speech*. Recently, he was guest editor of a special issue of *Slayage: The Online International Journal of Buffy Studies* titled *Beyond Slayer Slang: Pragmatics, Discourse, and Style in Buffy the Vampire Slayer*. His introduction to *Buffy* was accidental and a little pathetic, the story of a man with nothing to do but surf television channels while eating a solitary dinner. But, on about the same day as Rhonda Wilcox, he realized that *Buffy* was no ordinary television show. He wrote his first conference paper about Buffy in 1998, an expanded version of which was published in two installments in *Verbatim: The Language Quarterly* (fall and winter 1999).

Agnes B. Curry teaches philosophy and directs the Honors program at Saint Joseph College in West Hartford, Connecticut. Her essay "Is Joss Becoming a Thomist?" appeared in *Slayage* 16 and "We Don't Say Indian: On the Paradoxical Construction of the Reavers" will be in the forthcoming in a *Slayage* special issue on *Firefly*. She credits her husband with hooking her on *Buffy*.

Lynne Y. Edwards is an associate professor of media and communication studies at Ursinus College in Collegeville, Pennsylvania. She is the author of "Slaying in Black and White: Kendra as Tragic Mulatta in *Buffy the Vampire Slayer*" in *Fighting the Forces: Essays on the Meaning of Buffy the Vampire Slayer* (2002), "Black Like Me: Value Commitment and Television Viewing Preferences of U.S. Black Teenage Girls" in *Black Marks: Minority Ethnic Audiences and Media* (2001), and "On the Down-Low: How a *Buffy* Fan Fell in Love with Veronica Mars" in *Neptune Noir: Unauthorized Investigations in Veronica Mars* (2007). She currently is writing *The Other Sunnydale: Representations of Blackness in Buffy the Vampire Slayer*.

About the Contributors

Gregory Erickson earned a Ph.D. in English from the Graduate Center of the City University of New York, and currently teaches world literature, cultural studies, and writing at Mannes College and New York University. He is the author of *The Absence of God in Modernist Literature*, and the co-author of *Religion and Popular Culture: Rescripting the Sacred*. His possibly promising career as a scholar of Modernism was derailed by television in the late 1990s and shows no evidence of going back. He has previously published essays on *Buffy* in *Fighting the Forces, To the Quick,* and *Slayage: The Online International Journal of Buffy Studies,* and is working on a book about television and theorizing the future.

Carly Haines is a media and communications studies senior at Ursinus College in Collegeville, Pennsylvania. She is currently writing her senior honors thesis, which explores the relationship between twin mythology and the portrayal of clones and cloning in film.

Paul Hawkins is a writer and musician. He holds a bachelor of arts in scriptwrting for film and television from Bournemouth University and a master of arts in producing film and television from Royal Holloway, University of London. His interest in *Buffy the Vampire Slayer* comes simply from the quality and depth of the storytelling on the show.

David Kociemba is serving in 2008 as the president of the Affiliated Faculty of Emerson College union. He has taught at Emerson and at four other area colleges and universities for the past seven years. Past courses include introductory media history classes and seminars devoted to exploring topics like American film censorship, the representation of physical disability, video art, and *Buffy the Vampire Slayer*. In addition, he has taught talented 4th–12th grade students the principles and practice of parliamentary debate at College Academy and the Roxbury Boys and Girls Club. His writing focuses on the work of Todd Haynes, Joss Whedon, and Jane Espenson. David has previously written for *Slayage, Charming and Crafty* (forthcoming), and *Staking the Fandom* (forthcoming). He won the 2007 Short Mr. Pointy Award for his article, "'Actually, it explains a lot': Reading the Opening Title Sequences of *BtVS*."

David Lavery is an American, now chair in film and television at Brunel University in London. The author of numerous essays and reviews and author, co-author, editor and co-editor of over a dozen books on television, including (with Rhonda Wilcox), *Fighting the Forces: What's at Stake in Buffy the Vampire Slayer*, he co-edits the e-journal *Slayage: The Online International Journal of Buffy Studies*, edits *Intensities: The Journal of Cult Media*, and is one of the founding editors of the new journal *Critical Studies in Television: Scholarly Studies of Small Screen Fictions*.

Jennifer Lemberg is an instructor at the Gallatin School of Individualized Study, New York University, and serves as project coordinator of the Holocaust Educators Network. She received her Ph.D. in English from the Graduate Center, CUNY, where she completed a certificate in women's studies. She also holds a

About the Contributors 221

certificate from the International Trauma Studies Program. Although she has been an ardent fan since Season One, this is her first published essay on *Buffy*.

David Perry grew up in Arkansas, where he attended the Arkansas Governor's School in drama. He traveled to Memphis in 1984 to attend Memphis State University, where he received a degree in film and video production. He has worked primarily in that field for 20 years as a production assistant, sound mixer, video editor and, more recently, as producer. David has delivered a number of performances in Memphis community theater productions, one of which received an Ostrander Award for Best Supporting Actor in a Drama. He began watching *Buffy the Vampire Slayer* late in Season One and has been an ardent supporter of the show ever since. His dream job is to bring Marti Noxon coffee every morning and compliment her on her hair and shoes.

Elizabeth L. Rambo is an associate professor of English at Campbell University in Buies Creek, North Carolina, where she teaches medieval literature, Chaucer, and more. She has been watching *Buffy the Vampire Slayer* since episode 1.1 "Welcome to the Hellmouth" in 1997, but only discovered Buffy studies and Internet fandom in Season Five. Her essay "Yeats's Entropic Gyre and Season Six" took her to the first academic conference devoted to *BtVS*, "Blood, Text, and Fears: Reading Around *Buffy the Vampire Slayer*," 2002, at the University of East Anglia, Norwich, UK, and she has not looked back. Rambo and her husband also enjoy *Firefly* and own a cat called Xander.

Brandy Ryan is nearing the completion of her doctoral dissertation on elegies by nineteenth-century women poets at the University of Toronto. Although this is her first article on *Buffy the Vampire Slayer*, she has been an avid watcher of the text since the summer of 2001.

Anne Shull is an associate professor of developmental English and English-as-a-Second-Language at Quinsigamond Community College in Worcester, Massachusetts. In her free time she enjoys singing, but there is no truth to the rumor that she is planning to tour the U.S. performing the *Buffy* musical.

Ira Shull is a writer and a teacher who lives in Shirley, Massachusetts. He has taught writing in the School of Communications at Boston University (where he first heard about *Buffy* through a dean who taped it), and Franklin Pierce College. He is also the author of a nonfiction book, *For the Love of Teaching: And Other Reasons Teachers Do What They Do*. As with many things, Ira was a bit late to the party with *BtVS*, not watching the show until Season 4.

James B. South is associate professor of philosophy and chair of the department at Marquette University. His areas of research are in the history of philosophy, especially late medieval and renaissance philosophy, and philosophy and popular culture. His work in the history of philosophy has appeared in such journals as *Review of Metaphysics*, *History of Philosophy Quarterly*, and *Medieval Philosophy and Theology*. In the area of popular culture, he has edited *Buffy the Vampire*

Slayer and Philosophy (2003) and co-edited *James Bond and Philosophy* (2006). He has also published essays on movies, music, and comic books.

Josef Velazquez teaches philosophy at Stonehill College in Easton, Massachusetts. He became interested in *Buffy* and other Whedon creations through the bad influence of his long-time friend Agnes Curry.

Rhonda V. Wilcox, Ph.D., is a professor of English at Gordon College in Barnesville, Georgia. She is the author of *Why Buffy Matters: The Art of Buffy the Vampire Slayer* (2005) and the coeditor (with David Lavery) of *Fighting the Forces: What's at Stake in Buffy the Vampire Slayer* (2002). She is the editor of *Studies in Popular Culture* (now in its 31st year), a founding editor of *Critical Studies in Television: Scholarly Studies in Small Screen Fictions* (a new journal from Manchester University Press), and the coeditor (with David Lavery) of *Slayage: The Online International Journal of Buffy Studies* (a peer-reviewed quarterly now in its seventh year). She has published many articles and chapters in books on good television. Her collection *Investigating Firefly and Serenity: Science Fiction on the Frontier* (coedited with Tanya R. Cochran) was published in spring 2008. With Sue Turnbull, she is currently editing a collection on Rob Thomas's *Veronica Mars*.

Alissa Wilts is a singer-songwriter, freelance entertainment writer, and independent scholar who lives in Winnipeg, Canada, with her partner and their six pets. She writes regularly for the Winnipeg GLBT newsmagazine *Outwords Inc.* and has been a member of its board of directors since 2003. She is fascinated by the massive number of pop culture references in *Buffy the Vampire Slayer*, and used to fantasize about being a member of the show's writing team. Since she cannot write for *Buffy*, she writes about her all-time favorite show.

Index

ABC 136
Adam (*BtVS* character) 20, 99, 105, 111, 131
"After Life" (*BtVS* episode) 25, 29, 33, 36, 37, 68, 95, 97, 98, 99, 117
"All the Way"(*BtVS* episode) 48, 99, 100
"Amends" (*BtVS* episode) 92, 125
Amy (*BtVS* character) 17, 19, 54, 66, 71, 167, 192
Andrew (*BtVS* character) 23, 26, 30, 31, 34, 52, 55, 71, 75–82, 89, 90, 109, 123, 125–127, 172, 173, 179, 198, 199, 201, 202, 203, 205, 206, 207, 208, 209, 221
Angel 1, 9, 11, 15–22, 25, 26, 32, 38, 39, 62, 63, 65, 68, 71, 72, 78, 103, 112, 135, 139 144, 147, 150, 163, 165, 178–180, 182, 186, 194, 196, 197
Angelus (*BtVS* character) 63, 66
Anger 33, 34, 58, 100, 101, 155, 178, 196
"Anne" (*BtVS* episode) 169, 179
Anya (*BtVS* character) 2, 20, 21, 28, 29, 33, 36, 49, 52, 58, 65, 67, 69, 70, 71, 78, 87–89, 92, 97, 100, 108, 110, 126, 133, 145, 147, 150, 157, 163, 164, 171, 172, 175, 176, 183, 201–203, 205, 206, 208
April (*BtVS* character) 36
Arendt, Hannah 126
"As You Were" (*BtVS* episode) 177, 179
Autonomy 24–27, 125

"Band Candy" (*BtVS* episode) 25, 29, 34
Bargaining 5, 67, 71, 73, 115, 121, 130, 131, 169, 174, 179, 181, 183
Baron (*BtVS* character) 80
"Beauty and the Beasts" (*BtVS* episode) 17, 21, 139
"Becoming" (*BtVS* episode) 16, 34, 67, 73, 171, 180
"Beneath You" (*BtVS* episode) 89–91, 104
"Bewitched, Bothered, and Bewildered" (*BtVS* episode) 17, 18, 21

"Blood Ties" (*BtVS* episode) 6, 174, 179
blood sacrifice 101
"Blood, Text and Fears" 9
"The Body" (*BtVS* episode) 20, 22, 24, 62, 71, 73, 131
Bond, James 75, 76, 79, 222
bravery 33, 89
"Bring on the Night" (*BtVS* episode) 80, 81, 125
The Bronze 5, 16, 19, 35, 45, 53, 65, 71, 157, 167
Buffy (*BtVS* character) 1–3, 5–8, 15–21, 23–26, 29, 31–37, 48, 49, 57–59, 62–65, 67–72, 77–79, 81, 83–94, 95–108, 109–112, 114–128, 130–135, 137, 139, 140, 143–145, 147–158, 161–165, 167–179, 183–196, 201, 205–209
Buffy the Vampire Slayer 5, 7, 8, 13, 14, 20, 24, 41, 57, 63, 83, 84, 95, 134, 135, 139, 140, 143, 145, 149, 162, 167, 183, 189, 191, 194, 198
Buffyverse 2, 6, 8, 14, 19, 25, 37, 45, 48, 58, 62, 67, 69, 71, 85, 90, 93, 99, 108, 146, 164
"Buffy vs. Dracula" (*BtVS* episode) 17, 91, 105
"Bunker" (*BtVS* episode) 7

Caleb (*BtVS* character) 1, 92, 106, 109
Candide (*BtVS* character) 80–82, 209
Catherine (*BtVS* character) 71
CBS 136
Charmed 169
"Choices" (*BtVS* episode) 57, 69
"Chosen" (*BtVS* episode) 1, 7, 54, 91, 110, 128, 130, 133, 152, 155, 165
Chosen Family 143–151, 153, 158–165
Clem (*BtVS* character) 34
comedy 25, 26, 29, 31, 33, 35, 36, 38
"Consequences" (*BtVS* episode) 18

223

"Conversations with Dead People" (*BtVS* episode) 34, 75, 91, 107, 108
Cordelia (*BtVS* character) 15, 17, 18, 20, 33 90, 91, 132, 133, 144, 147, 161

Darla (*BtVS* character) 163
Dawn (*BtVS* character) 1, 2, 6, 30, 34, 59, 68, 71, 72, 85–87, 90, 93, 98–102, 116, 118, 127, 145, 156, 157, 164, 165, 167, 169, 170, 174, 175, 177, 179, 186, 192, 194, 204
"Dead Man's Party" (*BtVS* episode) 20, 29
"Dead Things" (*BtVS* episode) 98, 100, 103, 123, 172, 173, 176, 192
D'Hoffryn (*BtVS* character) 49, 50, 90, 150, 164, 172
"Dirty Girls" (*BtVS* episode) 91, 106, 109, 110, 122
"Doppelgangland" (*BtVS* episode) 72, 178
"Doublemeat Palace" (*BtVS* episode) 29, 31, 35, 36, 177
Dracula 20, 96
Dru (*BtVS* character) 15–18, 106
Drusilla (*BtVS* character) 15, 16, 18, 20, 106, 163

"Earshot" (*BtVS* episode) 7, 23, 26, 30, 137
Ellen 25, 44, 48
emotion 3, 16, 17, 38, 49, 59, 61–63, 67, 71, 83, 97–99, 145, 148, 155, 158, 160, 161, 168, 169, 171, 172, 178, 179, 184, 189
"Empty Places"(*BtVS* episode) 1, 79, 85, 109, 152, 157
"End of Days" (*BtVS* episode) 1, 78, 91, 127, 133, 157
"Enemies" (*BtVS* episode) 90
"Entropy" (*BtVS* episode) 121, 167, 171, 172, 175, 176
erotic love 17, 19
Espenson, Jane 2, 6, 14, 17, 23–38, 76, 198, 220
Evil-Dead Lesbian Cliché 41, 46, 48–51, 58, 60, 61, 64, 70–72, 179

faith 18, 19, 71, 72, 79, 91, 92, 108, 122, 133, 135, 152, 154, 157, 164, 165, 189
"Family" (*BtVS* episode) 48, 149
Family Guy 31
"First Date" (*BtVS* episode) 34, 91, 125
"Flooded" (*BtVS* episode) 5, 25, 27, 64, 67, 76, 155, 164, 170, 172, 174, 175, 184
"Fool for Love" (*BtVS* episode) 95, 96, 106, 188, 193
"Forever" (*BtVS* episode) 20, 30, 68
Fox 85, 135, 136, 140

Freud, Sigmund, 122, 156
friendship 83, 92, 95, 147
FX 85

Gellar, Sarah Michelle 106
Genesis 109
"Get It Done" (*BtVS* episode) 81, 89, 100, 105, 163
"The Gift" (*BtVS* episode) 5, 67, 130, 131, 207
Giles (*BtVS* character) 5, 15–17, 20, 25, 28, 34, 57, 59, 67, 68, 71, 79, 85, 88, 94, 96, 98, 102, 106, 135, 131–133, 144, 145, 147, 155, 157, 158, 163, 170, 171, 179, 186
Gill Men 20
"Gingerbread" (*BtVS* episode) 36, 136, 188, 192, 194
Glory 67, 71, 100, 131, 169
"Go Fish" (*BtVS* episode) 20
"Gone" (*BtVS* episode) 103, 177, 191
"Graduation Day" (*BtVS* episode) 7, 133, 137
"Grave" (*BtVS* episode) 172, 175, 177, 178
grief 36, 62, 68, 133, 178
Guardian 109, 173
"Guise Will Be Guise" (*Angel* episode) 25

Halfrek 71, 87
"Harsh Light of Day" (*BtVS* episode) 32
"The Harvest" (*BtVS* episode) 131
Helford, Elyce Rae 188
Hellmouth 15, 80, 83, 93, 117, 125, 126, 189
"Hell's Bell's" (*BtVS* episode) 107, 134 171, 176
"Help" (*BtVS* episode) 91
"Helpless" (*BtVS* episode) 95, 179
"Him" (*BtVS* episode) 91, 127, 150
"Hush"(*BtVS* episode) 21, 68

"I Killed Tara" (*BtVS* episode) 64, 65
"I Only Have Eyes for You" (*BtVS* episode) 17, 21
"I Was Made to Love You" (*BtVS* episode) 36, 38, 64, 123
"Inca Mummy Girl" (*BtVS* episode) 20
inhibition 177
The Initiative 17
"Innocence" (*BtVS* episode) 16, 21, 63
"Intervention" (*BtVS* episode) 25, 131
"Into the Woods" (*BtVS* episode) 21

Jenny (*BtVS* character) 17, 20, 61, 66, 68, 71, 147
Jesus 112, 143

Jonathan (*BtVS* character) 23, 26, 28, 71, 76–78, 80–82, 100, 123–125, 172, 173, 206, 207
Joyce (*BtVS* character) 30, 34, 62, 71, 131, 136, 140, 148, 157, 163, 164, 177

Kathy (*BtVS* character) 71
Katrina (*BtVS* character) 64, 77, 78, 100, 123, 124
Kendra (*BtVS* character) 15, 16, 132, 133, 135, 189
Kennedy (*BtVS* character) 42, 51, 53, 54, 91, 108, 153
"The Killer in Me" (*BtVS* episode) 50, 91

Lavery, David 9, 38
Legion of Dim 172
"Lessons" (*BtVS* episode) 70, 89, 91, 95
Liebniz, Gottfried Wilhelm 82
"Lie to Me" (*BtVS* episode) 57
"Lies My Parents Told Me" (*BtVS* episode) 87, 106–108, 148
"Life Serial" (*BtVS* episode) 25, 34, 60, 76, 176, 191
"Living Conditions" (*BtVS* episode) 20

Marcie (*BtVS* character) 140
Martin (*BtVS* character) 81
The Master 15, 19, 24, 95, 131, 132, 187
metaphor 6, 18, 19, 50, 61, 65, 66, 86, 87, 96, 114–116, 119, 120, 127, 128, 130, 131, 138–140, 151, 163, 165, 169, 186, 196
Mill, John Stuart 202
Millennium 59
Mutant Enemy writers 6–8, 14, 16, 17, 21, 178, 179

National Review Online 7
NBC 136
Nerds of Doom 169, 172
"A New Man" (*BtVS* episode) 25, 179
"New Moon Rising" (*BtVS* episode) 17, 21, 47, 101
Nietzsche, Friedrich 127
"Nightmares" (*BtVS* episode) 15, 187
"No Place Like Home" (*BtVS* episode) 174
"Normal Again" (*BtVS* episode) 118, 119, 177
Noxon, Marti 2, 6, 8, 14, 16–21, 25, 36, 52, 86, 96, 167, 221

"Older and Far Away" (*BtVS* episode) 69, 175
"Once More, with Feeling" (*BtVS* episode) 6, 9, 48, 83, 86–89, 92, 93, 97, 104, 130, 170, 175, 179, 187

optimism 33, 36, 80, 82
Ostiris (*BtVS* character) 59, 67, 171
Owen, Susan 8, 192
Oz 6, 15, 17, 19, 20, 47, 49, 50, 71, 99, 147, 171

"The Pack" (*BtVS* episode) 71
"Pangs" (*BtVS* episode) 34, 85
Parker (*BtVS* character) 137
persuasion 75, 165
pessimism 76
Petrie, Doug 5, 6, 14 25, 27, 76
Plato 200, 203
Postmodernity 8
"Potential" (*BtVS* episode) 79, 90, 91, 126
"Primeval" (*BtVS* episode) 98, 111
"The Prom" (*BtVS* episode) 18, 90, 103
"Prophecy Girl" (*BtVS* episode) 130–134, 168, 187
Prosperpexa 102
punishment 62, 71

Rack (*BtVS* character) 19, 67, 71, 134
radical evil 126
Rambo, Elizabeth 17, 44, 64, 68, 79, 114, 123, 199
Razor (*BtVS* character) 71, 116, 117, 120, 121, 123
Rayne, Ethan 71
reality 42, 52, 55, 77, 87, 102, 107, 118, 121–125, 127, 131, 136, 140, 159, 174, 187, 192, 207
reality shows 135
redemption 7, 778, 81, 205–208
"The Replacement" (*BtVS* episode) 25
"Restless" (*BtVS* episode) 99, 105, 158, 171, 179
Revelation 177
Riley (*BtVS* character) 17, 18, 21, 65, 72, 99, 147, 177, 188, 192

"Same Time, Same Place" (*BtVS* episode) 34, 102, 103
The Scooby Gang 59, 61, 67, 76, 81, 83, 85, 88, 89, 92–94, 98, 145, 147, 149, 155, 157, 161, 163, 168, 193
Seal of Danthalzar 80, 81
"Seeing Red" (*BtVS* episode) 7, 49, 62–64, 66, 67, 71, 77, 101, 121, 173, 176, 193
"Selfless" (*BtVS* episode) 49, 75, 87, 90, 126, 150, 163
Shakespeare, William 91, 127
"Showtime" (*BtVS* episode) 79, 90–92
The Simpsons 31
Slayage Conference 6
"Sleeper" (*BtVS* episode) 127

"Smashed" (*BtVS* episode) 53, 66, 133, 167, 176, 177
Socrates 204, 208
"Something Blue" (*BtVS* episode) 50
Spider-Man 191
Spike (*BtVS* character) 2, 6,-9, 15–20, 26, 34–37, 58, 69, 71, 72, 77–79, 81, 84, 86, 87, 96–100, 103–111, 116–118, 120–122, 124, 126, 127, 132, 133, 145, 147–149, 154, 163, 165, 167, 169, 170, 172, 174–178, 183, 184, 186, 188, 190, 192, 193, 196, 205
Star Trek 75, 135
"Storyteller" (*BtVS* episode) 23, 25, 29, 32, 34, 78, 79, 81–83, 88, 127, 198, 203–205, 208, 209
Suárez, Francisco 200
Superman 191
"Superstar"(*BtVS* episode) 23, 25, 31, 173
"Surprise" (*BtVS* episode) 16, 17, 21
swerve 67, 68

"Tabula Rasa" (*BtVS* episode) 49, 70, 170
Tara 2, 6, 17, 18, 20, 21, 41, 42, 44–55, 57–71, 86, 93, 96, 97, 99–104, 111, 121 134, 140, 145, 147, 149–151, 156, 163, 165, 167, 170–172, 174, 179
"Ted" (*BtVS* episode) 48
The Three 122, 123, 125, 126
"Touched" (*BtVS* episode) 1, 51, 108, 111, 152, 153
"Tough Love" (*BtVS* episode) 43
The Trio 76, 79, 80, 100, 116, 122–125, 127, 131, 139, 169, 172, 173
Troika (*BtVS* character) 2, 64, 88, 172, 173, 192, 193
"Two to Go" (*BtVS* episode) 48, 68, 77, 172, 173

unconscious 64, 154–156, 158, 172
UPN 2, 5–7, 9, 79, 85, 114, 130, 131, 134–136, 139, 140, 183

vampires 43, 44, 47, 118, 122, 125, 132, 133, 140, 147, 152, 154, 170, 186, 188, 191, 201, 20, 19, 497
Veruca (*BtVS* character) 17
villains 18, 19, 71, 79, 80, 121, 122, 134, 178
violence 17, 46, 72, 77, 88, 115–117, 121, 124, 125, 139, 153, 165, 176

Walsh, Professor Maggie 179
Warren (*BtVS* character) 19, 36, 50, 62, 64, 71, 72, 76–78, 80, 100, 101, 121–125, 172–174, 206, 207
Watchers 89
Watchers Council 105, 109, 179
WB 5–7, 13, 14, 85, 130, 131, 134–136, 139, 140
Webster, Holden (*BtVS* character) 107, 154
"Welcome to the Hellmouth" (*BtVS* episode) 61, 139, 221
Wesley (*BtVS* character) 18, 25, 57, 69
"What's My Line" (*BtVS* episode) 14–17, 67, 135
Whedon, Joss, 1, 2, 5–7, 9, 13–15, 18–21, 23, 24, 26, 27, 58, 60, 61, 63–65, 69–71, 86, 87, 92, 93, 98, 107, 110–112, 134, 159 160, 163, 164, 167, 174, 179, 184, 185, 196, 209, 222
Whedonverse, 1, 160
"When She Was Bad" (*BtVS* episode) 130, 132, 140, 168, 177
"Where the Wild Things Are" (*BtVS* episode) 65
"Who Are You?" (*BtVS* episode) 47
Wilcox, Rhonda, 1–3, 9, 23, 24, 26, 38, 93, 179, 185, 187, 194, 209, 219, 220, 222
"Wild at Heart" (*BtVS* episode) 17, 19, 21, 49
William (*BtVS* character) 91, 106, 163
Willow (*BtVS* character) 5–7, 9, 15–21, 33, 34, 41, 42, 44–55, 57–72, 85, 86, 88, 91, 93, 96–104, 108–111, 115, 117, 119, 121, 122, 128, 132, 134, 145, 147–151, 153–156, 158, 163–165, 167, 170–173, 175, 178, 179, 183, 189, 192–194, 206
"The Wish" (*BtVS* episode) 18, 19, 21, 187
Wood, Robin (*BtVS* character) 83, 87, 89, 106, 108, 148, 154, 163
Woods, Nikki (*BtVS* character) 148
Worm Guy 15

Xander (*BtVS* character) 15–20, 25, 59, 30, 32, 33, 35, 52, 58, 62, 65, 70, 72, 77, 81, 85, 87, 89–91, 96, 98–101, 108, 111, 132, 133, 145, 147, 150, 154, 157, 158, 161, 163, 164, 171, 173, 175, 176, 183, 193, 194, 196, 205, 206, 221

"The Zeppo" (*BtVS* episode) 18, 29, 137

www.ingramcontent.com/pod-product-compliance
Ingram Content Group UK Ltd.
Pitfield, Milton Keynes, MK11 3LW, UK
UKHW041949140426
5217IPUK00014B/721